Extending the Boundaries of Care

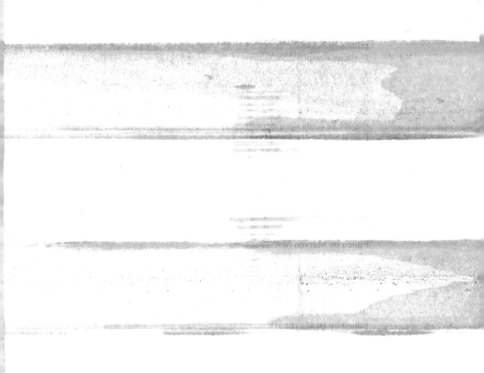

Cross-Cultural Perspectives on Women

General Editors: Shirley Ardener and Jackie Waldren, for The Centre for Cross-Cultural Research on Women, University of Oxford

ISSN: 1068-8536

Extending the Boundaries of Care

Medical Ethics and Caring Practices

Edited by
*Tamara Kohn and
Rosemary McKechnie*

BERG

Oxford • New York

First published in 1999 by
Berg
Editorial offices:
150 Cowley Road, Oxford, OX4 1JJ, UK
70 Washington Square South, New York, NY 10012, USA

© Tamara Kohn and Rosemary McKechnie 1999

All rights reserved.
No part of this publication may be reproduced in any form or by any means
without the written permission of Berg

Berg is the imprint of Oxford International Publishers Ltd.

Library of Congress Cataloging-in-Publication Data

A catalogue record for this book is available from the Library of Congress.

British Library Cataloguing-in-Publication Data

A catalogue record for this book is available from the British Library.

ISBN 1 85973 136 8 (Cloth)
      1 85973 141 4 (Paper)

Typeset by JS Typesetting, Wellingborough, Northants.
Printed in the United Kingdom by WBC Book Manufacturers, Bridgend,
Mid Glamorgan.

Contents

Acknowledgements

With the exception of the chapters by Okely and Dembour, the contributors originally presented papers at a one-day workshop on the Ethics of Care, organized by the editors and Shirley Ardener at the Centre for the Cross-Cultural Research of Women, at Queen Elizabeth House, University of Oxford. The participants at the workshop approached problems of 'care' from a number of different disciplines and experiences, and the excitement generated from such debate led to the construction of this volume. One paper from the workshop, written by Len Doyal on the universality of human needs and patients' rights, is unfortunately not included in this volume, but we would like to thank him for the contribution he made at the workshop stage. We are extremely grateful to the members of the Centre for the Cross-Cultural Research of Women who supported this venture and contributed to the workshop. Key among these is Shirley Ardener, a founder and previous director of the Centre, and a wonderful mentor and friend. We would also like to express our gratitude to Kathryn Earle and her staff at Berg Press for their patience. Finally, we would like to thank our families, who allowed us to keep things in perspective and often gave us cause to reflect on the multifaceted and multidirectional experiences of 'care'.

Tamara Kohn
Rosemary McKechnie

Notes on Contributors

Vangie Bergum is a Professor in the Faculty of Nursing and Co-Director of the John Dossetor Health Ethics Centre, at the University of Alberta. She has been involved in establishing interdisciplinary courses on health care ethics at graduate and undergraduate levels. She is currently principal investigator of research entitled 'Relational Ethics. Foundation for Health Care'. Her interest in ethics developed from her work in community health, especially childbirth education. She has published *A Child on her Mind* (1997).

Marie-Bénédicte Dembour has a degree in law (Belgium) and a doctorate in anthropology. She lectures on human rights in the Socio-Legal Centre of Sussex University. She has published several papers on the topic of human rights and also on issues related to death and dying.

Tamara Kohn is a lecturer in anthropology at the University of Durham and teaches Human Sciences and Health and Human Sciences at the University's Stockton Campus (UDSC). She has conducted fieldwork in the Inner Hebrides of Scotland, East Nepal, and the north-east of England. Her research has focused on identity change, interethnic marriage, and the anthropology of the body. Her interest in interdisciplinary exchange led to her involvement in this project at the Centre for the Cross-Cultural Research of Women, where she has been active since her DPhil studies in Oxford.

Helen Lambert is a lecturer at the London School of Hygiene and Tropical Medicine. She has carried out fieldwork in India, and is currently involved in research there, setting up local human immunodeficiency virus (HIV) prevention programmes. She is also taking part in research in Britain looking at the way health inequalities among ethnic minorities are concept-ualized.

Rosemary McKechnie is a lecturer in Social Sciences at Bath Spa University College. She has been involved in research on changes in sexual behaviour in relation to HIV, and also anthropological research on the meaning of irregular menstrual bleeding, comparing the way this is framed by medical professionals and by women.

Judith Okely is Professor of Social Anthropology at the University of Hull. She was formerly a Professor at the University of Edinburgh. She is the author of *The Traveller-Gypsies* (1983), *Simone de Beauvoir: a Rereading* (1986), *Own or Other Culture* (1996) and co-editor of *Anthropology and Autobiography* (1992). She has published articles on the aged in rural France and England. She is completing a book on ethnographic research entitled *Anthropological Practice* and a Study of Visualism and Landscape.

Frances Price holds a research post at the Institute for Child Development, University of Cambridge. She organized and carried out a national study of multiple births, which focused both on the needs of families and the provision of support and care by medical and social services. She has also carried out research on egg donation, looking at the experiences of professionals, donors and recipients. She is involved practically as a member of an ethical committee that is considering questions raised by new reproductive technologies.

Andrew Russell is a lecturer in the Department of Anthropology at the University of Durham, and is involved in teaching on the Human Sciences and Health and Human Sciences degrees at its Stockton Campus (UDSC). His research interests are in social, medical, environmental and applied anthropology, and he has conducted fieldwork in East Nepal and northeast India. He is currently involved in a number of health-related projects in the north-east of England, and is convener of the Centre for the Study of Contraceptive Issues at Durham and UDSC. He is the editor (with Iain Edgar) of *The Anthropology of Welfare* (1998).

Jan Savage is a Senior Research Fellow at the Royal College of Nursing Institute, London. Her work applies the insights of anthropology to increase understanding of nursing practice, with a view to improving patient care. Her current research looks at areas of nursing culture in the health services, including issues of sexuality, gender, kinship and the body. She is the author of *Nursing Intimacy: An Ethnographic Approach to Nurse–Patient Interaction* (1995).

Introduction: Why Do We Care Who Cares?

Rosemary McKechnie and
Tamara Kohn

This book has emerged out of a workshop held at the Centre for the Cross-Cultural Research on Women in Oxford attended by people from a number of different fields who needed to speak clearly to each other in order to foster an active and fruitful debate. The chapters presented here draw together diverse and overlapping points of view on a constellation of issues around a common theme: they question the way 'care' is conceptualized and practised. Rather than trying to construct an abstract argument that characterizes ideal-type solutions to ethical issues related to care, this book explores the different ways in which individuals and groups are grappling with very real practical difficulties and draws out the underlying themes that are being problematized. We do not aim to construct spurious consensus, only to clear some ground for cross-disciplinary discussion through which we can come to see the ways in which the boundaries of 'care' are being extended and refined in popular as well as professional understanding.

'Caring' is, at least on the surface, fairly unambiguously associated with things positive. It is in one sense a practical term which refers to actions that 'carers' in the broadest sense (nurses, doctors, relatives, friends, etc.) carry out for the benefit of other individuals. There is more to care than this, though. Care may be carried out in a variety of contexts, including domestic, institutional and community-based. Care may be conceptualized in a variety of ways – as a duty, as a responsibility, as a professional task, as a labour of love. Care is affective as well as effective.

Understanding the meaning of care is not straightforward. Thus, the starting-point of most texts concerned with describing or defining care is to try and frame care in relation to particular needs.[1] However, 'care' is very resistant to such clarification because of the taken-for-granted, practical and yet highly emotionally charged nature of caring practice.

1

The boundaries of care have been constituted in such a way as to marginalize care within the medical, academic and political world and to maintain its low and devalued profile. They have likewise tended to separate different actors' roles in the caring world when such classifications are increasingly questioned. It is very important to look at the ways in which 'care' and caring practice have been socially constituted and evaluated over the years. Understanding how boundaries of care have been constructed in different fields and how recent debates have worked to dissolve these boundaries is what this book begins to explore.

'Care' is coming to the fore in many contemporary debates. Understanding why this is the case is an interesting question to explore, and to do so one must, we believe, approach it comparatively and at several different levels. Specific issues (from euthanasia to abortion, multiple births from new reproductive technologies to genetic testing, etc.) feed into more general debates (such as changing the funding of health care, global differentials in health care provision, the ethics of testing new treatments). Across the board, it appears that questions relating to care give rise to contestation between groups who feel that they can define it, or that their experiences outline the boundaries of care. For example, what 'caring' is culturally, socially or morally acceptable, and in what contexts? Who are best positioned to judge these sorts of things: people in traditional 'caring professions', such as nurses and midwives, who have day-to-day 'hands-on' experience, or recipients of care (the old, the young, their relatives, the mentally ill, the physically disabled, the dying, etc.), who feel they know what they need; doctors, who take their cue from medical science, or believers, who take their cue from a religious credo; lawyers, who may situate any case within a set of socially prescribed rules, or philosophers, working within an intellectual framework?

One thing is clear, and that is that these problems of definition and authority are played out in texts, legal battles, media debates and pronouncements of committees, etc., in a way that creates and reifies disciplinary islands. Models of 'care' are socially constructed in separate closets. Sociologists generally only write with and for other sociologists, nurses with and for other nurses, etc. Part of the problem is that they all speak separate languages, which are at best uninviting, and at worst inaccessible to people outside their disciplines and experiences. It is one aim of this book to go some small way towards dissolving a few of the disciplinary boundaries that disperse and fragment issues surrounding care.

It is important to note that we (the editors) approach this subject as anthropologically trained 'outsiders' to many of the disciplinary and/or topical worlds that are represented in the various chapters that follow.

We are entering into some of these domains for the first time and are thus writing less as 'experts' (or natives) than as ethnographers. Within the ethnographic process we are attempting to step back from the particulars of debates to see how they have been bounded and defined. Contemporary dilemmas and debates concerning care indicate that social, cultural and technological changes have brought into question different assumptions intrinsic to the way care has been conceptualized. One of the most pronounced of these assumptions was (and still is) the notion that certain members of a population are 'natural' carers.

It's Natural that Women Care Best (Assumption 1)

Until feminists began to critically unpack ideas about femininity, the work that women do and their position in society, practical caring had been relatively undefined and untheorized. Much caring was rendered 'invisible' and classified as 'private', often happening in the home. Many important feminist texts focused on the gendered division of labour in society, the polarization of public and private and womens' role in domestic reproduction (Chodorow 1978; Burman 1979; Delphy 1984; Walby 1986). Others looked at how women's social position was underpinned by cultural values associating women with nature and men with culture (Ortner 1974; MacCormack and Strathern 1980; Moore 1988).

Not only were women expected to care for children, for the physical and psychological well-being of families, for the aged and for the dead, but their labour was devalued because it reaped no economic gain. Caring was seen as something women did naturally – intrinsic to their femininity (Finch and Groves 1983). This naturalized vision of women as carers transferred to the workplace as women took on paid roles as nurses, social workers and care assistants, etc. (Holden and Littlewood 1991). Meanwhile, within health care institutions, professional and academic disciplines developed which set apart the aspects of care associated with medical science. Professional closure progressed during the nineteenth century and the practice of medicine became an exclusively male pursuit (Witz 1992). The polarization of masculine and feminine roles within health care became institutionalized and hierarchical. The work involved with 'care' was associated with menial and polluting tasks, on the one hand, and an emotional supportive disposition, on the other – in opposition to the intellectual, rational, scientific work of doctors. Care could remain associated with female nurturance, while at the same time be assumed to develop with universal progress and science in a dependent role. Since caring was 'natural', it was secondary to the progress made by rationality. Thus, while medical and bureaucratic aspects of caring were set in progressive time (medical science moves on), the more intimate 'hands-on' aspects of caring were set in static time (nurturance is timeless).

'Care', therefore, has been defined by conceptual dichotomies which have ordered a division of labour, naturalized moral responsibilities, maintained the low status of 'caring', and bracketed it off from the wider issues of medical technology and curing. Understanding who is involved in caring work is very important for the way care is thought about – 'who cares' is not a facetious question. Carers and recipients of care have found that their actions and experiences have been bounded by professional hierarchies and cultural beliefs. Judith Okely (this volume) demonstrates this beautifully in her reflexive narrative account of her own mother's illness.

Dalley has shown how the concept of care can be broken down into 'caring for' and 'caring about' (1996: 13–15). The first involves the work of tending to another's needs while the second is about how one feels about another person. The two, she suggests, have become inextricably linked in the way in which women's caring roles are conceptualized, whereas they have not for men (ibid.).

> This raises the issue of ideology and the internalizing of values. A view that holds women to be caring to the point of self-sacrifice is propagated at all levels of thought and action; it figures in art and literature, it is the prop of official social welfare policies, and it is the currency in which the social exchanges within marriage and the domestic sphere are transacted. It means that women accept the validity of this view as readily as men do. Once this central tenet – of women's natural propensity to care (in contradistinction to men's nature) – is accepted, the locus for that caring then becomes determined. With woman as carer, man becomes provider; the foundation of the nuclear family is laid. It becomes the ideal model to which all should approximate. (Ibid.: 21)

Understanding the ways our ideologies of care are socially constructed is the first step in deconstruction. The historical and theoretical unpacking of moral and ethical issues raised by caring practice may not solve dilemmas, but it allows people to question patterns of thought and behaviour and thus initiate change. The implicit beliefs that have shaped the way practical care is organized have been brought to light by recent analyses, particularly feminist research concerned with the 'naturalization' of the association of women with care. This has led to a shift in the evaluation of 'care' within the nursing profession. As well as giving rise to historical and critical work (Mackay 1993), nursing theory has blossomed, as professional carers have begun to reconstitute 'care', finding language to talk about the practicalities of their craft, the carer/cared relationship and the politics within which care is delivered. The communicative role of nurses in translating medical knowledge to patients and assuming the position of advocate is another new focus. Vangie Bergum (this volume) provides an example of the new ideas that nurses are grappling with in an attempt to radically transform the way 'care' is conceptualized and evaluated. The way 'care' is thought about does alter the way care is given and received (Dalley 1996). Jan Savage (this volume) illustrates this by using ethnographic material from a hospital ward to show how theoretical framings of care (taken from an increasing diversity of models of care available to practitioners) have shaped the relationships that nurses form with those they care for. It may be significant to note that there is a tendency for women to write about the conceptualization of care in relation to caring practice. This book reflects this academic division of labour: as the reader will notice, all but one of the contributors are women.

As 'traditional' roles are challenged and care relationships are consciously considered, so nurses are moving out into research and some areas of treatment hitherto reserved for the doctor. The boundaries between 'caring' and 'curing' are being dissolved from inside as well as outside. Some doctors are starting to re-evaluate and contest the hierarchical ordering of their profession, recognizing the importance of communication with patients, of 'biographical work', of listening to patients (Armstrong 1983; Kleinman 1988)

Part and parcel of attending to patients is taking into account cultural and ethnic diversity. Ethnographic work exploring the relativity of knowledge about health and illness has revealed the cultural diversity of ways of thinking about health and illness. Epidemiological and specific researches aimed at marginal communities and non-Western groups (often in terms of their non-compliance with the medical model) have shown that differences in what patients think is important to their care and is related to cultural context.

The Homogeneity or Diversity of Patients (Assumption 2)

Another assumption that is coming to be questioned relates to the regimentation of those receiving care. Western biomedical models until recently focused on 'disease' rather than 'people' (Comaroff 1982). Health care provision was, especially in Britain, further shaped by the way society as a whole was imagined and organized. Just as the state was comprised of individual citizens, so the welfare state provided medical care for individuals according to their needs, not because of who they were or what they possessed. The ethical principles allocating scarce resources were shaped by a dominant ideology which presupposed equality as a cardinal principle (Elster 1994:5). That care should be provided for those who need it – whether they are too young, old, sick, physically or mentally incapable of looking after themselves – has been a tenet of the modern welfare state. The deliberations involved in the setting up of health and welfare provision reify concepts of responsibility for the provision of care through the allocation of resources, setting up of institutions and defining of legal and institutional responsibilities. They also institutionalize inequalities and discriminatory practices while maintaining a veneer of impartiality. These inequalities are then 'naturalized' in daily discourse. For instance, Hockey and James (1993) have looked at the ways in which people who are unable to work are identified by society at large in terms of metaphors of childhood, which in turn reflect and reify their dependent state and shape the way they are cared for by others.

As mentioned in the section above, within the world of care, there is a growing awareness of cultural diversity. Comparative work on the health care received by different groups as well as morbidity/mortality researches increasingly show that, in contrast to the ideals of ethical practice we have just discussed, everyone does not receive the same kind of care, nor can they expect the same results (Townsend and Davidson 1982). The health care system has inbuilt biases, which have not been overtly addressed because the institutions within it are viewed as rational and above such discrimination (see Savage (1992) on the neglect of 'Cinderella areas' of medical care, such as the gynaecological problems of older women). As more becomes known about the relationship between health care in the West and elsewhere, different questions about diversity and care are being raised and debated. One is about the appropriateness or inappropriateness of people trained in one country and practising in another. Another regards the role played by capitalist companies, especially pharmaceuticals, in reifying inequalities in care on a global scale or even endangering people by 'testing' on vulnerable populations (see Abraham 1997). Andrew Russell (this volume) illustrates quite clearly in his chapter on Depo-Provera how debates in the West may dominate care provision on a global scale. Rosemary McKechnie's contribution (this volume) looks at how public health responses to the unequal distribution of HIV Aids in society has given rise to new conceptualizations of social and cultural diversity in terms of people's relative risk.

Passive Patients (Assumption 3)

A view of recipients of care as passive subjects is being challenged on several fronts. One is represented by a subtle but powerful shift in perception which casts the patient as consumer. This is particularly clear in the USA, where paying patients and suing patients are more active and can expect different kinds of care. Insurance companies there wield tremendous power, too, in deciding what patients can and cannot expect *vis-à-vis* their caring needs and wishes. The framing of the patient as consumer is largely constructed by market forces. In addition, it ties in quite naturally to a discourse on individual 'rights' to care. Marie-Bénédicte Dembour (this volume) discusses this at some length from a legal perspective.

As greater and greater emphasis is placed on the care of the self, the public health model sets up a paradox: if you give people information and expect them to be active in keeping themselves healthy, you also empower them to question the kind of health care they require. Such concern and assertiveness often challenge the status of doctors, as does a growing patient interest in alternative courses of action and thought (e.g. self-help groups, alternative health care, etc.). However, this is not a simplistic move towards patient autonomy and empowerment (Sharma 1996). As Helen Lambert (this volume) shows, such alternative groups cannot be entirely independent from particular ties to the status quo, e.g. funding and a certain level of deference to expert knowledge. An even stronger challenge to the aims of doctors has come about, in part, through HIV activism, where identity politics and radical critiques of power relations shape patients' demands for particular kinds of care and counselling.

Challenges to the Boundaries of Care through Technology

Technological innovation is perhaps one of most important factors constantly pushing against the boundaries of care. As it becomes possible to work at the margins of life and death, so ethical issues merge into issues of how people should be cared for. Is it care to 'cure' infertility by bringing about a multiple pregnancy (see Frances Price, this volume)? Is it proper caring practice to keep very sick babies alive, or revive those who are terminally ill and suffering?

Medical technology itself has created areas of uncertainty where old boundaries are no longer easily accepted (e.g. reproductive technologies, genetic manipulation and transplantation). The questions raised by new technologies take 'medical' issues into the social, cultural and political domain, and the repercussions of medical intervention are seen to have many different dimensions. Interests and moralities are no longer straightforward – some of the key binary relationships which underpin our visions of our own society, e.g. parent/child, man/woman, animal/human, human/ machine, are challenged by technological advances. The more issues that are considered, the more complex they become. Diprose points out that technology does not simply fix a body part, it constitutes social categories of people: reproductive technologies constitute ideas of womanhood (1994). She considers that ethical codes need to be created which recognize this (ibid.). For instance, women need to recognize that simply assuming that they have the right to control their own fertility is not enough. They need to think about the ethics of how that control is used. Calls for the rethinking of ethical codes and their extension into areas of care are now commonplace (see, for example, the chapters by Price and Bergum in this volume). Health service planners, providers, doctors, nurses and patient advocates are implicated in this activity.

Boundaries of Care and Problems of Ethics in a Runaway World

In the West, 'care' has, until recently, remained a relatively underdefined area, and one which has not generally been theorized in terms of ethics. Ethics arise from the perceived need for a universal, expoundable set of rules and norms which should guide human conduct. As Bauman points out, the dynamic nature of modern society gave rise, on the one hand, to hitherto unknown levels of social change and, on the other, to an increasingly complex organizational system, in which ethics played a key role (1993). As people were individualized, their lives fragmented into different aims and functions. The need for a unitary vision of the world grew, giving rise to the aim to try and compose an all-inclusive unitary ethics, a cohesive code of morals that people could be taught or forced to obey (ibid.: 6). The practice of medicine was associated with ethical codes, which developed to deal with new interventions and professional hierarchy, and were associated with the rationalization and standardization of treatments. 'Care', however, fell largely outside these codes, and was considered to be governed by principles of 'common sense', policed by superiors and regulated practically rather than abstractly. Care was a safe area, a domesticated space in the tumult of modern society. Bauman views

the universality of the modernist project as a 'challenging campaign to
... eliminate all "wild" – autonomous, uncontrolled – sources of moral
judgement' (ibid.). It might come as something of a surprise that wild
autonomous uncontrolled sources of moral judgement have reared their
head in such numbers in relation to care. It is only now that the constraints
which have naturalized the control of care are being challenged.

The sections above have outlined some of the social shifts that have
given rise to questions about the meaning of care. Ideas about women's
work have changed, women are moving into the workforce in unprec-
edented numbers and the role of women in domestic reproduction, in caring
for families, is a matter of theoretical, personal and policy concern.
Demographic changes are giving rise to debates about resourcing and
providing care for older members of the population. The provision of
health and social care is being radically rethought in most Western nations,
as the relationship between state and private provision of services is
renegotiated. While governments increasingly reject collectivist solutions
to private problems, bureaucratic regulation of care is extended, and at
the same time individuals are increasingly viewed as having more
responsibility for their own health and well-being. This is associated with
the individualization of responsibility and sequestration of experience.
The importance of choice, of consumption, of self-care and self-help is
creating new kinds of ways for individuals to experience and participate
in their own care. This is interpreted by some academic theories as arising
from processes which increasingly question the authority and knowledges
of experts (Giddens 1991), exacerbated by the increasing awareness of
risk (Beck 1992; Gabe 1995).

Care, in becoming visible, has acquired radicalized carers and active
patients. A whole host of voices are contesting the boundaries of care,
trying to defend their vision of what it means to give and receive care.
New ways of thinking and acting in relation to care are to be found at a
variety of levels – in personal lives and relationships, in caring institutions,
at the level of legislation and policy and at the abstract level of theoretical
and philosophical debate. The following chapters are concerned with
discussions about care and caring practice at different levels, and they
touch on many of the issues we have alluded to above: the consequences
of new technologies, of new health strategies 'caring for the well', of new
relationships between the different professionals involved in care. There
are no easy solutions to the problems that have come to be associated
with care. Although each chapter may look at the relationship between
abstract definitions and contextualized experiences in different ways, some
taking the perspective of 'top down' and others that of 'bottom up', all

emphasize the importance of linking the two. The chapters are presented in four sections, each reflecting a different aspect of this problematic, and we would direct the reader to the short introduction at the beginning of each part, which tries to show the relations between the chapters in that particular section, as well as the thematic continuities that link contributions.

Most of these chapters have been written by anthropologists or sociologists, who are looking at debates from the outside. It is probably not accidental that their accounts arise from trying to straddle boundaries, seeing care from the inside both of other disciplines and of people in different practical contexts. Their insights in a sense are tied to making links between the way expert knowledges frame care and the ways in which care is practically realized. In reporting from an international conference on ethics in medicine, Margot Jeffreys commented that

> the agenda and discussion indicated the need to involve more sociologists and social anthropologists in the ethical debates which are now surfacing more urgently and cogently than ever before, within and across national boundaries. I missed what I consider is an essential element of ethical debate, namely its cultural and social contextualization. It will require however, that social scientists themselves recognise the value of addressing ethical issues directly not just obliquely in their work. (1994:19)

New Voices, New Dialogues: The Integration of Lived Experience and Abstract Theory

One of the interesting aspects of care becoming visible is the way that hitherto 'muted' perspectives on care, particularly the perspectives of those practically involved in giving and receiving care, are now making themselves heard. One of the concerns of this volume is to emphasize the importance of their perspectives on caring practice. Another is to show how abstract ideas and changes in social organization at high levels do have very real consequences for people giving and experiencing care. This is never a simple task, however.

The new visibility of care and the debates surrounding care offer both possibilities and dangers. There are some measured success stories. For example, in Britain, feminist critiques of the medicalization of childbirth have had an effect on the way care during pregnancy and birth is conceptualized and organized. Deconstructions of the way women's bodies were envisioned by gynaecology and obstetric theory and critical examinations of practice and research on women's experiences of medicalized childbirth (see Martin 1987) have been mobilized by midwives, general practitioners, interest groups (such as the National Childbirth Trust) and women themselves. There is a new emphasis on patient choice and on active birth, in which midwives rather than consultants play a central role, where support is valued and interventions kept to a minimum (see Oakley 1992). As a result of contestation between competing views, new practices are more mindful of the experiences and knowledge of those being cared for and those involved in caring. New technologies and scientific knowledge can offer possibilities as a resource in women's lives (Lupton 1994).

In other health care contexts, such as private medicine in the USA, issues around childbirth have acquired quite a different profile. Several developments which might in theory have led to the empowerment of women as patients (a concept of rights, a litigation culture and the idea that the consumer should expect the best possible treatment) have apparently had quite the opposite effect. Having the best medical treatment (most expensive, scientifically sophisticated and safest) has led to increased medicalization. The status of some professional communities, such as doctors, lawyers and insurance brokers, has been improved. The increasing formalization of ethical and procedural rules in relation to childbirth in this context is not encouraging.

In this introduction, we have briefly outlined how contemporary social conditions and new technologies are leading to the questioning of previously accepted practices of care, throwing into relief existing power relations and the conflicting interests of different sections of society. The apparent chaos created by the fragmenting of old boundaries is creating new relationships of caring, new views about dependency, trust and responsibility. The vulnerability of those receiving care and the everyday effort and grind of care, as well as its rewards, can be thought about in new ways by recognizing the empirical constraints within which people are working. Making visible some of the ways that boundaries of care are socially constructed is just one step along this path.

Notes

1. For example, Gilligan's position on the 'different moral voice' of women (1982) has been developed by herself and others in terms of an 'ethic of care'. Graham (1991), Bubeck (1995), James (1992) and Dalley (1996) are just a few of the feminist writers debating how women's work as care can best be conceptualized.

References

Abraham, J. (1997), 'The Science and Politics of Medicines Regulation', in M.A. Elston (ed.), *The Sociology of Medical Science and Technology,* Oxford: Blackwell.

Armstrong, D. (1983), *Political Anatomy of the Body: Medical Knowledge in Britain – The 20th Century,* Cambridge: Cambridge University Press.

Bauman, Z. (1993), *Postmodern Ethics,* Oxford: Blackwell.

Beck, U. (1992), *Risk Society: Towards a New Modernity,* London: Sage.

Bubeck, D.E. (1995), *Care, Gender and Justice,* Oxford: Clarendon Press.

Burman, S. (ed.) (1979), *Fit Work for Women,* London: Croom Helm.

Chodorow, N. (1978), *The Reproduction of Mothering: Psychoanalysis and the Sociology of Gender,* Berkeley: University of California Press.

Comaroff, J. (1982), 'Medicine, Symbol and Ideology', in P. Treacher and P. Wright (eds), *The Problem of Medical Knowledge: Examining the Social Construction of Medicine,* Edinburgh: Edinburgh University Press.

Dalley, G. (1996), *Ideologies of Caring: Rethinking Community and Collectivism* (second edition), London: Macmillan Press.

Delphy, C. (1984), *Close to Home: A Materialist Analysis of Women's Oppression,* London: Hutchinson.

Diprose, R. (1994), *The Bodies of Women: Ethics, Embodiment and Sexual Difference,* London: Routledge.

Elster, J. (1994), 'The Ethics of Medical Choices', in J. Elster and N. Herpin (eds), *The Ethics of Medical Choice,* London: Pinter Publications.

Finch, J. and D. Groves (eds) (1983), *A Labour of Love: Women, Work and Caring,* London: Routledge and Kegan Paul.

Gabe, J. (ed.) (1995), *Medicine, Health and Risk: Sociological Approaches,* London: Routledge.

Giddens, A (1991), *Modernity and Self-Identity,* Cambridge: Polity Press.

Gilligan, C. (1982), *In a Different Voice: Psychological Theory and Women's Development,* Cambridge: Harvard University Press.

Graham, H. (1991), 'The Concept of Caring in Feminist Research: The Case of Domestic Service', *Sociology,* 25(1): 61–78.

Hockey, J. and A. James (eds) (1993), *Growing Up and Growing Old: Ageing and Dependency in the Life Course,* London: Sage.

Holden, P. and J. Littlewood (eds) (1991), *Anthropology and Nursing,* London: Routledge.

James, N. (1992), 'Care = Organization + Physical Labour + Emotional Labour', *Sociology of Health and Illness,* 14(4): 488–509.

Jeffreys, M. (1994), 'Ethics in Medicine. The Fifth International Conference', *Medical Sociology News,* 19(2): 17–20.

Kleinman, A (1988), *The Illness Narratives: Suffering, Healing and the Human Condition,* New York: Basic Books.

Lupton, D. (1994), *Medicine as Culture: Illness, Disease and the Body in Western Societies,* London: Sage.

MacCormack, C. and M. Strathern (eds) (1980), *Nature, Culture, Gender,* Cambridge: Cambridge University Press.

Mackay, L. (1993), *Conflicts in Care, Medicine and Nursing,* London: Chapman and Hall.

Martin, E. (1987), *The Woman in the Body: A Cultural Analysis of Reproduction,* Boston: Beacon Press.

Moore, H.L. (1988), *Feminism and Anthropology,* Cambridge: Polity Press.

Oakley, A. (1992), *Social Support and Motherhood,* Edinburgh: Edinburgh University Press.

Ortner, S. (1974), 'Is Female to Male as Nature is to Culture?', in M.A. Rosaldo, and L. Lamphere (eds), *Women, Culture and Society,* Stanford: Stanford University Press.

Savage, W. (1992), 'Gynaecology in Older Women', in J. George and S. Ebrahim (eds), *Health Care for Older Women,* Oxford: Oxford University Press.

Sharma, U. (1996), 'Using Complementary Medicines: A Challenge to Orthodox Medicine?', in S.J. Williams and M. Calnan (eds), *Modern Medicine: Lay Perspectives and Experiences,* London: UCL Press.

Townsend, P. and N. Davidson (1982), *Inequalities in Health: The Black Report,* Harmondsworth: Penguin.

Walby, S. (1986), *Patriarchy at Work,* Cambridge: Polity Press.

Witz, A. (1992), *Professions and Patriarchy,* London: Routledge.

PART 1

Embodying Care: Giving Voice to Experience

We can learn a tremendous amount about the relations and contexts of caring practice from the detailed reflexive observations of individuals immersed in a caring relationship. While some analyses of caring practice will make generalized 'sound-bite' reference to individual experience, the way in which that experience is shaped over time by relations of power and personal dynamics between the 'cared for' and different carers tends to remain hidden from view. The first chapter in this volume shows how important the individual narrative of caring experience is for the study of care. It gives a most moving and revealing account of an anthropologist's personal experience of caring for her own mother, who was, unbenownst to all until much later, dying from Creutzfeld–Jakob disease (CJD). It makes us step immediately and completely into the heart of the matter, and gives us an insight into the tenderness and bitterness that are generated through the caring process. By weaving together past anecdotes of a time when her mother was a vibrant young intellectual with a detailed account of her deterioration of memory, Judith Okely's narrative manages to do more than make us feel a tragedy of decline and loss. Indeed, it reveals how the medical community tends to remain oblivious of the intimate knowledge which is so significant for the close family carer. By starting at the experiential heart of the issue, we are compelled to attend closely when more general themes are raised in this and subsequent chapters about the socio-cultural construction of different classes of carers (doctors, nurses, etc.), of the devaluing of the ageing body, of the gendered division of labour in relation to care and of the disjuncture between expert advice and grounded knowledge and intuition.

There are many useful points of comparison to be drawn between Okely's chapter and the one that follows it. Frances Price also deals with very visceral examples of caring, this time embedded in the experience of having triplets as a result of *in vitro* fertilization treatment. Like Okely, Price highlights the constructed biases of the medical community against a backdrop of personal reflections on experience. In particular, she looks at how the 'problem' of multiple births has been framed by the medical community in terms of the birth process itself, and how it neglects to deal with the great problems the parents are left with in caring for the children afterwards. Larger attitudes about the normality of the child-caring process in the domestic sphere inform a network of social and medical services, which subsequently fail to support parents and stigmatize them as being unable to cope. In both chapters, relations of power in different caring contexts are revealed from the inside out. Both chapters also deal with highly topical subjects in popular and medical professional circles: the 'new' and frightening disease of CJD, in the first instance, and multiple births, which arise from the development of new reproductive technologies, in the second.

1

Love, Care and Diagnosis

Judith Okely

Anthropological fieldwork aims at participation, but, so long as the fieldworker is not an indigenous member, there is some degree of estrangement. This is something which the anthropologist is obliged to confront and work with. There are degrees of involvement and shared understanding. Renato Rosaldo powerfully discusses the links between his personal rage after the tragic loss of his wife, Michelle Rosaldo, in the field and the anger/rage in the huntsmen's tales recorded and previously analysed in earlier fieldwork (1984).

I present a parallel case from Europe, where I had done fieldwork among the aged, but which I had hitherto not related to my ageing mother. I had also read and studied cross-cultural contrasts in healing, death and misfortune. When I found myself as unpremeditated actor rather than researcher, my powers of ethnographic observation were engulfed in the drama of the events. As daughter to mother, a role which I could neither choose nor discard, my relationship with the cared-for subject mixed emotions of love with the practicalities of care and the consequences of medical diagnosis. Only after the drama can I distance myself for some ethnographic description and comprehension.[1]

There are several strands to my discussion and ethnography. In one, I explore the experience of care in the case where the anthropologist is one of the carers, and in a decidedly personal context. The 'researcher' writer, in the case presented here, can in no way sustain a detached observer standpoint, even if that had been the preferred stance. Indeed, such a personal experience as the care and death of one's parent is hardly embarked upon as research. Only retrospectively, after the death of Bridget, my mother, did the detailed material present itself as something to interpret and write about. It happens that the sensitivities developed in anthropological fieldwork become part of the anthropologist's being. Indeed, both carer and cared for brought insights along the way from the perspective of social science; my mother had been a university lecturer in sociology and social administration, and before that a social worker with the elderly. The author, as one of the carers, is an anthropologist. We were both making running observations about what was happening. I draw on some of those insights now that the events have run their course. What also emerges are the shifts in the relationship between mother and daughter. The mother/parent was the original carer. She had breast-fed, changed the baby's nappies, washed, clothed and guided the child. The mother had intimate knowledge and control of the infant's body and character. She had chosen to continue to be a carer in loving, subtle ways through most of the daughter's adult life. Then in a series of stark incidents, the daughter was confronted with the frailty, vulnerability and increasing helplessness of the parent. In this case, my mother's illness, although never diagnosed in her lifetime, began imperceptibly, but lurched from the bizarre to total disintegration.

Other daughters have written autobiographical accounts of aspects of their relations with their mothers (e.g. Stanley 1992; Brettell 1997). De Beauvoir wrote a pioneering essay in 1964 (1980). This was something from which I remained somewhat detached when I wrote my own study of de Beauvoir (Okely 1986a). But my book was dedicated to my mother, and there are now some resonances, although my mother was a very different person from Madame de Beauvoir and our relationship did not bear the same history of conflict and incompatibility.

Another strand of this ethnography reveals how there are consequences for diagnosis arising from the different relationships with the 'patient' or cared for. Those involved in day-to-day, time-extended contact will have detailed knowledge of nuanced changes which are inaccessible to a distant doctor and consultant. The 'expert', trained in largely generalizable techniques, may fail to comprehend the importance of individual personality and the grounded knowledge of others. Deemed unqualified, these 'others' are not called upon for information relevant to diagnosis. The scientistic dismissal of 'anecdotal' evidence is embedded in Western medical orthodoxy. Where a premium is placed on the generalizable from statistical thousands, then the contrasting and supreme relevance of the anecdote for the diagnosis of one individual's affliction and illness is scandalously cast aside. Yet anthropologists and others have recognized the crucial significance of individual narrative and experience among the afflicted (Good 1994), as well as among those who surround them.

My detailed and incidental perceptions of others' grounded knowledge are consistent with recent debates about the flawed power of experts who either deny or appropriate, without acknowledgement, the grounded knowledge of those who live a daily, informed context. For example, it was the local farmers who first expressed concern about the long-term effects of Chernobyl nuclear pollution for sheep in Cumbria. But the experts, with hopelessly scientistic tests, at first dismissed the farmers' working knowledge of pasture and grazing patterns. Similarly, it was the parents who first suggested children's leukaemia clustering around the Windscale nuclear power station. Eventually, an official government report claimed to have 'discovered' the information.

Brian Wynne brilliantly explores these contexts in an article (1996) published after I had tentatively recognized the disparity between grounded knowledge of close associates or carers of a potential patient and the experts. His critique is based, likewise, on the rupture between generalizable positivist science and local, specific knowledge. As Wynne suggests, 'farmers' specialist knowledge of local environment conditions and sheep behaviour was ignored by the experts . . . The scientific knowledge constructed out of field observations began life as highly uncertain and uneven' (ibid.: 66) Yet this 'was obliterated by the time knowledge returned to the same public as formal scientific knowledge in official statements' (ibid.). The conflicts 'centred on the standardisation built into routine structures of scientific knowledge' when the farmers 'knew and could articulate various significant differences' (ibid.). There was a conflict 'between central administration and bureaucracy and a more informal, individualistic adaptive culture' (ibid.).

There are parallels among farmers and individual sceptics who raised questions about bovine spongiform encephalopathy (BSE), long before the British government took the matter seriously. By a strange and hideous twist, I discovered, ten months after my mother's death, that our family tragedy was interconnected with those very agricultural questions. I wrote the sections of this chapter about nursing, carers and grounded knowledge after the death of my mother in 1992, but before I learned of the correct diagnosis of her illness, namely Creutzfeld-Jakob disease (CJD). I had merely been sensitive to the brutal intellectual and social inadequacies of the medical profession.

The detached expert, whether in agriculture, nuclear power or medicine, has been 'trained' to eradicate difference and to seek the Holy Grail of generality, cleansed of all specificity, in the name of a hopelessly inappropriate and unknowledgeable definition of science. The gulf between generalizable detachment and grounded indigenous knowledge based on practice is found between Ministry scientists and Cumbrian farmers, between medical experts and day-to-day carers, and between positivist social scientists, addicted to quantifiable generalities, and anthropologists, who privilege ethnographic knowledge grounded in participant observation.

This chapter also raises the question of the need, especially in recent times in Britain, to find blame and then acknowledgement by some original perpetrators of an apparently avoidable death. If there is a suspicion that the death was caused by negligence, financial stringency or prejudice, be it racism, sexism or ageism, then those closest to the deceased are compelled to follow through the chain of causation back to the originating perpetrators. Although many may seek financial compensation for loss and suffering, sometimes a simple acknowledgement of responsibility and apology may best satisfy the bereaved. The rational argument in the modern world that death may be accidental, an inevitable statistical event for some rather than others at a specific time and place, is not experientially convincing at the individual level.

This has unexpected parallels with Azande witchcraft practice (Evans-Pritchard 1937). For these people of Central Africa, there is no 'natural' death. Coincidence as cause is not sufficient explanation. It is important to ascertain who (involuntarily) caused the death through witchcraft. Once located through the witch doctor, the person responsible simply apologizes, and there's an end of the matter. The 'witch' may have felt envy or anger towards the victim, but is not accused of deliberately causing the discomfort or death (ibid.). Similarly, it could be the case in Britain that the quest for the perpetrators might be in part be assuaged if there were an admission of involvement, when ultimate loss of life was never intended. A simple and genuine apology eases the pain, whether among the Azande or among the inhabitants of the UK. The relatives of victims of the Lockerbie plane crash, the capsizing of the ferry *Herald of Free Enterprise*, medical errors, food poisoning and other disasters may be seeking financial compensation. But as important to these people is a public admission that the deaths were not freak accidents or some 'act of God' (according to insurance parlance), but locatable to human agency.

In the case of my mother, I found myself caught up in the chain of causation of CJD. It went all the way back to the Conservative government. Sometimes I felt like the journalists listening to 'deep throat' in the underground car park in the film *All the Presidents' Men*. One botched burglary, they were told, led all the way to the White House. One seemingly inevitable and almost natural death of a woman in her early seventies, it seemed, went all the way back to political and economic decisions and commercial greed in the meat-rendering business and the intensive industrialization of agriculture, with the blessing of the notorious Ministry of Agriculture, Fisheries and Food (MAFF). The illness turned out to be a topical and politically specific one which linked all the way back to the government in power.[2]

The 1978/9 Labour government had received a report which recommended that offal etc. for animal feed in the meat-rendering industry be heated at a higher temperature, which would have ensured the destruction of the BSE virus. When Thatcher came to power, the rendering lobby asked for and obtained the right to have a lower and hence cheaper temperature, thus ensuring the survival of the virus. Herbivorous animals fed with concentrates which consisted of recycled animal cadavers contracted BSE. The human equivalent is CJD. My mother regularly ate beef and Cornish pasties. Fortunately, I have been a vegetarian since 1984. For years, the government denied any possible links and failed to regulate the beef industry and abattoirs. Unavoidable attention is being devoted to links with the new variant of CJD, notably in the 1998 BSE Labour government inquiry. To date, it seems that the link between the classical CJD, BSE and beef consumption and production is still being 'rendered' invisible, even though the numbers of classical CJD victims also rose during the 1990s.

I may be in search of witches. Like others, the quest is not so much for financial compensation, but for acknowledgement of negligence, if not responsibility. In the case of CJD and the 'accidents' outlined above, recognition of agency by specific persons, however symbolic and ritual the act, is partly precluded by powerful commercial and political interests. As with others who have been bereaved, pain is diverted into thinking of the possibility that one's actions may in some small way lessen the chances of the same events being repeated in future.

Finally, the chapter focuses on the disparity between the perception and therefore treatment of the aged and, by implication, those of younger age categories. In mainstream Britain, an older woman's death could be passed over as just another demographic inevitability among the aged. There is a suspicion raised in this chapter and ethnographic evidence given to show that illness among the over-sixties can pass as 'natural'. Dramatic signs of sickness are systematically overlooked and even deleted without professional consequence, as was the case with my mother.

It appears that fatal illnesses receive more care and attention if suspected among the young. In 1996, the government and the media responded most dramatically to the diagnosis of a new variant of CJD, not only because it was a recent discovery, but, I contend, because it had been located among 'young persons'. The fatal consequences of *Escherichia coli* (E Coli) and *Salmonella* have had less ruinous consequences for food production than BSE and CJD for the British beef industry because, I suggest, the victims of the former have been largely persons of retirement age. The aged are, I can only conclude, more disposable in a society which privileges youth and where the aged are perceived as an economic burden. The years of financial contributions to the welfare state through the working lives of the aged are deleted from public memory and discourse. More importantly, the aged's continuing supportive place in the social and emotional lives of their friends, neighbours and descendants is obliterated in an ideology that cannot cost in financial terms the love and care which the aged give back to those who surround them. The aged are witness to our pasts and sometimes, with time on their hands, they give informed focus and point to the long-term priorities in the hectic lives of those younger than themselves.

Diagnosis

Not only 'untimely' death, but diagnosis of specific illnesses among the aged may be a casual, perfunctory affair for the recognized experts, while those on the ground who witness the minutiae of change and affliction may be crying otherwise. My mother's cause of death was not correctly diagnosed until I sent her brain tissue away for medical research. I knew that this would be the only way of obtaining a specific material diagnosis, and without cost, since researchers welcome the 'free' gift of body parts. For many of her final months and at her death-bed, my mother's doctors and consultants were content with the catch-all term Alzheimer's to describe her mental and physiological deterioration, although there had been some admission that the symptoms did not fit the usual pattern. It was for this reason that I wanted certainty. I had also found a donor card in her handbag, where she had poignantly written over her previous writing, offering her body for science. I interpreted her childlike writing as some 'sign'. She could no longer spell Edinburgh when she had rewritten my address. But I imagined her writing the instructions with forethought and serious intent. The rewriting must have been only a few months before her death, when she had recognized that 'the beast was at the gate'. I wanted to respect her wishes. As it happened, it was good that I never offered her corneas as transplants, as the card had suggested.

Ten months after Bridget's death, in December 1992, I received a letter informing me that she had died of CJD. Like the majority of the general population, I did not know what it was. I had to look it up in a medical encyclopaedia, where I read that only one in 5 million died of this rare disease. Thus my mother's chance diagnosis had dramatically altered the national figures. How many other people past retirement age had died of this without the medical profession having a flicker of doubt or curiosity?

I had already written the first half of this chapter through the months of 1992 after her February death and before the late-December Exocet letter. I had contrasted the differing knowledge, treatment and care found among the range of people associated with a deteriorating individual. The aim was to explore how physical illness in Bridget had been systematically denied by doctor(s) and consultants, whereas friends, siblings, her house-cleaner, neighbours, nurses, health visitors, social workers, tradesmen and daughters knew otherwise. When writing the first draft, I had not realized, although I had vaguely suspected, that the official diagnosis at death was also incorrect. So the chapter has developed in further directions. But the opening sections are still valid and retained below. I have made only minor corrections. The observations are even more poignantly relevant. While I concentrated on the failure of those with diagnostic powers to recognize that there was anything wrong with my mother for about a year, I was not to know until many months after that her fatal illness, which the authorities could no longer deny, was itself incorrectly diagnosed.

Objectified or Intimate Encounters

There are conflicts between the notions of caring within the medical profession, not just between alternative medicine and the prevailing paradigm. This conflict has been historically controlled by a strict division of labour and one which has rested on an ideological gender difference. Although there may be numbers of biological males or females in medical occupations associated with the opposing gender, i.e. male nurses and female doctors, the characteristics of the occupations have been affected by ideological constructs of the masculine and the feminine. This was made clear when nursing was finally recognized in nineteenth-century Britain as a distinct occupation demarcated from the role of the doctor, while also moving away from the benevolent, amateur role epitomized by Florence Nightingale. Eva Gamarnikow documents the founding of the nursing profession and suggests that the patriarchal family was the model for the doctor/father and the nurse/mother (1978). Once the doctors' medical association was reassured that the tasks of nursing were associated with caring, cleaning and domestic-type labour without usurping the medical monopoly of 'scientific' decision-making, the nursing profession was officially recognized.

Whether or not the gender division of labour reproduced in medical care was said to be equal but different, it is clear from the contrasting financial rewards and in the strict hierarchy of command that nursing was and still is undervalued relative to doctoring. Nursing has been associated with domestic labour, hygiene, supportive skills and the expressive or emotional ingredients of caring. The doctor's role has been associated with diagnosis, decision-making, science and reason (cf Holden and Littlewood 1991). Private, personal and emotional qualities are not traditionally associated with the British doctor. Indeed, the doctor is, from the start, encouraged to acquire diagnostic skills through the examination of dead bodies in the early weeks of training. Such a dramatic initiation ensures that the patient is first approached as an insentient, depersonalized and non-speaking object. As far as I know, nurses are not put through a similar brutalizing initiation. If they learn early via the emptying of bedpans, they are immediately confronted with all the nuances of having to reaffirm the dignity and personal identity of an embarrassed, living patient.

The differences between the meanings attached to nurse and doctor in British, if not Western, culture can be explored through cultural representations, as well as through empirical studies of medical and nursing practice. Participants are embedded in the ideological notions of the wider society. They are not entirely free to redefine and create as new their occupational images and tasks. Here dictionary definitions are important clues to cultural meanings. Nursing is a more familiar and comforting noun than doctoring. The former is an all-encompassing activity, whereas doctoring can carry suspect overtones. The *Collins Concise English Dictionary* defines 'nurse' as 'a person, often a woman, who is trained to tend the sick and infirm, assist doctors, etc.'. The verb 'to nurse' is variously defined as 'to tend (the sick) ... to feed (a baby) at the breast . . . to try to cure . . . to clasp fondly . . . to look after (a child), to harbour i.e. to nurse a grudge . . . to give special attention to, esp. in order to promote goodwill' (1982: 772–3). A doctor is defined as someone licensed to practice medicine. The intransitive verb is 'to practise medicine', the transitive is 'to repair or mend . . . to make different in order to deceive . . . to adapt' (ibid.: 328). Thus the common usages and definitions of the two professions carry evocative distinctions.

The nurse and nursing are associated not only with the role of doctor's assistant, but also with the female biological act of breast-feeding and its cultural associations with nurturing and mothering. The suggestion that to nurse may be only an attempt at curing hints at her limitations in power and scientific skills. The definitional representation of the doctor, by contrast, does not suggest scientific failure. But there is the more ominous association of the verb 'to nurse' with deception in common parlance. To nurse a grudge conjures up the association with a female witch. The gender contrast is most apparent in the expressive character of nursing as nurturing or breast-feeding, while 'to doctor' can include the more instrumental and mechanical act of repairing or mending. Here, then, we find the child's gender division between dolls and trains or *Meccano* sets, which, through contrasting demands of the intellect and imagination, facilitate the different gender roles entailed in the game of doctors and nurses.

I have reached out to history and to common cultural meanings to make sense of the experience of caring for and of witnessing the care and treatment of my sick and dying mother. At the end, my mother benefited from the class privilege of being in a luxurious nursing home, where doubtless the staff had better working conditions and were therefore not driven to impatience or even the increasingly apparent bullying in both public and private homes. Moreover, since my mother had been able to stay at home for as long as possible, she had been visited by nurses and others who had greater flexibility and autonomy in their working conditions compared with those who themselves are subject to the rigid and repetitive routines of institutions. Like de Beauvoir's mother's death, it was a relatively easy death, a middle-class death (de Beauvoir 1980).[3]

Experience in Research: the Example of Transport

Originally, the editors approached me because of my research into the aged in both France and England. Many months of participant fieldwork had, it seemed, given me insights into the experience of the aged (Okely 1986b, 1990, 1991, 1994, 1996a). The research had only marginally touched upon severe illness and death, in contrast, for example, to the work of Hockey (1990). I had concentrated on the physically active elderly, in addition to those with less autonomy in retirement homes.

Suddenly, some of the earlier stages in loss of autonomy in transport and personal space which I had meticulously plotted in my research subjects (Okely 1990, 1996a) took on first-hand significance as I witnessed them in my mother's life. What was later seen to be some form of dementia, but then only as some vague emotional disruption, had led the doctor to instruct Bridget to give up driving. Neighbours reported that she seemed absent-minded at the wheel. Some months earlier, she had taken eight hours to drive what should have been a three-hour journey to my sister's. All my earlier descriptions of the hardships for the unmotorized rural elderly in my research on transport were played out in my family. My mother could voice her protests with unbridled emotions, which no research subjects had ever conveyed to me. She hurled her body forward while voicing her frustration. My stomach twisted with anxiety at her despair. If she had been 'an informant', I could have detached myself more effectively from what instead became complete emotional involvement. This is in fact the position of the majority of carers who are relatives or close friends of those they care for. The Conservative government's introduction of 'care in the community' is a euphemism for the taken-for-granted duties of the daughter or spouse.

It was one thing to describe the fear among the elderly of East Anglia of losing their driving licences in conversations with relative strangers, but it was another to listen to my mother's angered protests. I identified utterly with her pain and anger as I faced a woman who had given birth to me at the height of bombing and the siege of Malta, who had crossed continents as an evacuee with two infants. As a young widow, with only lower school certificate and a pittance, Bridget had made a successful career, first as a social worker and then as a university lecturer. Her great indulgence was high-powered cars. Not for her the safe, lady driver's saloon. She devoured motor magazines for the latest souped-up models and was fixated on formula-one racing television programmes. She had something of Toad of Toad Hall when he saw his first motor car. When I was a lecturer at Durham University and living in a windswept mining village, my mother arrived on my doorstep at midday. She had driven all the way from Cornwall that morning. She immediately drove me into Durham city and bought me some basics, like a set of saucepans, for my unfurnished, stark abode. I was sleeping on a piece of foam rubber I had bought in the market. My mother, as was her wont, gave me a little luxury. She had cared for me in infancy and continued in some ways, as I lived as an exile, with all the anxiety of a nine-month temporary lectureship.

Now, confronted by her own frailty and diminishing autonomy, it was my turn to be strong. I had to witness her growing helplessness as fate and, what no one guessed, the fatal illness took their surreptitious course. Bridget's arguments were utterly reasonable. Her still powerful intellect responded with full force: she had had no accident, she drove slowly, whereas the young male tearaways who sped round the corner at the back of her house had caused several crashes. One had smashed into her huge stone wall. They were fast and reckless, but they had not been banned from driving.

I became quite convinced by the implications of her detailed observations. It seems that older women, classified as doddery, are penalized, while young men, perceived as activated by 'natural' masculine test-osterone, can get away with it. The aged woman is seen as unable to choose to drive correctly, while a young man's recklessness is seen as wilful and therefore changeable through intent. Here were glimpses into the way youth in Western capitalism, especially young men, are privileged actors and allowed relative murderous freedom. Few motoring deaths are caused by aged drivers, but they are increasingly the subject of medical panics and controls. Few drivers who have killed on the roads are subject to really punitive fines, bans and long-term prison sentences. Frailty and a slow pace, while innocuously combined with gentleness, are seen as more bothersome or threatening than aggression and egotism in young (male) bodies behind the wheel. There are parallels again with the quality of hard-edged competence idealized in doctors, while softness and gentleness in caring are undervalued morally, politically and financially.

In my East Anglian research (Okely 1991, 1996a), I found that the rural elderly often lived in terror of losing their licence, so afraid they were of being seen driving overcautiously or slightly distractedly. They chose to drive by the back lanes away from police surveillance and at hours when the traffic was minimal. The only major accident involving the elderly which occurred in my field area was when a speeding police car failed to stop at an isolated crossroads and killed an elderly couple who had the right of way and were driving correctly. The policeman got away with a caution. A ban, it was said, would ruin his career and he had had a lot on his mind!

Doctors in Collision with Grounded Informants

Standard handbooks of diagnosis for doctors have a section on Alzheimer's disease. In this, doctors are advised to take note of the comments and observations of relatives and friends of the afflicted. Despite this and some changes in medical practice, doctors are primarily trained to treat the patient as a body and object where evidence which cannot be physio-logically tested is suspect. The patient is unsurprisingly the last person to volunteer dementia. But the 'untrained' amateurs who surround her and who have known her intimately for years should be seen as a vital source of information. My sister and I responded to alarmed comments from friends in my mother's village, together with personal observations of illogical behaviour. We telephoned the doctor and registered our unease. She had already been seeing him regularly in an attempt to get a diagnosis for her loss of bladder control. She had waited months for various appointments with consultants. On one occasion she had to travel from Cornwall to Bristol for some complex tests with 'high-tech' equipment. No one seemed to come up with a specific diagnosis. The consultants were looking for material evidence of problems in the lower body. They were not concerned with the whole being. One possibility eventually suggested was a bladder operation. For this there would be several years on the waiting list. The alternative was to pay for it privately. It was still unclear whether this would be worthwhile, since, after the bladder was tightened, we were informed that there might be the need for daily extractions of urine with a catheter.

My mother's state of mind had become increasingly erratic. This was noticed by the weekly cleaner, friends and myself. Yet the doctor assured us that there was nothing wrong with her mentally. She just seemed to be 'rather emotional'. Her descriptions of strange tinglings in her legs were apparently inevitable at her age. His proof of her normality was the administration of a formulaic question-and-answer test for dementia, which included questions about the informant's age and the name of the prime minister. Bridget, who continued to read and study after her retirement (for example, she took up the study of archaeology and attended courses at Exeter University), came out with top marks on the doctor's test. Her general practitioner (GP) insisted to my sister and me that there was nothing physically wrong with her.

Bridget was both insulted and amused at the simplicity of the test. But, if doctors were not in thrall to such standardization, which they believe proves some magical scientistic replicability in laboratory-type conditions, more information would be there to be gleaned. My mother had developed brilliant strategies at not giving the day of the week. She declared that, as a retired person, these things were largely irrelevant. When asked who was the current prime minister, she blasted the doctor with her political and historical knowledge: 'Do you want me to talk about Lloyd George, Disraeli, Churchill, Macmillan, Heath, Wilson or do you mean the bitch?' Among her own video recordings of wildlife programmes and archaeology discussions, I found the recording of Thatcher's tearful departure from Downing Street, an historic moment which my mother must have wanted permanently on tape and replayed with glee.

But in dialogue with the GP it may have been that she could not have filled in the details. Could she still remember the year Thatcher was first elected? This was once a date she had engraved on her memory as the start of the destruction of the welfare state, which she had worked for and lectured about for decades. She had never been a Conservative, but, after years working in a Labour fiefdom, she was disillusioned and, as a feminist, had naïve hopes for a woman prime minister. She was soon to regret that one 1979 vote. Intellectual powers and knowledge in aged patients may become distracting to GPs who have not been alerted to their diversity. Moreover, others in good health and younger would not be deemed demented if they could not name the prime minister. I suppose my mother was even more of an exception in this rural retreat (yet in the sort of location to which the middle-class aged are retiring in increasing numbers). When the estate agents looked over my mother's property after her death, the only unequivocal advice was to remove all her books, as they devalued the property and would put off potential buyers! As it happened, the eventual buyers insisted that the fitted bookshelves remain.

In swapping notes with a friend whose father had been a leading editor at Oxford University Press, I found similar experiences about the way the aged are homogenized as simple-minded once they are no longer seen as earning their living. Delia's father had shown worrying mental deterioration but, like my mother, had passed the GP's little test and the daughter had been told there was nothing wrong. She said the real proof would have been if her father had been asked to translate, as was his usual skill, the day's copy of *The Times* into Greek.

More Testing

Some weeks before the bladder operation, of which the doctor had approved, in desperation, I demanded that he arrange an appointment with a psychiatric consultant in order to find out whether her agitated and distracted behaviour was caused by nervous distress at her incontinence or, incipient dementia, as I and others close to her continued to suspect. We felt that it was no good my mother spending over £6000 in a private operation, if she would in future be intellectually incapable of inserting a catheter. It was difficult to persuade her to agree. I telephoned the doctor from Edinburgh and he said she would have to agree to it. It would be possible for a home visit by the consultant. Bridget used every available argument to resist, and finally consented to an appointment, on the condition that I was there. When she finished our phone call, the visiting neighbour told me later that my mother wept inconsolably at the humiliation. Possibly, she was frightened at the implications of such an examination. She was, it became increasingly clear, fully alert to her deterioration.

In the middle of my university term, I rearranged my teaching hours and took a nine hours' train journey from Edinburgh to Cornwall. When I arrived by taxi from the station, for the first time not met by her in the car, she had taken considerable trouble to look elegant and in control. Retrospectively, I weep at the huge effort it must have entailed.

Wised up to her forthcoming ordeal, my mother had prepared her lines well.

> I shall go and pick a bunch of all the different flowers in my garden and ask him to tell me the Latin names for them. If, as I suspect, he won't be able to, I shall ask him why he thinks he ought to be testing me. I shall ask him to tell me how many angels can dance on a penny.

Already the famous philosophical phrase about 'angels on a pin' had been transmuted. Later, she could not remember even the word penny, but said she would ask the doctor how many angels could dance on 'one of those round things', and she drew a circle on the tea table. Her listeners on this subsequent occasion were visitors from the Women's Institute. They were baffled, never having heard of the original cultural reference. But again I now note the Herculean effort my mother was making to communicate ideas. Gesture replaced the word penny.

The next day, a Friday, the consultant arrived, accompanied by a student. I was appalled that, after all my delicate negotiations, he had taken such a risk. The young medical student's additional presence might jeopardize the whole venture, if my mother became alarmed at being treated as a specimen. The consultant said he would make just one request from my mother: that the student be allowed to accompany him at his work. Bridget reacted magnificently; she beamed with approval, saying that she had taught students for many years and appreciated that they needed to learn through practical experience. The nervous young man was treated to a welcoming handshake before what would turn out to be a humiliating two hours of tests for numerical, spatial, temporal and other cognitive skills. I was asked to wait outside in the garden.

The consultant was a sensitive and empathetic person. It seemed from the neighbour who went in to make the coffee that he treated my mother with care and gentleness. He had already asked me detailed questions about her condition and immediate circumstances. I respected his diagnosis because it was combined with desire for knowledge about the whole person, her past and present. My mother did not resent him in the way that she was suspicious of her GP. I reasoned later and somewhat cynically that specialism in geriatrics and this kind of psychiatry was one of the least esteemed in the medical hierarchy, so that it attracted those who were genuinely concerned, and not obsessed with the prestige and public adulation that comes with innovative, technology-driven medicine, such as transplants and fertility. There is no lasting cure for old age, so the geriatric specialist is not credited with an all-powerful scientific control.

The consultant emerged into the garden, took me aside and, in an agitated fashion, informed me that my mother had deteriorated in every sphere — abstract, concrete and other intellectual capabilities. The only notable qualities remaining, he said, were her social skills, which were used to conceal her incapacities. 'The good thing is that she doesn't recognize her difficulties.' He implied that she was blissfully ignorant and therefore content. Here was his most fundamental error in diagnosis. Others who had known her well or who had spent extended time with her had watched her torment of confronting the erratic minutiae of losses in once taken-for-granted knowledge and daily practices.

The consultant used the word 'Alzheimer's' to Sally, my mother's domestic cleaner, who had become a close confidante and friend. To me he used the word 'dementia', saying the former was just a catch-all term. Before his diagnosis, he had recommended that we persuade her to move into a home, but now, made aware, through the home visit, how much she liked the house, garden and independence, he declared that she was entitled, under the community care scheme, to have up to eight hours of visits and home support a day. At first, this seemed a great relief. My sister and I had wanted our mother to be able to stay as long as possible in her home. I made plans for a full support system and was informed of the procedures, via the GP, social services and home-help schemes. In practice, it transpired that these were only formal rights, and largely unavailable. The authorities increasingly targeted the aged for cuts in services, regardless of formal legal obligations. By the late 1990s, the social care of the aged has been silently wiped from the public agenda.

My mother emerged and walked around the garden. Sally, who had been told the diagnosis by the consultant, whispered the dreaded word 'Alzheimer's' with tears in her eyes. She was so shocked, she walked straight back to the village. Meanwhile, Mum came up to me, with a piece of honeysuckle: 'Isn't it beautiful,' she said. 'What's it called?' I asked. Instead of having to acknowledge her humiliating and frightening memory loss of this common plant, let alone the Latin name, she, until the previous year the County Organizer of the National Garden Scheme, thrust the honeysuckle under my nose with a disingenuous smile: 'Smell it,' she said. Thus she used her social intelligence to silence and divert me from a recognition in the public sphere of her alarming memory loss. For the rest of the day, little was said about the consultant's visit. I telephoned my sister and aunts discretely from the portable telephone. They cried.

Life, not Opera

That night, I was woken up by the noises of movement in my mother's bedroom below. I went down, asking why she wasn't in bed. 'I'm having a little weep,' she said. 'The consultant said there was a touch of Alzheimer's when he was testing me. If that's the case, I'm finished . . . The beast is at the gate. The beast is at the gate . . . I don't want to be a vegetable in an armchair. I've seen too many old dears in homes.' Before becoming a lecturer, she had been responsible for old people's welfare in a large London borough. She had read every postwar government report on the elderly, as well as sociological studies. They lined the shelves of her bedroom, along with studies of mental handicap, the disabled and the history of the welfare state. She had taught health visitors and nurses and lectured in social administration. She, like me, was confronting the agony of becoming a participant subject in a topic previously researched by her through observation rather than membership.

At 3 a.m. in my mother's bedroom, I felt that I was a performer in a tragic opera. She had brought us up on opera. My sister and I were taken to our first, *Cosi Fan Tutti*, at the Edinburgh Festival when we were both under fifteen. She had been to all the great performances in pre-war Berlin opera-houses. She had been a member of a choral group and sung in a performance of Tippet's *Child of Our Time* in Guildford Cathedral. Her drawing-room had complete sets of opera recordings, as well as many of the scores. She loved her 'state-of-the-art' stereo, on which Wagner, Mozart, Verdi or Tippett could be played at maximum volume, with no neighbours to disturb on the hill.

At the same time, in that dark night of her bedroom, I was telling myself that this was real life and the kind of drama which opera deals with, except that with opera there is aesthetic and emotional catharsis. There could be no other moment when the truth could be more directly faced. I had to talk to my mother about her future death. On the walls were photographs of my sister and me as babies. This time I had really grown up. Using the example of a friend, whose husband had developed dementia and from whom she had withheld antibiotics when he got pneumonia, I assured my mother that my sister and I would do the same if she had lost her mind and if it was ever in our power. She quietened down and seemed silently comforted. She was thinking hard. I also consoled her that this illness brought no pain, unlike cancer, and, however detached she was mentally, she would not suffer such horrors.

The next afternoon, Bridget found her recording of Britten's opera *Billy Budd* and pointed to the section in the text where Billy sings the night before he is to be 'hanged and then thrown overboard'. She asked me to locate it on the disc and she read the words with total concentration as she listened to the tragic theme. She said, 'This is what it's like now. When you have so many plans ahead and they are never to be.' She matched her emotions and conditions to the fate of the innocent in the opera.

'They'll lash me in hammock, drop me deep, Fathoms down, fathoms – how I'll dream fast asleep. I feel it stealing now, . . . roll me over fair. I'm sleepy and the oozy weeds about me twist.
. . . Farewell to this grand rough world! . . . no more sea, no looking down from the heights to the depths. But I've sighted a sail in the storm, the far shining sail that's not fate, and I'm contented, I've seen where she's bound for. She has a land of her own where she'll anchor forever. Oh, I'm contented. Don't matter now being hanged, or being forgotten and caught in the weeds. Don't matter now. I'm strong and I know it, and I'll stay strong, . . . and that's all . . . and that's enough'. (Foster and Crozier 1951)

She did not weep, but hunched forward at the table, a vulnerable figure. I had a fleeting image of her as the beautiful and wild young Englishwoman who danced the length of the beer tables in pre-war Germany, to ecstatic accompaniment. Thus she had captivated my father, also working in Berlin.

I could not begin to console her or pretend her future was otherwise.

Retrospectively, I take comfort in the fact that I was there as a witness and one who shared some of her suffering. However great her mental deterioration, she was imbued with the full comprehension of her destiny. The consultant had been curiously naïve to suggest that she was blissfully unaware of her depleted intellectual abilities.

Medical Care(lessness)

What was to be more bewildering were the consultant's ensuing errors after his home visit, followed by a failure to minimize the effects. The technical tests administered to my mother during that visit, which I had arranged with considerable difficulty, were destroyed. They had provided detailed evidence of the particular form of mental deterioration and, even if my mother was regarded as just another elderly patient, the material would, it now transpires, have been scientifically valuable for ongoing research. Having typed them up, the consultant 'accidentally' erased them from the computer before they could be stored and printed. It is extraordinary that no attempt was made to recall the material from memory of the two-hour face-to-face encounter. The handwritten notes had been destroyed. Comparable evidence among anyone under fifty, let alone under twenty years old, would have been more conscientiously written up, and certainly reconstituted from memory soon after the negligent deletion from a computer screen. The secretary I spoke to on the telephone seemed unembarrassed and showed no interest in my requests for the reconstruction of just a few shreds of the evidence.

After the consultant had informed me of my mother's deterioration, we discussed whether she should still go ahead with the bladder operation. I described how she had been geared up for this for months and that it might emotionally destroy her if, at five days' notice, it were to be cancelled. It would also confirm that somehow any improvement in the quality of her life would seem irrelevant. It was agreed that the operation could go ahead. Since it was private, there was probably not the same attention made to decision-making.

Again, there are consequences for the differential attention paid to illness among the aged in contrast to those of younger age. The casualness about permitting her operation has had grave consequences for others, whether or not people 'care' about the premature death of the aged. The fact that my mother had a transmissible illness may have had fatal consequences for others. I doubt if anyone has dared to follow this up. It is said that surgical instruments cannot be sterilized in the normal fashion to kill off the CJD organism. It is not at all certain as to whether the operating implements used on my mother were free of contamination by the standard sterilization techniques applied before use on any subsequent patient on the operating table. The elaborate precautions now shown to be necessary for dealing with BSE contamination in the laboratory and furnace are warnings enough. With a certain cynicism, I fear that interest in CJD among those aged over 65 may only emerge if it is thought that the young are put at risk from the bodies of the aged.

The operation on my mother proved to be a disaster; far from improving the mechanism of the bladder, it destroyed any vestiges of control. I was advised that a catheter was now essential. When I fetched Bridget after the week's convalescence, her mental state had deteriorated dramatically. I wonder now if that was due to the massive blast of anaesthetic affecting a brain already punctured by CJD. I told her I was picking her up in her car. She saw me in it and said that she had one like it. We filled up with petrol on the way. As we drove out of the garage, she advised me to fill up with petrol. There was a poignantly passive agreement when I pointed out we had just done so. As was to be the pattern for the ensuing months, she always conceded the argument without question. I think now that she was very frightened by any glimmer of the confusion with which she must have been struggling.

In Limbo

Much of the detail of the months of the summer with her are too painful to recall or write about. There was sweet gentleness as this once forceful, independent and energetic woman complied with every one of my increasingly impatient remonstrations. I had no idea that this was a rapid, fatal illness. The medical representatives, including the consultant who visited, assured me that her mental state was merely a temporary result of the anaesthetic, which would wear off in a few weeks. The catheter disaster was described as merely unfortunate.

Encouraged by these professional diagnoses, I began to believe in her eventual mental recovery. I behaved as if reasoned argument with her would correct her muddles. I was also trying to establish a simple routine which I imagined would be possible for her to adhere to, so that she could remain in her own home, once I had to return to lecturing. A county organizer for the home helps visited. I presented her with a detailed list of the possible hazards any incoming carer would have to watch out for in the company of my mother. For example, Bridget would amass all the keys to the interior and exterior doors. It would then be a desperate task to match the different keys to the various doors and then lock up the back, front, garden and patio doors. She would remove washing from the machine, hang it up on the line, then bring it in five minutes later and place it still wet back in the machine. A day or so later, I would discover it all mouldy.

Thus the years of routine and organization, for which Bridget had been renowned at work and home, were now speeded-up travesties of past purpose. She had always prided herself on her organization skills. She had travelled around the world, sometimes with husband and two daughters. 'I'm a brilliant packer.' And she was right, as she squeezed yet more perfectly folded items into my suitcase the night before I left home at nineteen to study in Paris.

Bodily Invasions and the Losing of Autonomy

That post-operation summer in Cornwall, the medical and caring complexities increased. I had respected my mother's privacy with regard to the catheter. The nurses at the convalescent home had said that she had been instructed as to how to use it, although they had expressed scepticism as to her competence. This observation I wished to underestimate, especially since the professionals further up the hierarchy had been so reassuring as to the merely temporary nature of her mental confusions. My mother convinced me in her quiet, dignified way that she was managing all right. I never checked up. I did not want to invade the privacy of my mother's body. The first alarm came when she showed me almost the entire collection of spare tubes stuck with strips of plaster on to her thigh. The tubes were totally unconnected to anything above. There was no sign of a urine bag. Again, I persisted with logical, and increasingly exasperated, reasoning that the catheter had to be connected to the tubes and urine bag. I was clinging to the doctor's reassurances that her problems were a minor aberration. It seemed odd, given the cognitive tests he administered before the operation. Perhaps he had forgotten his findings, once they had been erased from his computer.

Whatever her long-term prognosis, soon the carpets were being marked by watery trails. It was obvious there was no working bag for the urine. I had no idea how to connect the different tubes. I was alone and useless. It was a Saturday of the Summer Bank Holiday weekend. I telephoned the emergency number for the on-duty GP for advice. The doctor's wife answered the phone. She would not put me through to anyone else. I could hear excited children's voices; there must have been a special party going on. Was this another example of the welfare of (healthy) children having priority over the frail elderly?

The unidentified woman told me the request was trivial and suggested that I should drive my mother ten miles to the nearest casualty section of a hospital. I explained that she was emotionally and mentally distressed, that she denied there was a problem and that there was no way I could force her bodily into the vehicle, if she refused to move. I rang off in tears. Coming up from the village below were the multiple noises of the village fête. I was terrified by the contrast between summer jollities and the alienation of being a long way from anyone who could help. The position of those daughter carers who devote their entire existence to ailing parents became even more vivid (Lewis and Meredith 1988; Hockey and James 1993). At least I had a job, an alternative identity, I reminded myself, even though my plans for writing over the summer had disintegrated. It wasn't that Bridget was so domestically demanding, it was the unpre-dictability of her actions and the illogicality of her statements which became more and more distressing. The mother who had been so forceful, original and independent was disappearing behind what still appeared to be a strong body. She was living in different, strange worlds, and yet the professionals insisted otherwise. The intimate carers face their own madness when their intuitive experience is undermined by the experts who insist that all is well.

In desperation, I telephoned the local hospital and, in contrast to the doctor's wife, an unidentified and alert receptionist put me through to the matron of a geriatric ward. That matron saved me, saved my sanity. She told me to collect up the spare bits of the catheter and bring them to the telephone. Then she talked me through the fixing, step by step. She had soul as well as technical information. She urged me to be strong as I wept with relief. She told me that I had the right to ask for a district nurse through the GP. She advised me next time to pull rank and name myself as doctor. This voice of warmth without a face down the telephone kept me whole that day. I did not break down in front of my mother. Many months after my mother's death, one of her former colleagues in nursing studies advised me to write an official complaint about my treatment by the GP and spouse. But, as the authorities know too well, the carers have little heart to go through the ordeal of challenging bureaucratic indifference, especially when they are coping with new griefs.

The next day, my mother came to my bedroom very frightened. This time she had pulled out the balloon shape of the catheter from her urinary tract. She couldn't understand how it had been there in the first place and why it was so large. This time I got through to a male voice, another GP. I pulled rank as 'doctor' and demanded a health visitor. Here the title of expert worked like a charm with another expert. The humble daughter carer had no power. The health visitor came an hour later and had all the tenderness and care that was needed. My mother said how she trusted her. We were advised against the catheter altogether, if it came out again. It was the traditional kindness of nursing care that worked. Mother and daughter calmed down. The gentle health visitor also warned me of the seriousness of my mother's mental disability. She could not see any long-term future for my mother staying in her own home.

But the local doctor still adopted an optimistic stance. Both he and a visiting social worker insisted to me that she would not be obliged to leave her house, without her consent. My sister, whom I regularly telephoned, was baffled as to what to plan. My mother had objected to all the welfare visitors I was lining up. True to decades of life experience, she wanted to be on her own. She could not understand this need for such a disruption. I welcomed the visitors because I hoped the promised backup after my departure would extend the time for autonomy in her own space. By this stage, my mother could neither shop nor cook. When I prepared meals, she would forget midway and wander off. She had long been unable to key in numbers on the telephone. She could not understand the narratives and chronology of television programmes. Her fear of the television and hallucinatory response matched the subsequent observations of new-variant CJD victims. I would stand over her as she copied her signature for cheques in a childlike scrawl. Once she gazed at her writing and remarked how clumsy it looked. She recognized that there was an incompatibility between what she envisioned and that which the hand enacted. The bank began to query the signature.

'Faith in the possibility of individual freedom is always vulnerable to the harsh realities of human dependency, and to the tension between continuity and change' (Hockey and James 1993: 112). Bridget, I now more fully realize, was having to confront the abandonment of her principles and practice of autonomy. This was something which had once been demanded of her, especially after she found herself a widow with minimum money and education in the bleak 1950s – an era that idolized the nuclear family, demonized working mothers with 'latchkey' children and stigmatized the spinster or single mother. In those days, a lone woman, even with employment, could not get a mortgage. My grandmother, with some private income, acted as guarantor. All of a sudden, after years of work, a university pension and financial security, Bridget was having to be a dependent again. The invisible disease may have been taking control, but she was now subject to the social surveillance directed towards the aged. Medical surveillance is another matter and more likely to be available to those with younger bodies.

The visiting social worker showed brilliant initiative. At first, Bridget refused to come out of her room to meet him. Finally, she appeared in her dressing gown. She continued to remonstrate. I slipped in somewhere that my mother had once been a social worker. My mother recalled her overall responsibility for the elderly in an entire London Borough in the 1950s. The social worker then asked if, in her past experience, she would have thought it right to check up on someone who had just had a major operation. Bridget got the point, giggled, agreed and made friends.

Again, as with the health visitor and the ward sister on the phone, it was practical, grounded knowledge, combined with compassion, which eased both carer and cared for. Perhaps a case could be made for the long-term 'efficiency' of such informal encounters. Compassion in caring, dare I suggest to the health trusts, should be costed. It pays in the long run, even while to date it is rendered financially invisible on the bottom line.

Staying at Home

From my long-term research in both England and France, I believed that the aged should be allowed to stay as long as possible in their own familiar surroundings. Bridget loved her garden. She had spectacular views from every window. After she died, I found dozens of photos of the vistas taken in all seasons and at all times of the day. There were mists of dawn, oncoming night, summer splendour and winter austerity. One view I especially liked had the defunct tin-mine chimney at which I had often gazed as I completed my doctorate one long summer. Then my mother took entire responsibility for the domestic chores. She had just retired from her university post while I was facing my first university lectureship. Her care eased the anxiety.

My mother's garden had been a bumpy field fifteen years before. Her post-retirement years had created an extravagant, exotic Eden. There were meandering paths, a fish-pond and waterfall, wooded areas, fruit cages, heathers and roses and two special trees, each planted in celebration of my sister's sons born in Brazil. Her newly enhanced expertise brought her county-wide connections. We couldn't take her away from this dream place until all forms of community care had been tried.

The house, which she had designed, was also a mnemonic space. One evening, I got her to talk through her ornaments displayed in the hall. The immediacy of the objects triggered vivid reminiscences of her travels: this vase came from Estonia, there were souvenirs from China, Egypt and our shared rail trip around India. The remarkable narratives and her enjoyment in their telling convinced me, however ill-informed, that she could be mending, that she might at least return to the pre-operation level of abilities.

She certainly never forgot people's identities. The standard signs of Alzheimer's were not present. No one considered any other type of ailment. At the end of the vacation, I left her in the hands of the welfare state, believing that she would have a full backup. But there had already been signs of poor services. After I presented the home-help organizer with the lists of hazards for helpers to watch for, the woman phoned back, asking if I would consent to the list being presented to persons in the county hierarchy. She explained that it was increasingly difficult to convince them as to what community care actually entailed. She believed that my stark list might jolt them into some realization. Here again, we find the example of decision-makers as experts at the apex being divorced from day-to-day practice and grounded knowledge. My list could only have emerged from days, if not weeks, of experiencing the detailed duties of care.

Departure

My mother's increasing and dramatic deterioration became a subject of gossip and near scandal in the village. She would appear semi-clothed. She presented friends with bags of rubbish as presents. It was such eccentricity in the public sphere which encouraged gossip about the scandal of her not being put in a home much earlier. The meals-on-wheels deliverers would return the next day to find that the food had been uneaten and the cling film was still on her coffee cup. Her friend and house cleaner lived her own agonies watching the disintegration and taking the major responsibility. We telephoned regularly. One night my mother fell into the bath and lay there all night. Her body was severely bruised. Finally, one of the GPs, who had again applied the standard test, informed us that she really had deteriorated and that a nursing home was the only option. My mother informed the social worker that she had 2.5 children. This was the former sociology lecturer giving us a national family average. There was therefore a continuing intellectual struggle to hold on to some empirical truths.

My sister and aunt in her eighties found a wonderful, but extremely costly, private nursing home. I travelled from Scotland to drive her to Wiltshire. She had convinced everyone that she was packed and ready for this 'holiday'. In the suitcase, I found neatly folded old pillows, long discarded curtains and rags. As we were leaving, Bridget pulled helplessly at the patio doors. My first reaction was to refuse to go through the elaborate unlocking and relocking. We were terribly late. I now thank all the gods that I repressed my impatience. My mother had one long and intense gaze at the gardens and little hills to which she would never return.

On the long drive, she became increasingly terrified by the lights of oncoming cars and would attempt to get out. I now realize from others' symptoms that she was seriously hallucinating. The next day I had to prepare to fly to a conference in Chicago.

At the nursing home, the room was pleasant but stark, because I had grabbed only a few pictures. My sister and aunt had been astute in their choice of home. They had visited half a dozen. The staff were gentle and tender. They did not seem to infantilize her, as has been found generally among caring staff (Hockey and James 1993). I was proud that her declared years of teaching health visitors and mixing with anyone as equal endeared her to the staff. They uniquely brought her to join them for their morning coffee together. Most of the other relatively wealthy residents were less favoured, partly because they patronized the staff as domestic servants.

Neither my sister Elaine nor I knew in November that our mother had less than three months to live. We were engulfed by the financial commitments and the need to sell the house to pay for the fees, which began to overtake her university pension. Because Alzheimer's had been diagnosed, we envisaged years of blankness. In preparing her house for sale, I spent just two afternoons back and forth between Scotland and Cornwall with her. I returned with ornaments, rugs, pictures and photo albums. We spoke of each framed photo – of her mother, nanny, husband – 'It was so long ago,' she cried, as she saw the image of my father, who had died of polio in his mid-thirties. 'Do you remember Uncle Eric?' I asked, as I showed her the photo of her with him receiving an OBE at Buckingham Palace. 'How could I forget?' she cried. She recognized them all. It was a cathartic act of memory. When I showed her a Monet landscape painting with rich vegetation in southern France, she said that it needed 'cutting back' or pruning. We both smiled. Here was the gardener talking in transposed context. She said in all seriousness that she would be able to absail out of the window. The mind was working in subtle ways for escape from confinement.

My sister subsequently crammed the room with a familiar coffee table, paintings and Bridget's ornaments collected from around the globe. All this had an unexpected effect. The staff found her room a welcoming and interesting place to sit in. They were fascinated by the many photo albums, where they could see her in childhood with relatives, or in Berlin or the Black Forest, and then in Malta as a young bride. There were images of her with two infant daughters in southern Africa, then as a London social worker, or lined up with her university students. On the walls we hung the framed wedding photo of her on the arm of her father and then the more recent picture meeting the Queen Mother; the patron of the National Garden Scheme. When friends and relatives visited, the staff would try to spot them from the albums. Thus her individual and extended biography was reconstructed by strangers. The matron joked with me how my mother would confide in the staff, including the matron, about another certain nursing home (and she confusedly named the one she was in). She told them that she'd heard that the matron there was 'an absolute bitch' and that she was glad that she was not there.

At my last visit when I could engage in some conversation, however disconnected, she continued to recognize me. There was no loss of memory there, as is said to be the case with Alzheimer's. Her continuing subscription to *The Times* was no proof of ability to read. She commented on the pictures with incoherent phrases. With a gentle smile, she told me of little animals that she had seen climbing up the staircase. She stood at the window and delighted in the rooks and trees. I brought in my cassette radio and played arias of her favourite singer, Maria Callas. Bridget became entranced and swayed in an ecstasy I was forever comforted in giving her. Since that day, I have been unable to listen to the same tape. My sister purchased a player with automatic replay.

Bridget was still able to answer the phone weeks before the end, although she couldn't replace it. Months after her death, I received my Edinburgh phone bill with the date, duration and exact cost of what I learned later was to be the last time I ever conversed with my mother.

The days she lay dying, she had ceased to speak. It seemed that she chose to die by refusing all food and liquid. Now it may also be that her last days may have been marked by muscular incapacity to swallow and speak. The doctor and matron, with our consent, respected what seemed to be her wishes and we kept vigil in turn. Malcolm, a student of 25 years back, and his wife Mary also sat up with her. Mary, a physiotherapist, brought different-smelling herbs and to my surprise explained how she communicated with Bridget by getting her to respond with eye flickers. We had known nothing of this before. The matron and nursing assistants showed all the appropriate compassion and sensitivity. One showed tears when we asked for scissors to take a lock of her hair, as we sat by her, just recently dead. But how could the young male doctor stand with his back to my mother's body, swaying on his heels, and bellow bureaucratic instructions to us, as if the room were now his office? She had died just half an hour ago. So much for any recent 'training' in ethics and human relations at modern medical schools. No second-year anthropology undergraduate would behave with such abomination. Yet the dominant ideology values such medics over 'useless' social scientists, who are sensitized to alternative ways of being in many contexts. The doctor's words disrupted our last profound experience with our mother. Over and beyond his procedural violence, Elaine and I were fixated on the snow which had fluttered for a few minutes outside and was just as suddenly gone.

She's gone for ever.
I know when one is dead and when one lives;
She's dead as earth. Lend me a looking glass;
If that her breath will mist or stain the stone,
Why then she lives.

(Shakespeare, *King Lear*)

The death certificate gave the causes as pneumonia and Alzheimer's. It is possible the young doctor was uneasy about the fact that we had asked that she be given neither drips nor force-feeding at the last. The woman doctor (a gender coincidence?) on duty in the days before had sounded us out.

Although Bridget was closely watched over in this relatively luxurious nursing home, being seen by a consultant weekly and the doctors more often, no one suspected anything other than Alzheimer's. Soon after her arrival, we had to consent to her being given tranquillizers to stop her night wandering. Then the shaking increased. It was thought that this was a side-effect, so the medication was withdrawn. There was no way she could have walked far on her own by now. When I asked why she shook so much as they tried to take her to the bathroom, and when she was bedridden, I was informed that this was because the drugs were still in her system weeks later. There was one recognition; the consultant informed my sister that he had rarely seen such rapid deterioration. But there was no follow-up. By contrast, similar symptoms in persons under fifty have been a subject of medical curiosity, however inept in some cases. For example, one young woman with CJD was subjected to electric-shock treatment, thanks to private medical expertise.

The Aftermath

The notification, many months later, that my mother had died of the 'rare' CJD opened another Pandora's box. It locked into the scandal of the Ministry of Agriculture's permitted farming practices and BSE. Her death became part of a political agenda. It was more than an individual case of care but also cause and diagnosis. Thus, by a second irony, I have been interlocked with my earlier research, which not only covered the elderly but also the changes in farming brought about by the Common Agricultural Policy. My Kayberry lecture (Okely 1996b: 206–33), which in part honoured a Normandy farming woman who rejected modern and industrialized factory farming and concentrates for her cows, was attended by my mother in 1989. This was Bridget's last year when it could be said that she was still in control of her life as an active, intelligent and autonomous, healthy woman. But she was a regular eater of beef. Is there no escape from the way one's personal experience links up with larger political events?

I had the surrealist experience, as a member of the university staff, of being interviewed at the Edinburgh University CJD research unit in 1993. The relatives of everyone who died of this disease are interviewed. By then, I had done a fair amount of detective work and had accumulated a box full of news cuttings. All my suggestions that there were links with beef were vehemently denied, doubtless because of the fear of media intervention. I inwardly wondered about the political pressures from the financiers of this research. It was, of course, only three years later that the new CJD variant was first named from this unit. In the interview room there was a map pinpointing all the CJD cases in the UK in recent years. There was no mark where my mother had lived for fifteen years. I drew attention to their possible conflation of place of death with place of residence.

One of the researchers found it problematic trying to blind me with scientific arguments about why there was no link with beef. He insisted that I was mistaken to suggest that the elderly may have been consistently misdiagnosed. He cited some research in Switzerland from the 1950s or 1960s, where apparently every brain tissue of the aged in residential homes had been tested for CJD and the percentage was no greater. When I pointed out that this research had been conducted outside Britain and before the BSE crisis and was not therefore compelling evidence, he fell silent.

We swung between the personal, emotionally charged recognition of my daughter identity and my position at the university as a Reader and therefore in a higher position in the university hierarchy. As bereaved daughter, I was treated as an amateur and non-scientist. Again, then, in this different context, local knowledge or even that from another non-medical discipline is hardly taken seriously. More significantly, the death of an aged person draws less medical, scientific, and social attention than the death of the young.

> The weight of this sad time we must obey;
> Speak what we feel, not what we ought to say.
> The oldest hath borne most: we that are young,
> Shall never see so much . . .

> (Shakespeare, *King Lear*)

Notes

1. A more directly involved autobiographical case of illness is presented by David Brooks, (1993) who describes his experience of the anthropologist as patient.

2. The following is a copy of the full version of the letter which I sent to *The Guardian*, shortly after the announcement in 1996 by Dorrel of the link between the new-variant CJD and BSE. Part of the letter was published:

Sir,

The new strain of the CJD found among the 'young' does not exclude a connection between BSE and the traditional strain. We are reassured that the chances of getting CJD are 'one in a million'. I suggest that this reflects more the chances of the over 60s being correctly diagnosed. The aged are dismissed as 'naturally' frail. Their untimely and agonising deaths are not treated as seriously. My mother died of CJD in 1992 aged 73. This was only diagnosed because her two daughters acted against all the odds to have her brain tissue examined.

Eighteen months before her death, we repeatedly approached her G.P. insisting that something was wrong. As a former university lecturer, she outwitted him in answers to simplistic intelligence questions. Our misgivings were dismissed and she was encouraged to proceed with a bladder operation for incontinence. Eventually she was admitted to a residential home and seen weekly by doctors and a consultant. Despite other symptoms, her death certificate records Alzheimer's. It took many phone calls before I could find anyone who would accept her brain for research; the only way to get a correct diagnosis. How many other active, otherwise healthy people past retirement age have been conveniently omitted from the CJD statistics?

Professor Judith Okely

3. Thanks to Tamara Kohn and Brian Rigby for critical and encouraging comments.

References

Beauvoir, S. de (1980), *A Very Easy Death* (trans. P. O'Brian), Harmondsworth: Penguin.

Brettell, C. (1997), 'Blurred Genres and Blended Voices: Life History, Biography, Autobiography, and the Auto/Ethnography of Women's Lives', in

D. Reed-Danahay (ed.), *Auto-Ethnography: Rewriting the Self and the Social*, Oxford: Berg.

Brooks, D. (1993), 'Living with Ventilation: Confessions of an Addict', *Care of the Critically Ill*, Sept/October, 8(5): 205–7.

Collins Concise English Dictionary (1982), Edinburgh.

Evans-Pritchard, E. (1937), *Witchcraft, Oracles and Magic among the Azande*, Oxford: Clarendon Press.

Foster, E.M. and Crozier, E. (1951), *Libretto for Billy Budd, Opera by B. Britten*, London: Hawkes and son.

Gamarnikow, E. (1978), 'Sexual Division of Labour: the Case of Nursing', in A. Kuhn and A.M. Wolpe (eds), *Feminism and Materialism*, London: Routledge and Kegan Paul.

Good, B. (1994), *Medicine, Rationality, and Experience. An Anthropological Perspective*, Cambridge: Cambridge University Press.

Hockey, J. (1990), *Experiences of Death: An Anthropological Account*, Edinburgh: Edinburgh University Press.

Hockey, J. and James, A. (1993), *Growing Up and Growing Old: Ageing and Dependency in the Life Course*, London: Sage.

Holden, P. and Littlewood, J. (eds) (1991), *Anthropology and Nursing*, London: Routledge.

Lewis, J. and Meredith, B. (1988), *Daughters Who Care*, London: Routledge.

Okely, J. (1986a), *Simone de Beauvoir: a Re-reading*, London: Virago.

—— (1986b), *The Conditions and Experience of Ageing Compared in Rural England and France*, Report to the ESRC, Swindon.

—— (1990), 'Clubs for le Troisième Age: Communitas or Conflict', in P. Spencer (ed.), *Anthropology and the Riddle of the Sphinx: Paradoxes of Change in the Life Course*, London: Routledge.

—— (1991), *The Ethnographic Method Applied to Rural Transport, Planning and the Elderly*, Report to the ESRC, Swindon.

—— (1994), 'Vicarious and Sensory Knowledge of Chronology and Change: Ageing in Rural France', in K. Hastrup and P. Hervik (eds), *Social Experience and Anthropological Knowledge*, London: Routledge.

—— (1996a), 'Picturing and Placing Constable Country', in K. Fog Olwig and K. Hastrup (eds), *Siting Culture*, London: Routledge.

—— (1996b), *Own or Other Culture*, London: Routledge.

Rosaldo, R. (1984), 'Grief and a Headhunter's Rage: on the Cultural Force of Emotions', in E.M. Bruner (ed.), *Text, Play and Story: The Construction and Reconstruction of Self and Society*, Washington: American Anthropological Association.

Stanley, L. (1992), 'Process in Feminist Biography and Feminist Epistemology', in T. Iles (ed.), *All Sides of the Subject: Women and Biography*, New York: Teachers College Press.

Wynne, B. (1996), 'May the Sheep Safely Graze? A Reflexive View of the Expert–Lay Knowledge Divide', in S. Lash, B. Szerszynski and B. Wynne (eds), *Risk, Environment and Modernity: Towards a New Ecology*, London: Sage.

2

Triplets: Who Cares?

Frances Price

Caring for Triplets

Debby and Bruce Stevenson's exhaustion was highlighted recently in an article in *Woman* magazine: 'Our 4th Child was Triplets' (March 1998). Their triplets, Grace, Alistair and Timothy, new brothers and a sister for their three older children were delivered, prematurely, at 31 weeks' gestation in February 1997. Thereafter, accommodation, time, financial resources and energy were at a premium. What is more, the couple found it difficult to elicit help from other people to support them in the care of their children. 'Everything's just so difficult.' Debby, aged 35, is quoted as saying: 'We've had to sacrifice virtually everything.'

Such public airing of personal troubles serves to sell magazines, but neglects the larger picture – the social context in which the care of children, in this case three or more children, takes place. This chapter explores the wider social ramifications surrounding the conception, birth and care of these children, focusing on the role of medical interventions and the allocation of responsibility.

Human triplets are not a novel phenomenon; the triplets Useraf, Sakure and Kakai survived to become pharaohs in ancient Egypt in the fifth dynasty (*circa* 2500 BC). Yet, today, the Stevensons are unusual, because their triplets were conceived spontaneously. The increase in numbers of triplets (and also of twins and higher-order births, such as quads and more) in recent years is largely a consequence of the use of drugs and procedures for managing infertility. The widespread practice of ovulation induction in infertility treatment, ovarian stimulation and multiple embryo transfer in *in vitro* fertilization (IVF) programmes increases the possibility of a multiple gestation. Ovulation stimulation, designed to induce the maturation of several human eggs in a single cycle, has become a routine part of various infertility treatments, including IVF, and clinicians routinely transfer at least two and often three embryos (Human Fertilization and

Embryology Authority 1998). As a result, the incidence of triplet births in the UK has increased by more than fourfold since 1985. Over a third of IVF births are known to result in twins or more; there is, however, no central record of multiple births following the use of fertility drugs. Headlines about such higher-order multiple births in recent years has brought home the idea not only of medical assistance in multifoetal reproduction. They also raise the question of women and their partners presumably consenting to the possibility as an outcome of treatment. The press reported that Bobbi McCaughey, the mother of the septuplets born in November 1997 in Iowa, had been taking Metrodin, one of the most widely used fertility drugs. Nowadays, complete strangers may ask parents of triplets or more whether they had infertility treatment, with apparently less sympathy forthcoming for those who are perceived to have 'interfered with nature' or consented to medical intervention. There seems to be an assumption that once one has made such choices then one must accept responsibility for the consequences.

But there are difficulties with the idea both of choice and of informed consent in this situation.[1] The information given to women undergoing such treatments may include the statistical risk of multiple pregnancy and mention of the various associated complications. But it has not been the usual clinical practice to acknowledge the wider personal, social and political consequences of a higher-order multiple birth, which come into play once the children are born. In so far as there is any such discussion, this is usually overlaid with a mutual concern about the prospect of pregnancy as an outcome of undergoing the procedure (see Price 1993).

Yet it is an extraordinary situation to conceive, deliver, nurture and care for triplets, quadruplets, quintuplets or more. The familiar is rendered unfamiliar, and the effects may overwhelm. This is not only because of the sheer number of infants born, but also because, as parents discover, there is no structured provision for the cumulative consequences of caring for the children, once they are discharged from hospital. Such is the novelty of the situation and scale of the demands that, without sensitive planning and the flexibility to revise such plans in the light of what is perceived as priority by the parents, whatever help, support and advice is proffered initially may miss the mark.

Few parents can envisage what is involved in caring for a multiple birth in advance. This lack of understanding is also found among the organizations which might be expected to assist them in their task. The struggle of mothers to cope is all too often compounded not only by an administrative limbo but also by professional uncertainty and disunity.

Social workers, health visitors and volunteers, variously empowered to assist, may feel disturbed by their inability to provide or summon up the help and support required. As this chapter will show, how they 'care' matters.

For most people, the prospect of caring for three or more infants remains too remote to be imaginable. Ignorance therefore seems understandable. Few know of the problems faced by those responsible for their delivery, care and welfare. Yet, in the context of consent being given to procedures that increase the risk of multiple births, this lack of information becomes an issue.

The way that the practical everyday experience of child care should there be three or more babies is glossed over as an issue in consent to these medical procedures and is indicative of the way that 'care' is being framed. An acknowledgement of the long-term consequences of this eventuality should inform both the provision of care in this setting and also the way that the organizations which could support parents of higher-order births conceptualize care. The difficulties that arise concerning the extension of professional care into the domestic setting reflect many of the concerns that were raised in the previous chapter. This chapter could be seen as an example of the way that new technologies are raising new issues which make us think about the way care is put into practice. The principal aim is to take seriously the experiences of those who care for triplets and more. It is their experience of caring and being cared for that is missing from expert and organizational framings of care in relation to multiple birth children. Lorraine Code makes this point:

> The crucial difference as I see it, turns upon acknowledgement. There is no more effective means of creating epistemic dependence than systematically withdrawing acknowledgement from a person's cognitive utterances; no more effective way of maintaining structures of epistemic privilege and vulnerability than evincing a persistent distrust in a person's efforts to claim cognitive authority; no surer way of demonstrating a refusal to know a person *as* a person than observing her 'objectively' without taking seriously what her experience means to her (1992: 278).

The Birth of a Problem: Making Visible the Need for Care

By 1986, the rise in the numbers of multiple births became apparent in UK national registration data. Paediatricians increasingly gave voice to their anxieties about the neonatal consequences, and eventually persuaded the Department of Health to support a national study: the United Kingdom *Study of Triplets and Higher-order Births* (Botting *et al.* 1990). It consisted of surveys of obstetricians, general practitioners, paediatricians and parents, as well as interviews with the parents. I was responsible for the design, execution and analysis of the National Parents Study, which was, above all, intended to obtain information about the specific needs and problems of these parents and their sources of assistance, advice and benefits in kind. Parents' own views about the type, quality and timing of the help and support were central to the study. Triplet, quadruplet and quintuplet mothers' evaluations of and commentaries on the support and care they received before, during and after pregnancy and delivery were crucial to the entire project.

Shared child care was a necessity in these households. It is impossible to cope alone for any length of time. Few parents of triplets or more could depend on relatives to reliably provide the help that was required. So another important objective of the Parents Study was to suggest how the provision of care and support given to these families by health authorities, by local authority social service departments and by voluntary agencies might be better targeted. The remit of the study was extended in this direction when the Department of Health also requested a survey of both the health and personal social services, looking at the support they could provide following triplet and higher-order births and the problems that they perceived in providing this care. Both surveys revealed substantial variation in the level of service provision and highlighted the practical difficulties of finding resources to meet the specific needs of these households.

In addition, the Home-Start Consultancy undertook a questionnaire survey of all Home-Start schemes at my request during the last months of the National Parents Study. Volunteers from this agency 'befriend' mothers who have children under five who are feeling isolated or having difficulty coping. As such, many were called on to 'visit' the mothers of higher-order births. The scale of the task of attempting to meet the diverse needs and demands of mothers who were caring for their triplets and higher-order multiple-birth children, and some of the difficulties of voluntary agency involvement were all too evident in the responses.

The study was, then, fairly comprehensive. It was able to bring together the experiences of parents with an overview of the organizations which could support them in caring for their children. It was thus possible to discern the extent to which the needs of these families were under-estimated.

The Experience of Caring

The National Parents Study made evident just how few parents realized beforehand the extent to which their circumstances would change after the birth of their babies. For those who had sought infertility treatment, their desire to be parents had already taken them through uncertain, distressing and often costly treatments. The reality of the situation they faced after the babies were born far exceeded expectation. Financial costs are high for parents, as well as for the health service. Every family discovered the growing demands on their incomes. Some lost income as fathers changed jobs, or reduced their hours of working, to be at home more. Many families had to move house or to extend their home, and buy a larger car. Special prams and pushchairs are more expensive. Day-to-day expenditure on food, nappies and everyday items of equipment cost far more than expected.

Time costs are high as well. Feeds, baths, washing, changing nappies, not to mention the additional housework, consume not only time but energy. Moving, watching, chasing and holding three, four or more lively children is a constant drain. Many mothers are effectively imprisoned by the sheer logistics of arranging even the simplest outing. Even moving from room to room could be difficult. The needs of these mothers are both prodigious and distinctive. Coping with periods of ill-health of parent or child is particularly difficult. The practicalities of having to move so many babies and baby-related things around gave rise to minor accidents, increasing the strain. Untoward events, which might be manageable in normal circumstances, such as house repossession, job relocation or redundancy, are potentially overwhelming. Mothers were fixed in time (in the daily repetition of caring tasks) and in place, and they were tired.

The sheer physical exhaustion of everyday (and night) care cannot be overemphasized. Tiredness is not easy to define and treat as a medical problem (see Popay 1992), and yet 'just' being tired has a deep impact on subjective experience. While the National Parents Study was underway, junior hospital doctors complained vociferously about their sleep deprivation. An editorial in the medical journal *The Lancet* entitled 'The Dangers of Not Going to Bed' reviewed the legal controls and research findings for pilots, lorry drivers and soldiers (1989). Research had shown that soldiers on exercise are impaired by a single night without sleep, and that sleep-deprived doctors report mood changes, including anger, hostility and sadness. Mood changes, the editorial observes, reflect a wider stress syndrome attributed to sleep deprivation. The impact of caring on the physical and mental well-being of parents, especially mothers, was high.

Coping: Being Seen to Care

Mothers in particular have to be seen to be caring, and this can generate a pressure to be seen to be coping (Price 1992). It is profoundly difficult to admit an inability to cope, and to be believed, as one mother of triplets described:

> I said [to the health visitor] 'I cannot cope, I'm getting to the point where something's going to snap, and I don't know what to do.' And it took me two or three days to screw up the courage to tell her that I couldn't cope with my children. And she said, 'Oh, you're being very silly. There's nothing wrong with them. They are fit, healthy children and you are coping beautifully. You just don't think you're coping.' And then she went away.

It was difficult enough to maintain the appearance of being in control. Reports of a deceptive 'public' front featured large in interviews. A mother of quintuplets spoke of the front she knew she presented to the world outside her home:

> Well you appear to cope you see. And if you're organized like I am and you get on with the physical things . . . they're all turned out nicely, they're all behaved on the road because they jolly well had to. We were very strict with them so they [other people] thought 'Aren't they nice.' 'Isn't she coping well.' And *she* wasn't at all and they didn't see me go home and cry my eyes out and moan at [her husband] and say it's not fair. Nobody knows what it's like. [Mother's emphasis]

At the outset, a woman may not even be able to acknowledge to herself her inner turmoil, as one mother of quadruplets pointed out:

> everybody thinks – and still thinks – that I coped pretty well and that – you know – I've sailed through it all. Mainly because I wouldn't actually admit for a long time the way [I felt] . . . People were always saying – still now – saying: 'Gosh, you are amazing . . . I don't know how you do it.' Because I have no choice. Absolutely no choice. You either go under a bus, or you cope. One or the other. There is no alternative.

Help is only forthcoming if it is seen to be needed, if the mother's situation is perceived as sufficiently care-worthy. For some mothers, an added difficulty was how to even start to express the stress and strain they experience. Some women reported that they were incapable of crying in public. One mother explained that she could not cry in such circumstances, although she knew that was what was expected of her at meetings with local social services, arranged to discuss whether to continue funding the help she received. 'If you don't cry,' she explained, 'people think you are coping.' Nissel and Bonnerjea (1982) make a similar observation in relation to women who care for the handicapped elderly:

> Women had to interpret the situation as a crisis to themselves, then they had to present an acceptable definition of a breakdown to the doctor; then help would be provided. One interviewee offered some advice to others in her position: 'You have to be a damn good actress; if you're seen to be coping, you're left alone and there's no help, no share of responsibility. It's very unfair.'

As one mother of triplets remarked in interview:

> Until you actually break down in somebody's house and weep all over the place, they're really actually not going to recognize that you've got a need, because they can't understand . . . And I think what I found when – during the toddler stage particularly – was people just had no idea of what it was like. I mean, you'd recount these dreadful stories of – stories that to you were dreadful, of dreadful days you'd had, and people would think they were terribly funny.

Mothers wrote and spoke of the need to get some sleep, and to ensure that their children were fed with the minimum of stress. But some of these children will pose particular difficulties. Although information from replies to the survey of general practitioners in the National Study had to be interpreted with care, because of the poor response, they showed a raised prevalence of cerebral palsy, congenital malformations, pyloric stenosis (a gastric disorder requiring surgery) and hospital admissions among these children.

The social pressure on mothers, in particular, to cope with the situation and the stigma associated with 'not coping' shaped the way they could access support. Mothers caring for children within the family home are seldom conceptualized as needing help from statutory authorities unless the children are assessed as being 'at risk'. No mechanisms otherwise exist to set care in place.

Help with triplets or quads is vital from day one. The National Parents Study showed that it is impossible to cope for long without such assistance. In interviews, mothers have openly expressed their fears of, and in a few cases the consequences of, their own or their partner's lack of control under stress. Mothers who already had older children spoke of their altered behaviour: they felt their identity as mothers had been compromised in some alarming way. It was very difficult for women to put these feelings into words. One triplet mother said, 'I feel . . . it's made me a person that shouts and, all I do is shout and it wasn't the sort of person that I ever wanted to be and I never thought that I would be.' Reports of sleep deprivation and chronic exhaustion extending well beyond the first year are uppermost in many of the accounts.

Those interviewed made it clear that a strong motivation to participate in the Parents Study was the desire that others did not go through similar experiences. Women said to me over and over again, 'I love my babies, but I wouldn't wish this situation on my worst enemy.'

Sharing Caring: Caring about Primary Carers

So a major issue for the mother is negotiating help – the arranging and managing of support services. But who can help and when? While her partner may be able to help some of the time, she still has to negotiate supplementary assistance on a long-term basis. All of the mothers spoke of the need for regular time to themselves – if only to wash their hair or bath without interruption. As one mother of triplets remarked:

> I mean I wasn't able to go the dentist, go to the optician, go and have my hair cut. My husband couldn't take time off work for me to do that.
>
> *Interviewer*: So how did you cope with that?
> *Mother*: I just didn't do it.

Relatives are an obvious potential source of assistance. But it cannot be taken for granted that they will rally round. They may not be able or willing to help. Many relatives found the situation overwhelming. More than half of the parents in the National Parents Study reported that their relatives had difficulty providing assistance because of their age, infirmity, distance or lack of transport. About a third of the parents had no help at all from relatives, friends or neighbours in the first year after the birth. While for some mothers, relatives and friends could supply some assistance, all required the provision of additional responsible and reliable help on a day-to-day basis – as well as appropriate extra assistance in emergencies.

Difficulties arise when there is uncertainty as to who will reliably provide relief from the burden of continuous care, and at what cost. The identification of budgets to fund service provision to these households poses problems. A respondent to the UK survey of social services departments commented on the exceptional nature of these cases: 'Such cases do not easily "fit" in terms of local authority provision – i.e., not elderly, not handicapped, no real question of reception into care. Require some "imaginative" and liberal interpretation of guidelines and legislation.' Because of the hours needed, it often became necessary to set up a rota of volunteers, but it is difficult to find volunteers able to give the amount of time required at the time required, for example, teatime, bath time, bedtime. Ideally, volunteers should be on call to help mothers with triplets. It may well be that the local authority can provide professional oversight of suitable volunteers, but there have been as many difficulties as successes with such informal provision. In fact, the major criticisms raised by the mothers in the National Study were that the students, trainees or other volunteers recruited, usually by the health visitor or another health professional, were often unsuitable. Much of the time, these helpers themselves could not cope with the situation in which they found themselves. Some volunteers who offered to help with feeding, for instance, either cancelled at short notice or just did not turn up.

Also, several mothers made the point that busy mothers cannot supervise. Mothers under stress are vulnerable because when offered help they are more likely to accept. One set of triplets were sexually abused by their male carer – a community work student from a local school. The mother concerned had overridden her own initial qualms about his suitability because, at the time, it was the only help offered to her.

The Stevensons, the parents of triplets mentioned at the outset of the chapter, credited volunteers from their local Home-Start scheme as providing the only help on offer. Volunteers from this national charity visit and strive to support mothers with children under five in their own homes. Sometimes they worked as a team, sequentially or in pairs (to provide help with feeding, for instance). As many as five Home-Start volunteers had been involved with one household in the National Parents Study. Each volunteer provided an average of between six and eight hours per week, although two Home-Start organizers reported that, in specific cases in which they had been involved, volunteers had provided help for 18 and 20 hours per week, respectively.

The 26 Home-Start organizers who reported their volunteers' experience with mothers of triplets and quads described the help provided as, in the main, practical. Yet providing practical help alone, without 'care' directed towards the mother, could call into question the Home-Start volunteer's role, as volunteers are recruited to Home-Start to befriend mothers, not to act as surrogate home helps.

Of concern to several Home-Start organizers were the anxieties and pressures on the volunteer because so little other help was available to the mother concerned:

> Mother derives a great deal of support from volunteer whilst jointly involved in practical tasks, e.g. feeding, changing, shopping, visits to clinics etc. Volunteer has felt pressure on her time, as so little other help is available. A major difficulty for the mother, is her inability to devote sufficient time to older children who become increasingly jealous and difficult to handle. [There is a] lack of general support and understanding of difficulties. An assumption is made that if mother copes with initial stages she can manage and no help offered. This mother found earlier stages just manageable but stage of crawling onwards almost impossible. Volunteer and mother feel professionals too little understanding of practical difficulties e.g. pressure to attend clinics, but appointments made of periodic assessments of triplets on different dates! Mother felt very isolated. Much admiration of triplets but little practical help, support or advice.

The comments from organizers, as they described the experience of their volunteers, echoed the comments of the parents themselves and of the health professionals who cared for them.

It is difficult to envisage, in the light of the responses to the Home-Start survey, that any one volunteer can provide more than supplementary or complementary assistance and support over an extended period to mothers in these circumstances. Yet additional stress arises with the introduction of many different helpers in the confines of a home, however capable these people are and even if they do not all arrive at once. As one volunteer organizer noted, 'even coping with an army of different helpers is tiring'. Furthermore, such help is needed over several years. Assistance with child care is as necessary in the second as in the first year – although for different reasons. The combined efforts of three toddlers can push down safety gates, push heavy furniture in front of fires and initiate 'team' ventures unimaginable to those whose only experience is of singleton children.

Managing Uncertainty: Taking Care Seriously

Few women and men can envisage the prospect of a multiple birth. Nor can they imagine the magnitude of the responsibility, or the consequences and costs of involvement in caring for these children. Such is the novelty of the situation and scale of the demands that the help, support and advice available from the health and social services, and also from the voluntary sector, may not begin to meet the needs as perceived by the parents. Also these services are already stretched, as a consequence both of welfare policies transferring care to the community and of a shortage of volunteers. Since the publication of the report of the National Study, the parents of twins and triplets have campaigned for better state support, and in 1992 received the backing of the House of Commons Health Committee. However, the Department of Social Security refused to accept that the needs of such families were unusual, claiming that the costs for triplets are no different from those for three single children. This narrow conceptualization of the care of children and the needs of parents in terms of cost invalidates the experience of those concerned, and the negotiation of support for parents of higher-order births remains uncertain.

With the development of techniques for 'assisting' conception, reproduction is brought into the public domain and ever more prominently within a medical frame. Clinicians act in effect as both providers and moral and political gatekeepers of a new range of 'treatment services' which carry the risk of multiple birth. New reproductive technologies permit the prospect of a remedy – the facilitation of a pregnancy. In this context, the focus on and language of pregnancy in the clinic are significant. Effectively, the quest for a child becomes a quest for a pregnancy, and is deemed to be a medical matter, thereby narrowing the time-scale and focus of concern, to the neglect of possible consequences in the long term. Because decisions are made in a medical setting, people are inclined to accept that these judgements are 'expert'; thereby doctors are de facto given the licence to decide on the appropriate procedure.

Although information about the risk of multiple pregnancies is given to couples before starting infertility treatment, the overwhelming desire for a pregnancy makes it difficult for them to envisage the implications of having more than one baby. The National Study found that the quality of the information given varied considerably, and it recommended improvements in practice. Clinicians, however, remain resistant to any restrictions on their clinical judgement. Moreover, they practise in an increasingly competitive commercial setting, where there is pressure to achieve a high rank in the official league table of pregnancy rates. In addition, clinicians in the private sector are usually insulated even from the medical consequences of multiple births that occur in National Health Service (NHS) hospitals.

Far more than the facilitation of pregnancy is at issue here. These techniques potentially redefine relationships and may compromise anticipated parental roles (see Strathern 1992). Yet the framing of contemporary assisted conception as routine practice based on medical criteria consistently obscures this context, because it focuses on the individual case and birth as a biological event.

The significance of assisted conception extends beyond the prospect of pregnancy, birth and associated clinical risks and uncertainties. Birth is a social event, and women and men shoulder new kinds of risks and uncertainty concerning their future relationships, particularly if there has been a multiple pregnancy. We need to ask not only under what circumstances these new relationships can be sustained, but also how medically mediated multiple births can be avoided.

Notes

1. The issue of informed consent in relation to new reproductive technologies has been the cause of much debate (see Social Science Research Unit (1993) conference report).

References

Botting, B.J., Macfarlane, A.J. and Price, F.V. (1990), *Three, Four or More: A Study of Triplets and Higher-order Births*, London: HMSO.
Code, L. (1992), 'The Unicorn in the Garden', in E.D. Harvey and K. Oknihlik (eds), *Women and Reason,* Ann Arbor: University of Michigan Press.
Human Fertilization and Embryology Authority (1998), *6th Annual Report*, London.
Nissel, M. and Bonnerjea, L. (1982), *Family Care of the Handicapped Elderly: Who Pays?*, London: Policy Studies.
Popay, J. (1992), 'Sick and Tired?', in H. Roberts (ed.), *Women's Health Matters*, London: Routledge.
Price, F. (1992), '"Isn't She Coping Well?" Providing for Mothers of Triplets, Quadruplets and Quintuplets', in H. Roberts (ed.), *Women's Health Matters,* London: Routledge.
—— (1993), 'Beyond Expectation: Clinical Practices and Clinical Concerns', in J. Edwards, S. Franklin, E. Hirsch, F. Price, and M. Strathern (eds), *Technologies of Procreation: Kinship in the Age of Assisted Conception,* Manchester: Manchester University Press, pp. 20–41.
Social Science Research Unit (1993), *Consent and the Reproductive Technologies* (SSRU Consent Conference), Series No. 4.
Strathern, M. (1992), *Reproducing the Future: Anthropology, Kinship and the New Reproductive Technologies,* Manchester: Manchester University Press.
The Lancet (1989), 'The Dangers of Not Going to Bed', 1: 138–9.

PART 2

Controlling Care: Rights and Responsibilities

The chapters in this section shift the focus of concern from the previous section. The magnitude of the shift involved, from the personal experience of caring and the interface between those who need care and those provide care, to the analyses of global debates and abstract concepts, may seem large. However, despite the apparent distance between these two levels of concern with care, the points made by Dembour and Russell both illustrate, in different ways, that this distance is in itself produced by social and cultural relations which frame abstract ideas about care in specific ways. Both argue for the debates they touch on to be tied back into specific contexts, and grounded in experience.

Issues regarding care can generate a great deal of contestation. Andrew Russell's contribution considers some of the economic, social and political interests embedded in debates about the use of Depo-Provera. These condense into the conflict between the need for population control, in which procreation (and the procreation of specific groups in particular) is identified as problematic, and the need for birth control, which is identified in terms of individual decision-making. This raises a theme that reappears in later chapters – the evaluation of risks and benefits. Here, two models are in conflict. For proponents of Depo-Provera, health risks can be bracketed off and balanced by the global benefits associated with population control. For those who oppose the drug's use, risks are central to evaluations of the impact of the drug on women's lives and consideration of whether their well-being is improved by the drug. Depo-Provera provides a good example of how medical care is being extended by new technologies to looking after the 'well' (a theme taken up later to good effect by Lambert). This extension of the boundaries of care raises serious questions about the way we think of care.

The debates Russell analyses exhibit many of the themes recognized by Dembour in discourses about human rights. Efforts to get beyond the rhetoric of opposition seem doomed to failure. The contesting parties are intractably locked into completely divergent conceptualizations, which draw attention away from the significance of Depo-Provera for women in specific and often entirely different contexts.

Marie-Bénédicte Dembour looks critically at how human rights discourses are invoked in relation to health care. She enumerates the reasons why, for example, the human rights associated with health care cannot provide for legally enforceable rights. She points out that there are no institutional mechanisms for enforcing these rights, that the definition of concepts such as 'well-being' or 'good medical care' is deeply problematic, and that medical care cannot be evaluated without taking the social, economic and political context within which it is delivered into account. She goes on to argue that rights are fundamentally illusory, an ideal that cannot be realized within contemporary socio-legal structures. While Dembour does recognize that human rights discourses can be effective, she raises questions about the ways in which they are effective.

3

Taking Care? The Depo-Provera Debate

Andrew Russell

Introduction

This chapter looks at the meaning and implications of the word 'care' in the context of the debate concerning the injectable contraceptive, Depo-Provera. It is a study of policy-making in so far as I shall look at the history of decisions made over whether or not to license the contraceptive for use in the USA between 1974 and the present. I look at the cultural influences and ramifications of the debate and the decisions ensuing from it, both within the USA and worldwide. I shall investigate the moral viewpoints of proponents and opponents of the drug in this debate as they are reflected in the various meanings that can be attributed to the concept of 'care'.[1]

To say that 'care' is a problematic concept in Western thought is almost, in the context of this book, a truism. As McFarlane (1988) describes 'caring', it 'is a woolly concept and notoriously difficult of precise definition'. This is partly because 'care' is a multifaceted concept, with different meanings in different languages. In English, it is possible to differentiate three dominant meanings to the word. The first is 'care' in the sense of caution: to 'take care', to avoid risks, to be safe. The second is care as 'being concerned', often expressed in the negative 'I don't care'. The third is 'care' expressed in the need to 'look after' someone. These meanings all involve moral imperatives as well as the implementation, very often, of practical techniques. They offer three intertwined, and often dissonant, visions of Depo-Provera, configuring a debate in which 'science' has frequently been invoked to act as an arbiter of decision-making. Examining the different meanings of 'care' as they are played out in the debate uncovers the nature of the power relations between groups, and their assumptions about birth control/population control, risks and benefits, 'freedom of choice' and 'informed consent'. The anthropological approach enables us to look at these issues cross-culturally and holistically.

Contraception is one of the many areas of human life in which 'medicalization' (Illich 1976) is taking place. Contraception is part of the burgeoning medical domain. As Doyal reports, 'contraceptive management is by far the most common reason for women consulting their GPs, with an annual rate of 1406 visits per 10,000 women, compared with the next highest rate of 873 for acute respiratory infections' (Doyal 1997: 334). Yet to what extent does this make the Depo-Provera debate a subject for analysis via medical ethics? It is questionable how far notions of 'health care ethics', based on a premise of caring for someone who is 'sick', can be extended to the consideration of contraceptive 'care' for someone who is 'well'. Part of the reason for the Depo-Provera debate reflecting what Levine (1979) calls 'a clash of political, social and ethical values', it will be suggested, is because of the domination of medical science models in a situation where other models are seen by opponent groups as equally salient, but are 'muted' (Ardener 1975). Unpacking the Depo-Provera debate, then, provides an exegesis of the cultural contests surrounding women's reproductive health issues.

This chapter first looks briefly at the development and testing of Depo-Provera. I shall then go on to consider the debate as it developed in the USA over the 25 years between 1967 and 1992, focusing on the way the discussions about 'care/ethical' issues surrounding Depo-Provera in the USA developed during this time, and the relationship of the different issues to wider political-economic and cultural changes. The anthropological approach, I shall argue, 'extends the boundaries' by allowing for consideration of all three meanings of 'care' in the analysis of Depo-Provera as a compound used, not in isolation, but in a social context.

History of the Development of Depo-Provera

Products such as Depo-Provera (depot medroxyprogesterone acetate, sometimes shortened to DMPA) have a tendency to 'burst on to' the scene without a history, or rather, a 'constructed history' of orderly progress rather than a 'natural history' in which the process of pharmaceutical development is less ordered, less rational and, above all, less 'scientific' than is often presented or assumed.

The pharmaceutical technology to produce 'depot'[2]-type compounds was developed during the Second World War. Depo-Provera was the first contraceptive application of this new technology. The 'constructed history' has it that Depo-Provera was developed and first marketed by the Upjohn pharmaceutical company as a treatment for inoperable cancer of the endometrium and endometriosis in 1960. In this, it follows a pattern which can be observed in many other hormonal contraceptives developed out of hormonal drugs designed originally for the treatment of menstrual and menopausal dysfunctions (Oudshoorn 1994). Trials in Los Angeles and Jamaica showed that just one intramuscular 150 mg injection of Depo-Provera every three months gave contraceptive protection, with a 'failure rate' of 0.25 per 100 woman years, the lowest of any contraceptive then on the market.[3] Like Oudshoorn, we can query the ethics of doing trials of contraceptive technologies in places or among people largely unprotected by legal institutions and not fully informed about the nature of the product being tested or the purpose for which the tests were being carried out. As with the oral contraceptive pill (ibid.), the use of Depo-Provera for endometriosis in particular may have provided a useful 'smokescreen' for the development of the product for a much more lucrative role as a contraceptive in a social/religious context in which contraception was seen as problematic. In whose interests did this development take place, and what were the levels of 'care' extended to the different population groups involved?

The Role of the Food and Drug Administration

The Food and Drug Administration (FDA) is the US government agency most concerned with 'care' (in the sense of 'caution') about the USA's pharmaceutical formulary. Some writers have argued that the FDA is too cautious (e.g. Richard and Lasagna 1987). Depo-Provera is now often held up as an example of the prolonged length of time it takes some products to be approved: the Upjohn chemical company first applied to the FDA to have Depo-Provera approved for contraceptive use in 1967. Approval was finally granted twenty-five years later in 1992.

One cannot say that, with the evidence available to them in 1967, the FDA were wrong to be cautious. In animal studies, which the FDA insisted be carried out, autopsies were carried out on beagles that had been given 25 times the human dose of Depo-Provera. These revealed significantly greater numbers of benign and malignant breast tumours compared with controls (WHO 1982).[4] However, after further deliberations by its advisory committee on Obstetrics and Gynecology, in 1973 the FDA proposed approving Depo-Provera as a contraceptive for a limited range of women, based on the principle of informed consent. This was the first new product for which the FDA had proposed requiring informed consent as a basis for its use. According to the FDA, the significance to humans of the drug having caused tumours in beagle dogs had not been established. Nor was any other 'equally effective' injectable contraceptive then on the market. In view of this, it was considered that the potential risks were not certain enough to be reason for depriving the public of the special benefits Depo-Provera was perceived to have. In fact, the FDA considered that, if concern was appropriate over Depo-Provera, 'this concern should properly extend to all steroidal contraceptives' (US Government 1974a). On the other hand, the FDA took the precaution of proposing to establish a registry of all physicians administering the injectable so that they could be notified 'in the event that any of the potential carcinogenic hazards were confirmed' (US Government 1974b).

In 1974, Senator Edward Kennedy's Health Subcommittee held twelve days of widely publicized hearings on the drug, and strongly objected to approval being given. The FDA, regardless, announced its final form of approval for the drug to take effect on 15 October. Congress representative L.H. Fountain convened hearings on Depo-Provera, claiming that the FDA had ignored the findings of the Third National Cancer Survey, which had indicated a link between Depo-Provera and cervical cancer. The Secretary of the Department of Health, Education and Welfare halted approval of the drug (US Government 1974b).

The FDA convened further meetings of its advisory committees, including the Obstetrics and Gynecology Committee, which ascertained that no link between Depo-Provera and cervical cancer could be proved. Despite this, on 7 March 1978 the FDA anounced that the drug would not be approved as a contraceptive after all. It was quite surprising, given the recommendations of the various FDA committees beforehand, that 'caution' should have ruled in this case. An extended list of reasons for the decision were given, one of which was the safety questions raised by the beagle studies (still unresolved). In addition, the FDA saw no clear evidence of a patient population in need of the drug in the USA. It also raised the possibility that bleeding disturbances might necessitate the administration of oral oestrogen (with the risks that this would entail), and that the exposure of a developing foetus to Depo-Provera could lead to congenital malformation (a risk enhanced by the prolonged action of the drug). Upjohn had proposed a post-marketing study for breast and cervical cancers, but the FDA considered this unlikely to yield meaningful data. Finally, the probable as well as the proposed usage of the drug had to be considered, and the FDA thought it likely that the drug would be put to non-approved uses for which the benefits would not outweigh the risks.

However, in explaining his decision, FDA commissioner Donald Kennedy stated that it should not be taken as universally applicable, since, in his view,

The benefit–risk considerations are not the same in all countries of the world. In an economically developed nation like the USA, with an advanced health-care system, the disapproval judgment is appropriate. The opposite decision may be more appropriate, however, for nations with higher birthrates, lower physician–patient ratios, and less readily available contraceptive methods. (US Government 1978a)

This was the first time that developing countries had been considered in an FDA decision, and reflects an increasing awareness of the role of the USA on the world stage in such matters. The commissioner's statement can be seen as proposing the 'relativization of caution', in that he suggests the risks of Depo-Provera need to be considered not only in absolute terms but also relative to other risks and benefits (or their lack) in the particular national contexts in which it is found.[5]

Upjohn appealed this decision and requested that a public board of inquiry be appointed to review the issue. A board was appointed, another 'first' in the way a pharmaceutical product application was handled by the FDA. The board published its findings in 1984 (Weisz et al.1984). Their remit was to study a broad range of questions, based around the central question of whether the benefits of Depo-Provera outweighed the risks, under conditions of general marketing. As a result of its findings (which were critical of the long-term studies of Depo-Provera which had been undertaken up to that time), the board recommended keeping the ban until more was known about the effect of Depo-Provera on cancer rates. Finally, in June 1992, the FDA's Fertility and Maternal Health Drugs Advisory Committee voted to recommend approval of Depo-Provera for contraceptive use in the USA, a recommendation that was finally made law in December that year.

One reason for the length and, as we shall see, often vitriolic quality of the debate is the polarization of the social, economic and political interests each side saw the other as representing. Supporters of the drug included Upjohn, various population, health and development organizations, such as the International Planned Parenthood Federation (IPPF), United States Agency for International Development (USAID) and the World Health

Organization (WHO). They were further supported by the American College of Obstetrics and Gynecology. A variety of different interests and philosophies can be identified among the supporters, whose claims are backed up by favoured scientific approaches (Russell 1995/6: 15).[6] Similar variety characterized the opponents of Depo-Provera, who came from feminist and consumer organizations, such as the National Women's Health Network, as well as the FDA itself.

Supporters and opponents of the debate were at loggerheads not only because of their different interests and philosophies but because of what for them constituted 'evidence' for their point of view. We can see the Depo-Provera debate as a contest between different types of scientific knowledge as well as between scientific ('care as caution') and other types of 'caring' knowledge which, we shall see, were muted in the scientific framework within which most debate about the contraceptive took place.

Two Types of 'Caring': Population Control and Birth Control

An example of contested ideas of 'care' in the debate over Depo-Provera is the competition it represents between population control and birth control. The medicalization indicated in the introduction can be seen as a necessary precursor to the philosophy of population control, which, in its extreme form, sees women's procreation as a 'problem' to be 'cured', rather than a matter of individual decision-making, as it is regarded in birth control philosophy.

Gordon (1976) argues that the radical ideals of birth control were linked to the struggles of the suffragette and socialist movements of the late nineteenth century, struggles that have continued into the twentieth century regarding equality for women and men and 'the larger struggle to control our bodies and our lives' (Boston Women's Health Book Collective 1973: 181). In Gordon's view (1976), 'reproductive freedom cannot be separated from the totality of women's freedom'. The separation of birth control from this overall struggle is a pity, since it has

> led to an increasingly narrow definition of its goals, settling eventually for technological reform within the status quo rather than freedom. The majority of those who lack reproductive freedom experience the problem as part of a system of social and economic problems, in which, most often, lack of birth control is not the major one. (ibid.)

For Gordon, 'birth control has always been primarily an issue of politics, not of technology' (ibid.). It took the struggle of such organizations as Sanger's Birth Control League and Bennett's Voluntary Parenthood League to make birth control respectable, and only after this had been achieved could research take place aimed at improving technology.

Birth control, then, tends to be seen by opponents of Depo-Provera as a matter of social as well as physiological issues. Even the supposedly 'hard science' of contraceptive technology is not divorced from wider gender, ethnic and racial issues facing society today (Easlea 1983). In many respects, these form part of the wider power relations inherent in society, evidenced in the expressed disinclination of those (men) developing contraceptive technology to have it put into the hands of individual women.[7] The hesitancy about allowing total freedom of information about contraception and individual control over its use is to be perceived in Margaret Sanger's insistence in the 1920s that every applicant for birth control should first see a doctor.[8]

Population control came from very different roots from those of the birth-control movement. Gordon suggests that 'population control was the successor to eugenics in every respect – ideologically, organizationally and in personnel' (1976). Another point of origin was in the increasingly popular biomedical definition of birth as abnormal and in need of medical supervision. Indeed, one could argue that, in the case of population control, the sense of 'abnormality' in childbirth is semantically extended, so that childbirth becomes not only medically but also socio-economically abnormal, and fertility control can come to be viewed as a valid end in itself, extraneous to the desires (or 'cares') of individual women.

The ideological tensions between 'birth control' and 'population control' were fully active in the history of the debate about Depo-Provera, particularly in the 1970s. Concerns about women as individuals entitled to full reproductive health and the 'right to choose' jostled with concerns about women (particularly Third World women) as a group having a pregnancy problem to be 'solved'. The outcome of population-control ideology in policy statements is indicated by Dr Frederick Robbins's statement that 'the dangers of overpopulation are so great that we may have to use certain techniques of contraception that may entail considerable risk to the individual woman' (Robbins quoted in Seaman 1969).

Similar statements, if not so extreme, have been made by people who subsequently spoke in favour of Depo-Provera in public debate. Dr Malcolm Potts, executive director of the International Fertility Research Program (an Agency for International Development-funded agency) comments in a book written with John Peel that: 'Contraception is not merely a medical procedure; it is also a social convenience, and if a technique carried a mortality several hundreds of times greater than that now believed to be associated with the Pill, its use might still be justified on social if not medical grounds' (Peel and Potts 1969). In a later statement, at the 1978 hearings, Potts argued for 'adding every additional [contraceptive] option that it is responsible to add', because of his observation that 'every time a community is offered a new option in fertility regulation you get more users' (US Government 1978b). Similarly, because of a supposed 'gut feeling' about injectables being 'very important for a certain population', at a Congress Subcommittee of the Committee of Government Operations meeting convened to consider the use of advisory committees by the FDA, one doctor suggested 'that could be a justification for using a compound that happens to cause breast tumors' (US Government 1974a).

Such arguments highlight the fundamental difference in the notion of 'care' in the philosophies of birth control (helping the individual) and population control (assisting the nation or saving the planet), and in the way in which 'choice' and 'freedom' are likely to be exercised within them. This has an impact on how contraceptives are chosen and used. In population-control programmes in the mid 1970s, Gordon saw an increasing push away from voluntary control towards 'coercion', with a decreasing use of diaphragms and pills, and an increasing use of intra-uterine devices (IUDs) and operations not in the women's control (1976). Depo-Provera arrived at an opportune time for such a push to be maintained, particularly after legislative controls on sterilization in the USA became far more stringent in 1979.

Risks and Benefits: Debating the Domain of 'Care'

The FDA's 'care as caution' approach attempts to evaluate Depo-Provera from a 'scientific' perspective, in terms of 'risks' and 'benefits'. However, as we have seen in the previous section, the question of what risks are acceptable and what benefits are to be applauded varies according to the ideological and philosophical perspective of speakers in the debate. It is worth looking at the meanings attributed to 'risks' and 'benefits' by opponents and supporters of Depo-Provera, because they are the crux to understanding the dilemmas faced in assessing the safety of such products.

Articles supporting Depo-Provera seem to take the benefits of the product for granted.[9] For proponents, benefits are absolute, almost unquestioned. They are presented as a prelude to the fugue-like discussion of 'risks'. Benefits, write Rosenfield *et al.*, are 'worth reviewing' simply as 'the attributes that make it [Depo-Provera] worth the effort of continued controversy and evaluation' (1983: 2922). Yet benefits are less 'taken for granted' by opponents of the contraceptive. For them, benefits are strictly relative and distinctly troublesome. Indeed, they are sometimes hard to distinguish from 'risks'. The benefit of contraceptive protection for three months, for example, is placed against the likelihood of side-effects during this time, and the impossibility of reversing the procedure (and therefore any side-effects) should undesirable effects occur. In a medical, 'care as caution' perspective, side-effects are arguably of little concern. In the context of 'care as looking after', however, they are far more significant and salient to the debate.

Contrary to benefits, each group is far more explicit in its standpoint on risks, how they should be evaluated and what counts as acceptable. Risks discussed generally take the form of various types of sickness and disease, which (in the case of disease, at least) are far more amenable to scientific observation and discussion, and appropriate to the 'care as caution' approach. As Douglas and Wildavsky describe it, 'the notion of risk is an extraordinarily constructed idea, essentially decontextualized and desocialized' (1982). However, I would argue that it is the direction this decontextualization takes that leads to a large part of the acrimony of the debate. For the proponents of Depo-Provera, risk should be seen relative to other risks. For opponents, it is an absolute quality.

Part of the proponents' push to relativity is exemplified in their tendency to evaluate the risks of contraceptives in the same terms as those of drugs in general. According to Benagiano and Fraser, for example, 'all drug use entails some risk, and the relevant question for the user or the physician is whether such risks are commensurate with the benefits' (1981).

Opponents, on the other hand, seek to establish a sharp distinction between curatives and contraceptives. As one speaker at the 1978 Select Committee on Population hearings argued, contraceptives are given to women who are well. She argued for caution, because of the large numbers of women who take contraceptives, often in places not mediated by a personal physician (US Government 1978b: 191). The chairman of the committee, revealing his exclusively 'care as caution', 'scientific' stance, argued 'that is a philosophical position and a political decision that, in your judgment is correct' (ibid.).[10]

The side-effects question highlights the different perspectives on 'care' of the various groups involved in the debate. The 'care as caution' approach looks at 'risks' in absolute terms, as disease or mortality. From this perspective, lack of risk means lack of death or disease (i.e. a biomedical, health as absence of disease, model). Biomedical expertise is in the use of compounds and techniques to treat serious disease, side-effects being an unfortunate but necessary by-product of some of these efforts. In the 'care as looking after' or 'care as concern' approaches, on the other hand (which could be glossed as 'health as well-being'), side-effects are a much more serious issue, particularly in a recently medicalized field such as contraception, where no disease is being cured. The Campaign Against Depo-Provera considers that, because side-effects cannot usually be verified by doctors; 'in all the major surveys of the research literature on Depo-Provera they are called "subjective complaints". What this means is that they are often dismissed as unimportant' (Campaign Against Depo-Provera 1980). If we want to generalize, we could say that proponents tend to view side-effects and health risks as categorically distinct (reflecting the medical view of health as 'absence of disease'), while opponents tend to merge them (in their 'health and well-being' approach).

Unlike more rigorously defined 'diseases', furthermore, 'side-effects' are open to negotiation as to their severity and impact. Compare these two accounts of menstrual disturbances, the first from an article by influential proponents of Depo-Provera, the second by the Campaign Against Depo-Provera:

> The major side effect of all injectable contraceptives is disturbance of the menstrual cycle, and this is the rule rather than the exception. With DMPA there is a high incidence of amenorrhoea and irregular (but infrequent) bleeding, and a lower incidence of prolonged or heavy bleeding. Very few women will experience relatively regular bleeding approximating normal menstrual cycles. (Fraser and Weisberg 1981)

> The most common side-effect of Depo-Provera is menstrual chaos. It is quite impossible for a woman or her doctor to have any idea of when and how much she will bleed. Women react differently. Many experience irregular and prolonged vaginal bleeding, some may have persistent spotting. Some may cease to have vaginal bleeding at all and it seems that after a couple of injections, many women will be experiencing amenorrhoea. (Campaign Against Depo-Provera 1980)

There are important rhetorical differences between these two statements. Apart from the obviously more concrete, emotional nature of the second, the first is talking of women in a decidedly plural sense (as part of the 'care as caution', epidemiological approach, concerned with questions of 'safety', as well, perhaps, as the need for population control), while the second has the very significant, personalizing, singular 'woman' (line 2), which reflects the more individualistic, 'care as caution' and 'care as looking after' approaches.

Opponents also try to include cultural meanings in their accounts, as in this account of the cultural meaning of menstruation: 'In almost every culture, menstrual blood is highly charged with social and often religious significance. It also spells out a biological message which more often than not a woman is thankful to receive. The message is "you are not expecting a child"' (Campaign Against Depo-Provera 1980). Menstruation is not welcome in all cultures, however, and there may be variations in attitudes within one culture. In a country where amenorrhoea is interpreted as the amassing of 'bad blood' in the womb and is considered dangerous to health (e.g. Jamaica: Sobo 1993), Depo-Provera runs the risk of being culturally unacceptable. In other societies, where menstruation signifies impurity, women, once over the heavy bleeding stage (if they ever have one), might find Depo-Provera a preferable option. This may help to explain the popularity of Depo-Provera in some South Asian and Latin American countries.

The Upjohn company takes a less deterministic view of culture. It considers that 'women, once assured that bleeding and spotting are merely signs of the hormonal activity of Depo-Provera, seem to regard them as a minor inconvenience' (quoted in Campaign Against Depo-Provera 1980). Similarly, Fraser and Weisberg state 'counselling about side-effects before administration usually has a beneficial influence on patient tolerance' (1981). Benagiano and Fraser are confident that, if Depo-Provera were really so bad, 'information spread by word of mouth would rapidly dissuade women from using the drug' (1981).

Proponents and opponents differ in their ideas about epistemology. For proponents, only empirical evidence can be considered:

> A variety of side-effects and complications have been reported in clinical trials with DMPA, but many of these are difficult to link directly with the drug itself, with the major exception of the menstrual disturbances . . . It is well recognized from the results of carefully conducted placebo-controlled trials of hormonal contraceptives that most of the minor side effects are almost as common in the women taking the placebo. (Fraser and Weisberg 1981)

Or, in the words of Dr Coutinho, speaking at the Select Committee on Population hearings, 'it's so difficult to find a woman that doesn't have a headache in the period of 6 months or so with or without an injection' (US Government 1978b).

A WHO study did not find a random reporting of headache incidence through time, however, contrary to what Dr Coutinho's remark assumed. Out of a sample of 846 Depo-Provera users, 8.5% reported headaches three months after their first injection, a figure that had risen to 15.7% three months after the fourth injection. As far as spontaneously volunteerd complaints were concerned, however, the WHO considered that 'many events were either too nonspecific or too infrequent to permit detailed analysis' (WHO Expanded Programme1977). There were also no controls to compare with the 60% of Depo-Provera users who registered some complaint over the duration of the study.

Far from assuming over-reporting of side-effects, as Dr Coutinho does, the National Women's Health Network at the 1983 Public Board of Inquiry argued that the method of data collection used in most studies, relying on the patient to report her side-effects, was inadequate. In their view, women in developing countries were likely to be too scared, embarrassed or intimidated to report bleeding or other side-effects. Alternatively, they might not associate their condition with the use of the drug. They suggested that many doctors do not inform women about the possible side-effects of Depo-Provera for fear of encouraging just the psychosomatic symptoms Dr Coutinho seemed to think so common among women.

Opponents favour individual, case study material rather than large-scale surveys. For example, a report by the International Contraception, Abortion and Sterilization Campaign (ICASC) on the experience of a woman in South Africa runs as follows:

Offered Depo-Provera after birth of third child in 1975. Complained of bloated feeling, enormous weight gain and no menstrual periods. Was told by clinic that she would 'get used to it'. Physical condition deteriorated, experienced severe headaches and continuing weight increase. Clinic told her not to worry and that there was no necessity to see a doctor. Complained of severe abdominal pains at work one morning, haemorrhaged severely and died ten minutes later. The clinic denied any link with Depo-Provera and no investigation was carried out. Cause of death – Unknown. (ICASC quoted by Gordon 1981)

Opponents of Depo-Provera, then, consider risks in wider and more absolute terms than do supporters of the drug. The relativization and decontextualization of risk among proponents of Depo-Provera is further exemplified in the use of 'continuation rates' as a measure of the severity of the contraceptive's side-effects. Continuation rates are a product of many factors, of which side-effects are only one. Proponents tend to compare continuation rates for Depo-Provera with those for other contraceptive methods: the WHO task-force study found that 'the total discontinuation rates of about 50 per 100 women after one year . . . are comparable to those reported for oral contraceptives in similar trial settings' (WHO Expanded Programme 1977).

Opponents tend to look at continuation rates in less statistical, relativized terms. For example, a Kenyan midwife (a 'carer' in the sense of 'looking after someone') is quoted as follows: 'At first when women heard of the injection, they were very delighted – but later on they started complaining of many things such as raised blood pressure, disturbed menstruation, irritation of the nipples, and again growing too fat, and in fact most of the women using this method have since withdrawn' (quoted in 'E.B.' 1980).

Relativity in the assessment of 'risks' and 'benefits' is also apparent in the discussions about the safety of Depo-Provera at the global level. Dr Fred Sai, speaking on behalf of the IPPF at the Select Committee on Population hearings, pointed out that 'the maternal mortality rates in the less developed countries, particularly Africa, range from one to 10 per thousand births. This is 100 to over 200 times the comparable risk for the U.S.' Any assessment of risk for Depo-Provera, in his eyes, 'would have to be a comparison not only with other contraceptives but also with pregnancy' (US Government 1978b). Going further even than purely health risks, the IPPF representative at the 1983 Public Board of Inquiry said, with reference to the Third World, that 'in stark contrast to the risk/ benefit ratio . . . lies the catalogue of well-documented medical, socio-economic risks of the alternatives – repeated child-bearing, and the vicious cycle of unwanted pregnancy, abortion and deprivation' (quoted in Skurnik 1983). For opponents, in contrast, the 'risks' of Depo-Provera are absolute and comparing them with other types of (to them) categorically distinct 'risks' is unacceptable. Opponents point out that there are contraceptive alternatives to Depo-Provera which have less possible risk to women's health and well-being than the injectable. There are also alternative strategies to taking Depo-Provera as a 'drug' protecting one from the 'dangers' of pregnancy, abortion and deprivation. As Levine argues:

> The best results in population control do not depend on family planning programs alone, and certainly not on the availability of one contraceptive, but on a whole range of measures that improve income distribution, raise the educational level of women, provide better maternal and infant health care, better sanitation, more jobs, and more opportunities for meaningful choices in life (1979).

Or, as the Campaign Against Depo-Provera puts it, 'by developing Depo-Provera, manufacturing it and aggressively marketing it as the next best thing to sterilisation, the real problems facing women in the Third World are being deliberately and callously ignored' (1980).

It is interesting to speculate as to why the 'scientific idiom' (Gusfield 1981), in this case specifically 'risk–benefit analysis', has become the dominant discourse in the 'care' which is accorded to the evaluation of products such as Depo-Provera. There can be no doubt that 'science' has moral, social and epistemological status in Western society. Its position means that, if one can show one's opponents to be 'unscientific', one has a much better chance of winning the debate, regardless of wider moral and political implications the debate may conceal. As Gillespie *et al.* (1979) put it, in positivist science, facts are facts and disputes over facts can be 'explained in terms of political views, bias or irrationality of one or more of the disputants', the party exhibiting more bias being the less 'scientific' (and hence less valid) of the two.

This cultural sleight of hand might be convenient for proponent groups, such as Upjohn or the international population, health and development institutions with interests in Depo-Provera for economic or legal/practical reasons. This trend can be observed in the ways in which proponents attempt to establish their authority by arguing for their higher scientific status and creating a dichotomy between their 'science' and their opponents' 'populism'. Rosenfield *et al.*, for example, talk of 'medical reports with responsible discussions of . . . potential risks and benefits, and reports that use selected evidence and biased interpretations to make a particular point' (1983: 2922).

However, the anthropologist cannot be so judgemental in his or her analysis of the debate. I would argue that, while 'risk-benefit' analysis has appeared the most important method to use in 'taking care' of decision-making concerning the licensing of Depo-Provera, such an approach alone does not adequately address the 'care as concern' and 'care as looking after' aspects of the contraceptive. Arguments seeking to 'extend the boundaries of care' in such directions have in many respects been 'muted' (Ardener 1975) through the need to stick to issues within the 'risk–benefit' analysis associated with the FDA's 'care as caution' approach. Partly this is because, as McFarlane writes, 'the lack of scientific precision in the concept of caring . . . fails to provide a blueprint for scientifically based professional action in modern health care and a basis from which the efficiency and effectiveness of such action can be judged' (1988:10). However this does not mean that, in a more holistic account of the debate, wider issues of 'care' can be ignored.

Conditions of General Marketing: 'Care as Concern' and 'Care as Looking After'

I have argued that the assessment of Depo-Provera in terms of 'risks' and 'benefits' is an inadequate vehicle for the consideration of wider 'care' issues that discussion of new contraceptive technologies requires. The FDA importantly required the consideration of the 'risks' and 'benefits' of Depo-Provera 'under conditions of general marketing', and it is in this sphere that issues of 'care as concern' and 'care as looking after' come to the fore. However, it is also an area that has been consistently marginalized throughout the debate. For example, a memorandum from a WHO meeting trying to establish the 'facts' about injectable contraceptives stated that, while the potential for misuse was acknowledged 'as an area that should be addressed both by international agencies and by countries using the drug,' 'the topic was not discussed in detail at the meeting' (WHO 1982).

The FDA's proposal in 1974 that only a limited population of women could and therefore should 'benefit' from using Depo-Provera has always been a controversial issue. Levine argues that

> Although Upjohn vehemently denies the allegations made by women's health groups, health activists, and others that Depo-Provera is intended for poor women or for 'second class citizens', it is difficult to avoid the conclusion that the drug's target population in the United States would be those or other similarly vulnerable groups, such as institutionalized mentally ill women and the mentally retarded (1979).

At the 1983 hearings, while rejecting the concept of limited use, Upjohn and other supporter groups did single out certain groups of women for whom they thought Depo-Provera would be most appropriate. These included women over 35 for whom the risk of pregnancy was too great to rely on barrier methods, women who smoked and therefore increased their risk from the pill, women not planning to have more children, women contemplating sterilization or for whom sterilization was unacceptable, women with certain disorders, including substance abuse, for whom a regimen of birth control was difficult, and the severely mentally retarded (for whom Depo-Provera had the added 'hygienic' advantage of inducing amenorrhea).

Opponents argued that the nature of the population to whom Depo-Provera will be prescribed makes the concepts of 'informed consent' and 'freedom of choice' problematic. In the words of the National Women's Health Network and Health Research Group at the 1983 inquiry:

Subjecting poor and mentally retarded women to the risks would create a double standard which is morally offensive and unacceptable. Moreover, these groups of women are the least likely to be able to weigh the benefits and the risks of the drug and give true informed consent. They may also be more susceptible to pressure from physicians anxious to prescribe the drug, and may be less likely to identify early warning signs of serious side effects and take steps necessary to discontinue drug use. (Quoted in Skurnik 1983)

The anthropologist can contribute cross-cultural data on the questions of 'informed consent' and 'freedom of choice'. In a study conducted in the UK, Dr Wendy Savage found that, in the prescription of Depo-Provera in Tower Hamlets, a deprived London borough, in only 20% of cases investigated did the doctor discuss the drug with the women involved, usually poor and often illiterate Bengali immigrants. Porter (1990) gives evidence of doctors in the UK limiting the range of contraceptive options they offer women not only through their stereotypes of 'ideal type' or 'suitable' patients (for whom a particular method might be considered preferable on sometimes rigid, non-medical grounds) but also by prescribing favoured methods in such a way as to deny women choice (Porter 1990: 201). Riley *et al.* (1994) in a study of Depo-Provera use in rural Bangladesh found that less than half their sample of 200 first-time Depo-Provera users had been counselled about possible menstrual changes before accepting Depo-Provera. Just over a third were counselled after they had already 'accepted' (been injected with?) Depo-Provera, and the rest had received no counselling (ibid.).

In Thailand, Depo-Provera has been in use since 1965, and is currently one of the most popular forms of contraception. The McCormick Hospital in Chiengmai is the headquarters of the largest family planning programme in the world, and has played an important part in the testing of Depo-Provera. However, it is unlikely Depo-Provera is given in such rationally controlled conditions as the Chiengmai Hospital. One reason for this is the high value placed on injections as an effective and powerful form of ingesting 'modern' drugs, reflected in the role of 'injection doctors', who were proliferating when Cunningham wrote about them in 1970. Although they might be charged as much as seven to eight times more per treatment by 'injection doctors' than if they visited a rural health facility, Cunningham found many people preferred to go to such practitioners, who, while having no formal qualifications and only at best tolerated by local officials, spoke a language their patients could understand and offered remedies they wanted to have. Cunningham gives a sketch of one 'injection doctor', Dr Chi'id, who, although able to identify foreign drug labels, could not read the instructions on them because they were written in English. During the year of study, some 'injection doctors' started administering Depo-Provera, in addition to their usual range of sulpha drugs, penicillin, streptomycin, camphor, vitamins, saline and glucose. The ethical issues in provision of contraceptive services ('care as looking after') are as serious, potentially, as the ethical issues in the safety evaluation of particular drugs ('care as caution'). In other countries, the chief dispenser of Depo-Provera may be the chemist. Despite the Colombian Society of Obstetrics advising against the use of the drug, the *El Tiempo* newspaper of Bogota is reported as saying that Depo-Provera is 'freely sold in our drug stores for 80 pesos, and the package does not specify any contraindications at all' (quoted in 'E.B.' 1980).

Contraceptive provision takes place in the context of power relations in which the ethical concept of 'care', in any of its forms, may be severely lacking. In June 1980 the story broke in the US newspaper the *Philadelphia Inquirer* that a voluntary organization called Community Based Emergency Relief Services (CBERS), 'almost solely a birth control promotion group' (Nordland 1980), was conducting an aggressive birth control programme among Khmer refugees, in which the distinction between voluntary and compulsory contraception (let alone 'informed consent' and 'freedom of choice') was very blurred.[11] Dr Judith Greenberg, a US relief worker in the Cambodian refugee camps, linked the aggressive nature of the CBERS programme to the long history of ethnic and political conflict between Khmer and Thai people. She saw vans touring the camps, spreading propaganda about Depo-Provera – telling women that it would make them fatter and hence more beautiful, or that it was harmless. She also wrote of another doctor whom she says was thrown out of Thailand for insisting too vehemently that women should be screened before receiving their injection (Greenberg 1981).[12]

Similar power relationships can be seen in South Africa, where again Depo-Provera administration has to be seen in a social and political context. With medical literature in the apartheid era containing articles with titles such as 'More White Babies: What Hopes?' (Walker 1981) and articles such as Bloch (1971) pointing out the benefits of Depo-Provera for '"problem" patients with "problem" families who will not, or who cannot, use other methods of contraception reliably', people for whom 'motivation is usually lacking or very poor', the issue of 'care' in the administration of Depo-Provera becomes a haunting question. Rall *et al.* note the 'popularity' of Depo-Provera . . .

. . . as a means of fertility control among patients from lower socio-economic groups because of its simplicity of administration. The migratory nature of some populations in the Western Cape area of the country is conducive to a preference for longer-acting contraceptives, and DMPA is therefore viewed [by whom is unclear] as an eminently suitable method of birth control. It also has the advantage of considerable cost saving in scattered population groups, who must often be traced for follow-up injections. (1977: 55)

While the head of the Family Planning Association of South Africa, Dr Elin Hammer, is quoted as saying that the policy of the association as regards contraceptive choice is 'to explain the different types and let women (and their men, who are also welcome) decide for themselves what they feel is best suited for them' (Gordon 1981), what is questionable is how far, in the social and political circumstances (both macro and micro) in which it is administered, such ideals are actually put into practice. The ICASC argued that, in South Africa, 'For many women it [Depo-Provera] is the only contraceptive offered them. No follow-up appears to be being done on complaints of side effects . . . very few women are aware of the link between the drug and the medical complaints that it brings' (quoted in Gordon 1981).

What these examples show is the broad spectrum of places and power relations where the provision of contraceptives such as Depo-Provera is riven with problems for those concerned with the ethical issues of care as 'looking after'. Such issues have been marginalized in debates about the drug. Yet questions about the nature of the contraceptive services provided should also be of relevance to those concerned with safety issues ('care as caution'). The evidence presented supports Levine, who argues that, in many places,

The capabilities for screening high-risk users from the general family planning program population are likely to be very limited, particularly in rural areas. The information about risks is likely to be presented in skimpy fashion, given the program planners' commitment to the drug. Medical capabilites for follow-up are likely to be restricted to the most severe side-effects. If Depo-Provera is to be used at all, in very special circumstances, it seems to require the most careful kind of individual medical attention, a situation that is very rare in poor countries (1979).

Such concerns extend as legitimately to the implantable contraceptive Norplant, which came on to the market in the USA and Britain in the early 1990s without the acrimonious and lengthy debates that accompanied the passage of Depo-Provera into the marketplace. However, concern has been raised at the incorporation of Norplant into the punishment system (Grant 1993), and studies of its use in Egypt and Thailand offer stories of women being refused the right to have implanted rods removed.

Conclusion

Arguments about Depo-Provera and other long-acting hormonal contraceptives which seek to extend the boundaries of care into issues of care in service delivery do not fit into the 'care as caution' model, which has framed the mode of discussion about Depo-Provera. However, recent work in the 'total reproductive health' field seeks to bring such issues to the forefront of the agenda. Perea, for example, argues for the need to find ways of ensuring 'that provider–user relations are equitable and that decisions about reproduction take place in democratised spaces' (1994: 17). This is a far cry from the 'care as caution', risk–benefit concerns that have characterized FDA discussions of Depo-Provera. With the licensing of Depo-Provera for use in the USA, in some ways the debate has moved on from questions of 'whether or not' to 'how'. Elsewhere I argue that medical knowledge has also developed (the 'realist' approach), which has subsequently changed the terms and concerns of the safety aspects of the debate (Russell 1995/6). The issues that people are concerned about in the field of contracepion have changed, and yet the power relations and ideologies that underlie decision-making at global, national, service delivery and user levels remain the same.[13]

This chapter has looked at the notion of 'care' and its ethical implications when applied to the development of, discussion about and use of the injectable contraceptive Depo-Provera. It makes the point that, in a field like contraception, questions concerning 'care' need to be applied beyond what is the traditional domain of 'health care' for the ill. In the family planning arena, the meaning of 'care' fuels debates about the ethics of testing, evaluating and disseminating injectable contraceptives such as Depo-Provera. This chapter has questioned the ability of scientific risk–benefit analyses to take into account the ethical issues of 'caring' which offering Depo-Provera either on its own or as a 'suite of contraceptive options' involves.

Notes

1. Some of the material on which this chapter is based has appeared in altered form in an article in the *British Medical Anthropology Review* (Russell 1995/6). However, this chapter is intended to complement the other not only by expanding on some of the themes it contains, but also by incorporating recent work on ethical issues in women's reproductive health, which is a focus characteristic of much contemporary writing on this topic.

2. Slowly dissolving, microcrystalline compounds injected into muscle tissue in suspension. Depo-Provera contains progesterone, in the form of an esterifed progesterone alcohol, which is released into the bloodstream slowly, offering contraceptive protection for at least three months.

3. This accolade has since been taken by the implantable contraceptive Norplant, which typically has a tenfold lower 'failure rate' in the first year of use than Depo-Provera. For a discussion of Norplant, a contraceptive that raises similar ethical issues to those analysed here, see Mintzes *et al.* (1993).

4. As a result of these findings, Provest (an oral contraceptive containing medroxyprogesterone acetate and ethinyl oestradiol) was taken off the market and the FDA called off further US trials of Depo-Provera. This decision was justified, in the case of Provest, because 'other equally effective oral contraceptives were available which did not exhibit tumorogenicity in these dogs' (US Government 1974a).

5. However, his relativism did nothing to allay the fears of governments in many developing countries, and, because of their concerns, Kennedy sent out letters to over 60 of them explaining the FDA's decision in more detail.

6. Upjohn, for example, can be seen as having an interest in profits and a philosophy of free-enterprise capitalism. Sun (1982) writes, 'information about the contraceptive market suggests that the economic stakes are tantalizingly large', with contraceptives being 'amongst the most profitable of all the pharmaceuticals'.

7. Kennedy (1970) quotes a researcher from Edinburgh, who, in reporting the first synthesis of a hormone controlling ovulation to an early symposium on contraception, suggested 'it is doubtful whether we shall ever wish to obtain a point where these dangerous weapons will be at the disposal of man'.

8. This led to the 'Doctors Only Bill' (violently opposed by the Voluntary Parenthood League), which proposed that only doctors be allowed to

impart information about birth control, and to dispense it only when medical indications showed it to be necessary (Gordon 1976).

9. The benefits invoked can be listed as follows:

Highest use-effectiveness of any reversible method.
The only injectable contraceptive effective for as long as three months.
Effectiveness continues even if the user is a few weeks late in obtaining next injection.
As an injection it is especially desirable for those women who prefer injections over other forms of contraception.
Not used in relation to coitus.
Requires infrequent administration.
Requires no supplies to be kept around the house.
Gives the user a high degree of privacy.
It can be administered by any person who normally gives injections in a health care system.
Does not necessarily require a clinic setting for its administration.
Few harmful metabolic side-effects.
Good for women who have special medical/psychosocial needs contraindicating the use of other methods and for whom sterilization is not legal, available or desirable.
Does not suppress lactation, and may even increase milk volume.
Development of oligomenorrhoea and secondary amenorrhoea may alleviate iron-deficiency anaemia.

10. A pressure group campaigning against Depo-Provera asserts that these hearings 'took place in a context full of assumptions about the need for population control' (Campaign Against Depo-Provera 1980).

11. Nordland (1980) reported that every woman in Khao I Dang holding centre who agreed to take the drug was given a chicken, an inducement that did not exist for other birth-control methods. Furthermore, in another camp, there were a number of compulsory injections. The Red Cross medical coordinator was reported to have interviewed 100 women, of whom 61 had taken the drug. Of these, 36 said they had been given no information regarding the purpose of the injection. Only 15 of the women had been asked beforehand about their menstrual history, despite the fact that this is important if the drug is to be appropriately administered. Nordland wrote that 'informed consent is not obtained for the majority of women receiving Depo-Provera contraception' and that 'no precautions were taken to ensure that Depo-Provera is not given when women are pregnant or suffering

from amenorrhoea' (ibid.). There were also indications that Depo-Provera had been given as a prerequisite for marriage. In Kamput (another camp), seventy-four of the women interviewed had been married in the camp and, of these, fifty-six (76%) had received Depo-Provera. Of the 26 women interviewed who had married beforehand, only three (16%) had received Depo-Provera.

12. According to Nordland (1980), the director of a French medical group was also threatened with expulsion if he did not stop his criticisms of the CBERS campaign.

13. Ulin *et al.* plot the changing focus of family planning policy and goals from the reduction of fertility rates in the 1970s, through the Safe Motherhood Initiative of the 1980s, to the decade of the woman in the 1990s, concerned with 'women's total reproductive health, quality of life, and women's rights and status in society' (1994: 6). While I would agree with these broad categorizations, it should be remembered that the issues, concerns and power relations of earlier decades have not disappeared, but have become more muted, their salience diminished in the current scene.

References

Ardener, E. (1975), 'Belief and the Problem of Women', in S. Ardener (ed.), *Perceiving Women*, New York: John Wiley.

Benagiano, G. and I. Fraser (1981), 'The Depo-Provera Debate. Commentary on the Article "Depo-Provera, a Critical Analysis"', *Contraception*, 24(5): 493–528.

Bloch, B. (1971), 'Depot Medroxyprogesterone Acetate (Depo-Provera) as a Contraceptive Preparation', *South African Medical Journal*, 45: 777–80.

Boston Women's Health Book Collective (1973), *Our Bodies, Ourselves*, New York: Simon and Schuster.

Campaign Against Depo-Provera (1980), *Depo-Provera*, London: International Contraception, Abortion and Sterilization Campaign.

Cunningham, C.E. (1970), 'Thai Injection Doctors', *Social Science and Medicine*, 4(1): 1–24.

Douglas, M. and A. Wildavsky (1982), *Risk and Culture: an Essay on the Selection of Technical and Environmental Dangers*, Berkeley: University of California Press.

Doyal, L. (1997), 'Gendering Health: Men, Women and Well-Being', in M. Sidell, L. Jones, J. Katz and A. Peberdy (eds), *Debates and Dilemmas in Promoting Health: a Reader*, Basingstoke: Macmillan.

Easlea, B. (1983), *Fathering the Unthinkable: Masculinity, Scientists and the Nuclear Arms Race*, London: Pluto Press.

'E.B.' (1980), 'Upjohn Birth Control Drug Causes International Controversy', *Kalamazoo News*, 10 January: 1–4.

Fraser, I.S. and E. Weisberg (1981), 'A Comparative Review of Injectable Contraception with Special Emphasis on Depot Medroxyprogesterone Acetate', *The Medical Journal of Australia, Special Supplement*, 1: 1–20.

Gillespie, B., D. Eva and R. Johnston (1979), 'Carcinogenic Risk Assessment in the United States and Great Britain: the Case of Aldrin/Dieldrin', *Social Studies of Science*, 9: 265–301.

Gordon, L. (1976), *Woman's Body, Woman's Right: A Social History of Birth Control in America*, New York: Grossman.

Gordon, P. (1981), 'Banned Drug Used in South Africa', *Southern Africa*, September–October: 14–15.

Grant, L. (1993), 'Where Contraception is Used as a Punishment', *Marie-Claire*, No. 58, June: 79.

Greenberg, J. (1981), Diary, unpublished mimeograph in the offices of the American Friends Service Committee, Philadelphia.

Gusfield, J.R. (1981), *The Culture of Public Problems: Drinking-Driving and the Symbolic Order*, Chicago: University of Chicago Press.

Illich, I. (1976), *Limits to Medicine*, London: Marion Boyars.

Kennedy, D.M. (1970), *Birth Control in America: the Career of Margaret Sanger*, New Haven: Yale University Press.

Levine, C. (1979), 'Depo-Provera and Contraceptive Risk: a Case Study of Values in Conflict', *Hastings Center Report*, August: 8–11.

McFarlane, J. (1988), 'Nursing: a Paradigm of Caring', in G. Fairbairn and S. Fairbairn (eds), *Ethical Issues in Caring*, Aldershot: Avebury.

Mintzes, B., A. Hardon and J. Hanhard (eds) (1993), *Norplant: Under Her Skin*, Amsterdam: Women's Health Action Foundation and WEMOS.

Nordland, R. (1980), 'Birth Control: Injections of a Drug Banned in the U.S.', *Philadephia Inquirer*, 24 June: 9A.

Oudshoorn, N. (1994), *Beyond the Natural Body: an Archeology of Sex Hormones*, London: Routledge.

Peel, J. and M. Potts (1969), *Textbook of Contraceptive Practice*, Cambridge: Cambridge University Press.

Perea, J.G.F. (1994), 'The Introduction of New Methods of Contraception: Ethical Perspectives', *Reproductive Health Matters*, No. 3, May: 13–19.

Porter, M. (1990), 'Professional–Client Relationships and Women's Reproductive Health Care', in S. Cunningham-Burley and N.P. McKeganey (eds), *Readings in Medical Sociology*, London: Tavistock/Routledge.

Rall, H.J.S., W.A. van Niewerk, B.H.J. Engelbrecht and D.J. van Schalkwyk (1977), 'Comparative Contraceptive Experience with Three-Month and Six-Month Medroxyprogesterone Acetate Regimes', *Journal of Reproductive Medicine*, 18(2): 55–60.

Richard, B.W. and L. Lasagna (1987), 'Drug Regulation in the United States and the United Kingdom: the Depo-Provera Story', *Annals of Internal Medicine*, 196: 886–91.

Riley, A.P., M.K. Stewart and J. Chakraborty (1994), 'Program- and Method-Related Determinants of First DMPA Use Duration in Rural Bangladesh', *Studies in Family Planning*, 25(5): 255–67.

Rosenfield, A., D. Maine, R. Rochat, J. Shelton and R.A. Hatcher (1983), 'The Food and Drug Administration and Medroxyprogesterone Acetate. What are the Issues?', *Journal of the American Medical Association*, 249(21): 2922–8.

Russell, A.J. (1995/6), 'Depo-Provera: Cultural Controversies in Contraceptive Decision-Making', *British Medical Anthropology Review (N.S.)*, 3(1): 4–15.

Seaman, B. (1969), *The Doctor's Case Against the Pill*, New York: Peter H. Wyden.

Skurnik, J. (1983), 'Depo-Provera: FDA Hearings Raise Questions', *Off Our Backs*, 13(2): 5–6.

Sobo. E.J. (1993), 'Bodies, Kin, and Flow: Family Planning in Rural Jamaica', *Medical Anthropology Quarterly*, 7(1): 50–73.

Sun, M. (1982), 'Depo-Provera Debate Revs Up at FDA', *Science*, 217: 424–8.

Ulin, P.R., K. Hardee, P. Bailey and N. Williamson (1994), 'The Impact of Family Planning on Women's Lives: Expanding the Research Agenda', *World Health Statistics Quarterly*, 47(1): 6–8.

US Government (1974a), *Use of Advisory Committees by the FDA*, Subcommittee of the Committee of Government Operations, 93rd Congress, 6, 7, 8, 12 and 13 March, 30 April and 21 May.

—— (1974b), 'Patient Labeling of Medroxyprogesterone Acetate Injectable Contraception', *Federal Register*, 39(178): 32907–11.

—— (1978a), 'Upjohn Co.; Depo-Provera Sterile Aqueous Suspension', *Federal Register*, 43(127): 28555–6.

—— (1978b), *The Depo-Provera Debate*, Hearings before the Select Committee on Population, US House of Representatives, Ninety-Fifth Congress, Second Session, 8, 9 and 10 August.

Walker, A.R.P. (1981), 'More White Babies: What Hopes?', *South African Medical Journal*, 59(9): 285.

Weisz, J., G.T. Ross and P.D. Stolley (1984), *Report of the Public Board of Inquiry on Depo-Provera*, Rockville, Maryland: Food and Drug Administration.

WHO (1982), 'Facts about Injectable Contraceptives: Memorandum from a WHO Meeting, *Bulletin of the World Health Organization*, 60(2): 199–210.

WHO Expanded Programme of Research, Development and Research Training in Human Reproduction (1977), 'Multinational Comparative Clinical Evaluation of Long-Acting Injectable Contraceptive Steroids: Noresthisterone Enanate and Depot-Medroxyprogesterone Acetate. I. Use-Effectiveness', *Contraception*, 15: 513–33.

4

Medical Care as Human Right: The Negation of Law, Citizenship and Power?

Marie-Bénédicte Dembour

In the contemporary world, it is common for political claims of almost any kind to be phrased in the language of rights. In this language, the expression 'human rights' enjoys a special aura. It is therefore appropriate for a book that questions what kind of care one can or should expect to pay attention to the way the human rights discourse has been invoked in various discussions about 'care'.

Human rights are a construction of Western political thought.[1] Their antecedent can be traced to natural law, a branch of jurisprudence which already attracted passionate debates in ancient Greece. Their modern origin can be traced to the eighteenth century, especially in the American Declaration of Independence, the US Constitution, and the French Declaration of the Rights of Man and of the Citizen. These documents declared rights such as freedom of speech and association, personal liberty, access to a fair trial, etc., i.e. rights that belong to the civil and political category. These probably remain the human rights with which we are the most familiar today through the work of organizations such as Amnesty International. They only constitute, however, one 'generation' of human rights, the first one. Since then, two other generations have come to be recognized. The second generation embraces social and economic rights, and the third refers to collective rights.[2] Compared with the first generation rights and perhaps even some of the third, the second generation has received very little international implementation. Thus, violations of the rights it encompasses do not give rise to complaints before the United Nations (UN) or other international institutions set up to deal with human rights violations.[3]

Medical care is one right that is generally accepted to belong to the second generation of human rights.[4] It is specifically mentioned in the

Declaration on Human Rights, which the UN signed in 1948. In this chapter, I question what it means to say of medical care that it is a human right.

I begin by arguing that the proposition which determines that medical care is a human right cannot be taken at face value. The Declaration guarantees rights in the abstract, outside any defined context. This means that its provisions are not readily applicable in practice. But some would argue that this does not matter. After all, human rights are not meant to be legal rights (Milne 1980). Indeed, the main characteristic of human rights is that they are supposed to be above the law of the government; they are conceptualized as binding and setting limits to what a government can do. Thus, in some ways they are at their most useful when they are invoked in the absence of a national framework that can guarantee them. It could therefore be said that, while legal rights are 'real' rights, human rights typically represent promises for the future, claims which have not (yet) been granted (Dembour 1996a). Human rights, however, are often talked of as if they were 'real' rights. This is problematic. 'Rights talk' is problematic in other ways too. Most importantly, it arguably leads to the loss rather than to the stimulation of a sense of active citizenship. Human rights claims typically come to be fought on an individualistic basis, rather than being based on collective political involvement. Also, human rights talk generally fails to highlight the existence of relations of power which underlie not only the denial but also the granting of a (human) right. Some people benefit from the human rights discourse directly to the detriment of others.

At one level, this chapter is a critique of the human rights discourse. My aim, however, is not to dismiss the language of human rights altogether. Although it is riven with difficulties, we may have no better language available today to express our protest in the face of what we regard as morally and politically unacceptable situations. Thus, we can and should keep the principle and ideal of human rights with us, but we need at the same time to contextualize them, think about the way we wish to implement them in practice, i.e. in particular circumstances. In other words, one key to resolving the largely fruitless debate on the universalism or relativism of human rights is to remain in between these two positions. In the field with which this book is concerned, this means envisaging the right to medical care as a good, but one with which we, as recipients and givers of care, need to engage with and define, rather than one which we can take for granted as something to be received from the medical establishment and the government.

An All-too-abstract Declaration

Article 25 (1) of the Universal Declaration of Human Rights provides:

Everyone has the right to a standard of living adequate for the health and well-being of himself and of his family, including . . . medical care.

This language is deceptively simple. It may give the impression that the Declaration provides for things which are simple to comprehend, but difficulties abound. I shall identify four problematic areas. (1) Is anyone responsible for enforcing the declared right when it is not spontaneously respected? If not, is it still worth talking of a right? (2) According to which criteria does one (who?) decide that a standard of living is 'adequate'? (3) Even more fundamentally, who can say what constitute health, well-being and (good) medical care? (4) Finally, why are women implicitly conceived of as necessarily part of a male-headed family? I shall say a few words about each of these questions, addressing them in the reverse order to that in which I have listed them.

The last question, at least, may seem disingenuous, only signalling a historical lapse long taken care of. After all, the Declaration was signed in 1948, at a time when one could hardly expect feminist claims to be taken on board by representatives of state governments in the UN. This, however, is precisely part of my point: human rights propositions are the product of particular, identifiable, circumstances. They are not valid in the abstract.

Human rights specialists might well accept my last point. They talk in terms of various generations of human rights, and they generally agree on the fact that the definition of particular human rights evolves through time. Most would readily admit, to return to our topic, that what counts as proper health care depends on social circumstances. In considering the latter, they would reserve special consideration for the level of 'development' achieved in any particular region. I would retort, however, that, on the whole, human rights activists and scholars do not doubt that what counts as proper care in given circumstances is definable. In other words, they do not see that the concepts they elevate to the status of human rights are problematic. Other contributions to this volume show how wrong this presumption of straightforwardness is, as far as health and medical care are concerned. These concepts lose their supposed transparency as soon as one begins to discuss or attempts to apply them; one is then forced to realize that there is very little agreement on exactly what they mean.[5] Ultimately, the question of who can define what constitutes health, well-being and good medical care is a political one, for which there exists no neutral answer. This ties in with the objection that the Declaration is ethno-, Western-, élite- or within-a-particular-view-centric. There is more. The question of defining what 'adequate' medical care consists of remains pertinent, even if we leave aside controversies and uncertainties about the merits of various health approaches and/or specific treatments. Is the question of defining what 'adequate' care is to be answered by reference to state-of-the-art scientific achievements at any one time, or do other considerations, such as costs, need to be included? One may be tempted to say that only scientific medical progress should provide the answer. Such a view, however, is an unrealistic one. Doctors, but also policy-makers and active patients, know only too well that deciding which level of care is adequate, on the one hand, and examining which means are available in the health-care field, on the other, are not independent issues. This is an increasingly topical issue on the public agenda, evident in the media, and one which will give rise to more controversy.

Let me take the example of the report of a doctor's outrage at the denial of radiotherapy for terminally-ill cancer. To quote the article where the report appeared:

> Dying patients in urgent need of pain relieving radiotherapy treatment can expect only 'second-rate' care from the National Health Service unless the Government commits extra funds to cancer services, a leading specialist [Dr Victor Varley of the Bristol Oncology Centre] warned yesterday . . .
> Those with curative conditions were receiving radiotherapy, while scores of terminally ill patients were being prescribed painkilling drugs instead of palliative radiation treatment, he said.
> 'This is less than the optimum treatment,' Dr Varley said last night. 'A single radio-therapy treatment to a painful bone can bring relief for several months. To achieve the same effect with drugs requires large doses which make the patient drowsy and affect quality of life.' (*Guardian*, 17 February 1996, p. 4)

Cancer that has spread from a primary tumour to the bone can be very painful. Because the Universal Declaration talks of health but also of well-being, the practice of not providing terminally ill patients with radio-therapy, which Dr Varley asserts has negative effects on the patients' quality of life, can be seen as a glaring violation of the Declaration. Failure to provide the advocated treatment sounds even more scandalous, as it is referred to as 'second-rate care'. Such qualification offends the ideal of equality on which the Universal Declaration explicitly rests, and on which many in the Western world like to think their democracies are based.

Delivery of rights, including that of medical services, depends upon the existence of an infrastructure that allows for such delivery. This, in turn, requires social vision, effort and execution. To continue with our example, the right to medical care cannot be seen in isolation from the social context in which it is enacted. One can criticize, of course, how resources are allocated in a particular society to achieve (or not achieve) a particular level of health care. However, one cannot speak of a right to medical treatment without addressing the question of its resourcing. Any other view is theoretical and fails to encompass the constraints of practice. Incidentally, it is only when the resource question is addressed that one can start tackling the question of how to remedy failure for the right to medical care to be 'spontaneously' respected.

The right declared in the Universal Declaration suddenly appears all too evanescent. Is it worth talking of it being violated when an (arguably) unsatisfactory medical treatment becomes the norm? Asking the question brings us to the main flaw in the human rights discourse as a whole. The fundamental problem with this discourse is that it is abstract, set out of context and is therefore unrealistic. Perhaps this does not make it altogether useless, but one consequence is that it cannot possibly provide for legally enforceable rights.

Would-be Infinite, Hence Legally Incongruous, Human Rights

Discussions about the difficulties relating to transforming human rights, especially those belonging to the socio-economic category, into real 'rights' abound (see, for example, Garibaldi 1976; Berenstein 1981; Henkin 1981; Peces-Barba 1981). With the exception of Maurice Cranston (1964), however, few have argued that such an enterprise is inherently faulty (see especially Golding 1984; Donnelly and Howard 1988; Donnelly 1989, chapter 2). The eminent French legal philosopher Michel Villey is one scholar who attacks not just the idea that economic and social rights can be human rights, but the very concept of human rights. He is of course not the first person to have done so. Predecessors in this radical critique include Jeremy Bentham, for whom human rights were 'non-sense upon stilts'.[6] None the less, such a complete rejection of the concept, which is rare, tends to rest, when adopted today, on the rejection of the claimed universality of human rights. For Villey, however, the problem with the concept of human rights lies elsewhere. The leitmotif of his book *Le Droit et les droits de l'homme* (1983) is that the concept deceptively refers to 'rights'. For him, human rights are fundamentally alien to the legal process; they rely on a false concept of right. His argument, which he bases on an analysis of Greek and Roman texts, is relevant here. I shall thus review some of the themes that run through his book, numbering them for the sake of clarity (i.e. such numbers are mine, not Villey's).

1. Human rights consist of promises that are infinite (*infinies*). Interestingly for us, Villey takes the example of health: 'equal health for everyone: a heart transplant for all those with cardiac problems? The right "to health" of every French person would suffice to empty the French budget, and one hundred times more!' (p. 11).[7] Human rights, by making infinite promises, have nothing to do with law and legal rights, for law is not interested in infinity (p. 115). Law and rights are always about apportioning things that are finite and measurable, i.e. about establishing proportions and deciding who gets what (p. 45). Legal rights are never infinite.

2. Fundamentally, human rights entail promises to something (for example, medical care). Having a substantive content is of their essence. In contrast, law is primarily relational – it is about establishing relations (p. 47). This Villey says and repeats. For example, he notes that there is always a plurality of litigants to a lawsuit (p. 96).

3. Human rights claim to derive from the subject. This is clearly suggested by the definition, according to which they are those rights which one has solely by virtue of being a human being. This, for Villey, again reveals them to be outside the legal process: how could one infer from a single term (man, the subject) something with a legal bearing, which by nature is relational and therefore covers more than one term (p. 154, see also previous points)? Villey incidentally observes that, in law, legal rights are never self-assigned; the claim to a right always needs to be confirmed by an external body (p. 46).

4. The previous points highlight the different nature, object and basis of human rights and legal rights, respectively. It therefore comes as no surprise that human rights have not been invented by lawyers. Locke is generally credited with having laid down the political philosophy allowing for the development of the concept of human rights a few years later in the French and American declarations. Villey remarks that Locke had no legal training whatsoever (p. 144).

5. Human rights are conceived as rights to things (point 2). The idea of having rights to things (i.e. the idea of the *droit subjectif*) has come to be regarded very much in a Kantian way, as if it were impossible to live in a world without rights in the sense just outlined, as if it constituted – to borrow Kant's expression – an eternal category of the human mind

(p. 70). Contrary to what is generally believed (and taught to law students), the notion of *droit subjectif* was nevertheless unknown to the Romans and, according to Villey, it could not have been accommodated in the Roman (apportioning) conception of law. Looking at the idea of having such rights as a permanent human feature entails both a misreading of history and an ethnocentric vision. It is entirely possible to live in a world where one does not base one's claims on the idea that one has a right to this or that.

6. Human rights are nothing but false promises. Villey qualifies them as, in turn, unreal, illusory, untenable, unworkable, contradictory, useless. They seem to announce an earthly paradise where everyone would have the same things, without limits. But the implementation of such a philosophy would lead to chaos. Seen in this light, it is hardly surprising that in reality only a few benefit from the human rights discourse (p. 153; see also Dembour 1996a). In contrast, Villey suggests that 'true' law is always very clear on the fact that it does not achieve equal distribution (p. 50): the debtor, for example, does not have the same right as the creditor, or the criminal the same right as the innocent (p. 99).

7. The concept of human rights is also flawed in that it has no place for notions of responsibility, duty and solidarity (p. 97). Let us pursue the example of the right to health beyond Villey's short allusion to it, which I have quoted. If we want to be entitled to sophisticated medical care, be it a heart transplant, radiotherapy or any other costly treatment, we must also be ready to contribute and make such a health system a reality: the system will neither fall from the heavens nor materialize through verbal declarations. This, in turn, requires us to take a social, rather than an individual, stance: we as individuals may never directly benefit from the efforts we have invested in building up the system.

In conclusion, Villey's analysis suggests that the gap between theory and practice in the field of human rights is structural rather than amenable to closure through better practice. Many human rights activists would take this analysis to indicate that a gap exists between theory (the Declaration) and practice (the failure to provide radiotherapy); they would argue that the gap needs to be reduced through better practice (ensuring that radiotherapy is available). Villey's analysis, however, suggests that the gap will not go. It is there to stay, because human rights constitute illusory promises. Not only the practice but also the theory needs to be revised.

Waiting for the Impossible to Happen Effortlessly

The concept of human rights has been invented in societies which, to a greater or lesser degree, employ the concept of constitutional rights. In other words, the former takes for granted basic ideas, such as the existence of a division between civil society and government, the necessity to limit the powers of the government and the idea that citizens are entitled to certain guarantees, called rights. Villey may well be right in thinking that the concept of 'human rights' relies on a mistaken notion of what a 'right' is. The idea of rights is none the less fundamental to the concept. It may therefore be useful to analyse the wider rights discourse when one tries to tackle what the human rights discourse is about. In what follows, I turn my attention to the analysis of the American political scientist Mary Ann Glendon, who has focused on rights talk in the USA and argued that such talk impoverishes political discourse (1991). Contrary to the author's own suggestion, I think her analysis need not be restricted to the American case. Certainly I do not find the comparative material she presents strong enough to justify her elevating (or should I say downgrading) the 'American rights talk' to a specific dialect within the worldwide rights discourse. While Glendon discusses rights talk in general, rather than human rights as such, the propositions she makes are consonant with those of Villey. Reviewing them will help me to consolidate my own critique of health care as human right.

Glendon starts from the observation that, in the USA today, individuals constantly assert rights – to this, that, anything and everything. The same happens on this side of the Atlantic, as a cursory reading of any newspaper will demonstrate. Here is one illustrative statement of such rights talk: '[T]he Policy Studies Institute has found that British children are increasingly being denied a *basic right* – to get around on their own without adult surveillance – as traffic and abduction fears take hold of parents (*Guardian Education,* 17 October 1995, p. 8, emphasis added). Not only do individuals assert rights, but they do so as if the rights they claim for themselves were absolute. But, as Glendon observes, a right is never unlimited. Even the right of property, fundamental in American ideology, is limited by the duty to use it in a way that is not dangerous, not illegal or simply not inconvenient to neighbours, by rules on forced sale in the public interest, and by a series of other constraints which American citizens generally do not think about. Thus the illusion of absoluteness persists, with a number of negative consequences. I shall go through these and, for the sake of clarity, I shall number them, as I did for Villey's propositions. The examples I shall use for illustration will not necessarily be Glendon's.

Instead, I shall also draw on European situations, to show that Glendon's analysis applies to this side of the Atlantic too.

1. Individuals constantly assert rights. Each of these rights demands respect, but all cannot be simultaneously granted, as they come into conflict with each other. Abortion is a case in point: one cannot respect both the woman's right to her body and the foetus's right to life (Glendon 1991: 11). Freedom of expression is another classic example. If the right to expression is absolute, how can one reconcile it with the right to physical integrity, privacy, respect of the person of others (think of the problems which emerge from incitation to racial hatred, pornography, blasphemy, etc.)? The chaotic situation anticipated by Villey (point 6) emerges.

2. The more a right is thought of as absolute, the more likely a conflict is to emerge, and the less negotiation, dialogue and mutual understanding will be represented as key values (p. 45). The way in which the issue of female circumcision has been tackled in France is typical of this logic (Dembour 1996b). There, various female circumcision practices are generally seen as violating the right of a girl/woman to bodily integrity. The opposite and minority view is that the right that one's culture should be respected demands that they be tolerated. The phrasing of the issue in two conflicting positions eliminates the possibility of a dialogue and the discovery of any common ground. One result of the absoluteness of the respective claims is that migrant mothers who had an operation performed on their daughters were sentenced to imprisonment by the French judiciary, which subsequently realized that something was wrong in its approach and found a way not to send these women to jail.[8]

3. Following from the previous point, Glendon remarks on the number of cases raising crucial political issues which have been dealt by the US Supreme Court in the past few decades. She notes: 'To many activists, it seemed more efficient, as well as more rewarding, to devote one's time and efforts to litigation that could yield total victory, than to put in long hours at political organizing, where the most one can hope to gain is, typically, a compromise' (p. 6). This situation is not exclusively American. In Britain, the action by two mothers who wanted their children to be able to play on the local beach is an example of a policy issue being 'resolved' in a judicial way; the women managed to have the High Court condemn their local council to ensuring that sewage was removed (reported by Tom Leonard in the *Daily Telegraph*, 4 April 1996, p. 8).[9]

4. The assertion of individual rights tends to lead to the development of what Glendon calls hyperindividualism. One claims one's rights because it is one's due, irrespective of social and long-term implications (p. 171). As Villey also noted (point 7), a sense of sociality and of responsibility is

missing. Citizens come to consider themselves as individuals who act alone
and who consider the rights they claim as their due, without perceiving
that they need to contribute to the system from which they feel entitled to
benefit. Thus, the parents of Richard Wilding, a 13-year-old disruptive
pupil excluded from school, brandish their son's right to education. But
what their child needs to do to avail himself to this right is a question
which they should not ignore (see the *Guardian*'s leader, 24 April 1996).
 5. Rights claims are expressed in a sound-bite form, which glosses over
the complexity of the claim (p. x). This fits with what I have said above
about Article 25 of the Universal Declaration, whose wording makes the
right to medical care appear deceptively simple.
 6. For Glendon, the recourse to rights talk can degenerate into the
affirmation of unbounded desires which deny, almost pathologically, the
contingency of human life. To quote her:

'Claims of absoluteness . . . tend to downgrade rights into mere expression of
unbounded desires and wants. Excessively strong formulations express our
most infantile instincts rather than our potential to be reasonable men and
women . . . When we assert these rights in an absolute form . . . we are
expressing infinite and impossible desires . . . There is pathos as well as bravado
in these attempts to deny the fragility and contingency of human existence,
personal freedom, and the possession of worldly goods. (Glendon 1991: 45)

This echoes Villey's denunciation of (human) rights as representing the
promise of an earthly paradise (point 6). It also ties in with his cynical
remark about each case of cardiac illness receiving a heart transplant in
the name of 'equal health for everyone'. Perhaps human rights talk
makes us dream of a world where everything would be possible. This is
characteristic of a society that prefers to ignore death and serious illness,
rather than to face its reality (Mellor and Shilling 1993; Dembour 1999),
a society which likes to think that suffering should have no place, that our
lives should run easily and smoothly. We need to ask whether such a mode
of thought is really beneficial, or whether it is simply naïve and ultimately
unhelpful.
 By asking the last question, I am not denying that many claims phrased
in the language of rights and/or human rights are legitimate. I believe, in
particular, that it is worth fighting for clean beaches, children's access to
school, and heart transplants to be readily available. I suggest, however,
that all these things need to be fought for. We cannot just sit back and
wait for 'the world' to deliver them to us. We need to ensure that they
happen by investing our time, energy and resources; we need to think

about how we wish to resolve conflicts of interests; finally we must adopt a holistic and long-term perspective. To borrow from Glendon's vocabulary, we need to act as responsible citizens. Then rights talk will stop impoverishing political discourse and, on the contrary, enhance it, in the best of our political traditions. In the field of care, this also means that one must have an active vision of what care entails and recognize that it is a relational practice that involves choices and negotiations between all actors involved. In particular, one must abandon the idea that all groups and all individuals require the same thing. Imagining a standard of care to be applicable anywhere and everywhere around the world, as the human rights discourse tends to do, in its search for a globalized vision, too easily overlooks the necessity to ground rights in locally diverse realities and quests.

Revolutionary Rights Turned Power Enforcers

Rights talk is triggered by the perception that something is going wrong. Otherwise there would be no need to think that a right is being infringed and, therefore, no need to claim the existence of a right in the first place. To return to earlier examples, the basic right for children 'to play on a safe beach' or 'to get around on their own without adult surveillance' has only come to be identified (respectively) after pollution rendered beach play on some coastal stretches unadvisable and after the 'danger of raising a generation of paranoid children who believe the world is out to get them' had been envisaged (*Daily Telegraph,* 4 April 1996, p. 8; *Guardian Education,* 17 October 1995). The same is true of more readily recognizable basic rights, including the Universal Declaration of Human Rights, which was signed in 1948 in an effort to ensure that events comparable to those which had taken place in the Second World War would never happen again. Similarly, Locke's *Second Treatise of Government,* generally regarded as having laid down the foundations on which the concept of human rights was allowed to develop, can only be understood in the context of its time, as a theoretical contribution undermining absolute monarchy and supporting a change in the constitution towards (some) people being represented in the government (see Laslett 1970: Introduction).

Neil Stammers is one of the few academics who advocate against examining and discussing human rights as if they were an abstract concept. He also explicitly links human rights with power relationships and argues that 'conceptions of human rights have both challenged and sustained particular forms of power, thus playing a highly ambivalent role' (1993: 70). Basically, Stammers proposes that human rights initially challenge power relationships but subsequently tend to sustain the newly achieved status quo.[10] To quote him at some length:

> The claims to 'natural rights' and 'the rights of man' put forward by John Locke and Tom Paine and codified in the American and French declarations clearly had something to do with challenging the status quo . . . The notion that sovereignty derived from the people challenged the divine right of kings. The right of resistance or rebellion was predicated on the notion that government was legitimate only insofar as it served the interests of the people. The idea of individuals having rights challenged the idea that individuals only had duties to their masters and betters. The claim of a right to private property challenged the prevailing belief that all property was ultimately vested in the crown . . . But [with the passing of time], the doctrine of natural rights ceased to be a revolutionary challenge. Instead it came to sustain the highly unequal economic power relations inherent in developing capitalist societies. (Ibid.: 73–4)

As Donnelly, quoted by Stammers, remarks: 'the original and largely bourgeois proponents of natural rights gradually moved out of political opposition into control' (Donnelly 1989: 29).

In his article, Stammers successively applies his idea that rights talk historically transforms itself from a challenging tool into an instrument for sustaining existing power relationships to the three generations of human rights, i.e. to the rights belonging to the civil and political, economic and social, and collective categories. I find this idea extremely useful and pertinent. I think, however, that it should not be used just to comment in a broad and therefore simplistic way on long periods of history and mega-categories (the fictional dichotomy between the public and private realm, the bourgeoisie, postcolonial societies . . .), but that it can equally be used by reference to relatively small-scale situations. Let me take one in the field of medical care.

Nancy Scheper-Hughes traces rumours, widespread in Brazil, South Africa and elsewhere, of child abduction and mutilation for the purpose of international trade in organs to 'poor people's perceptions . . . that their bodies and those of their children might be worth more dead than alive to the rich and the powerful' (1996: 7). She does not want to get too much engaged into the debate on whether these rumours reflect actual cases of kidnapped children for organ transplants. Rather she concludes that '[t]he stories are told, remembered, and circulated because they are fund-amentally, *existentially* true' (ibid.: 9). Typically it is the rich who benefit from the organs 'donated' by the poor, because of the economic and political difference between the two groups (civil unrest and political disappearances are not without implications for the availability of organs). On this basis, Scheper-Hughes criticizes the proposal approved by the Brazilian Senate in February 1996, which established a medical norm of 'presumed consent' with respect to organ donation. She writes:

'Opting out' systems of organ donation based on presumed consent can and do operate quite well in countries where civil society is strong and where democracy is consolidated, such as in Belgium and Austria. But in large, complex, and conflict-oriented nations like Brazil, the United States and South Africa, where sharp social, ethnic, and class-based inequities divide the nation into almost predictable 'classes' of likely organ donors and likely organ recipients, and where the risks and the benefits of medical technology are not randomly distributed, presumed consent can only generate a kind of existential terror and ontological insecurity in the already fragile sense of 'ownership' over one's own body. (Ibid.: 9)

She denounces the abomination of organ transplantation practices within health-care systems which are not reasonably fair and equitable and, in so doing, she has recourse to the language of human rights (not very surprisingly, as she identifies a seriously wrong situation). For the present discussion, what is interesting in her account is that it situates the claim to the (human) right to a transplant (a conceivable assertion; remember Villey's remark on cardiacs and heart transplants) in a particular context. Rights cannot be declared 'good' or 'bad' in the abstract. They must be assessed within the context in which they are/would be exercised. A transplant system may be wonderful in Belgium but terrible in Brazil.

The idea of 'challenging rights turned power sustainers' highlighted by Stammers must teach us not to approach rights talk in a single-minded way. We cannot assume from the outset that, because a right (including a human right) is being invoked, there must be a scandalous situation underlying it which we wish to see transformed for the benefit of those who claim this right. Conversely, we cannot assume either that relying on a right necessarily means that the person who seeks to assert her right is just trying to maintain her powerful position; perhaps she is fighting for a change that we wish to support. Finally, we should be aware that rights claims can both challenge and sustain power relationships at the same time. In other words, each situation of a rights claim needs to be analysed on its own terms.

Looking at human rights from such a perspective helps to resolve the vexing debate on universalism and cultural relativism.[11] Rather than trying to decide which of these two positions is valid, we should consider the benefit of agreeing to remain in between them. The universal appeal of human rights allows us to think of what kind of world we would ideally like to inhabit; it gives us useful ideas for political engagement, including with regard to health care. The universal position, however, is unsatisfactory as soon as it leads us to overlook the need to problematize medical care (and other rights). Care cannot be decontextualized, it always requires social engagement. The relativist position compensates for the defects of universalism by paying attention to the needs and wishes of particular people, living in given circumstances. Relativism, however, is not helpful if it prevents the development of a vision that goes beyond local circumstances. The in-between position combines the strengths of universalism and relativism by making it possible to invoke a general principle for specific purposes. It encourages people to fight for the practical care they wish to see established in the name of an abstract ideal, found, for example, in the Universal Declaration.

Conclusion

The UN Declaration of Human Rights has provided the starting-point of this chapter. I have noted that the vague and abstract character of the provision dealing with medical care empties this presumably universal right of any effective meaning and I have teased out the implications of this rather simple observation through reviewing three powerful critiques of human rights and/or rights. I have first paid attention to Michel Villey's proposition that human rights have nothing to do with a properly understood concept of law: in this perspective, human rights represent unsubstantiated promises to unlimited goods. I have then discussed Mary Ann Glendon's warning that rights talk lends itself to producing individualistic members of society who consider the fulfilment of (legitimate) claims as their due rather than as something that requires collective action. Finally, following Neil Stammers, I have observed that human rights do not necessarily challenge the status quo, but can serve to sustain unjust power relationships. My aim in linking these critiques together is not to dismiss the language of (human) rights altogether, but rather to sound a note of caution: rights talk can be both used and abused. It is for each of us to be aware of its multiple character and to exercise our intellectual and moral judgement to decide which situation is which.

In the field of care, it is therefore of paramount importance not to be satisfied with the proposition that one is entitled to medical care. This is so because this proposition, which fails to grasp the inherently relational nature of medical care, does not in itself mean anything. We cannot take for granted a so-called right to medical care as if it were an unproblematic good to which we are entitled. Instead, we must work out what we want it to mean in practice. Failing this, the reality will fall away from the Utopia, and not just in the Third World. To avoid finding ourselves oppressed by the medical care we receive, we must think of what we want it to be. While we can welcome Article 25 of the Universal Declaration as a valuable political ambition, we should not rest and fool ourselves into believing that 'human rights' provide definite solutions. These do not exist. This is why we should always fight for better practices in the field of care, as in other ones.

Notes

1. For a classical view on what human rights are, see, for example, Pennock (1981).
2. Whether some human rights are more fundamental than others is a question that has tantalized scholars (see, for example, Van Boven 1982; Meron 1986).
3. On the United Nations Human Rights regime, see Alston (1992).
4. Another second-generation human right is education. For an interesting approach to this and to human rights more generally, see Rendel (1997).
5. The same goes for other notions central to the Universal Declaration, such as cruel punishment, impartial tribunal, family, education, etc.
6. See Bentham's essay on the 'Declaration of Rights' (reproduced in Parekh 1973). Since then, however, efforts have been made to reconcile the concept of human rights with a utilitarian political philosophy (e.g. Gibbard 1989).
7. All translations from the French are mine.
8. For more on these trials, see Winter (1994) and Lefeuvre-Déotte (1997).
9. Incidentally, the action also illustrates how pervasive the language of rights has become. One mother explained: 'Children have been denied their right to play on a clean beach. That was ultimately why we brought and carried on with the case . . . This is a nationwide problem. Hopefully others will now take action, too, to have clean beaches.' This way of explaining the action refers to a notion of a child's right which

is not a legal one: I have never heard of a child's legal right to play on a clean beach. The discourse is nevertheless effective. However baffling to a lawyer's ear, speaking in terms of the violation of a right makes sense in view of the present tendency to refer to rights to put forward all sorts of claims. We may see many of these as legitimate, as in this case; however, the danger is that, as we assert our rights, we forget to listen to each other because we see ourselves engaged in a battle where total victory is the aim. Note also the end of the quotation, which exhorts other people to follow suit, supporting Glendon's observation that what is sought is a judicial, as opposed to a legislative, solution.

10. He could thus be seen to follow in the steps of the young Karl Marx, who, in his early writings, had offered a powerful critique of the concept of human rights (see his essays 'On the Jewish Question' and 'The Holy Family' in Marx 1975). For a useful contemporary reading of human rights theory that adopts a Marxist approach, see Szabo (1982).

11. To get a feel for this debate, compare, for example, in an extensive literature, the approach adopted by Pollis and Schwab (1979) with that of Panikkar (1982), and the position of Renteln (1988) with that of Hatch (1997). For two recent collections of essays specially devoted to this debate, see the issue of the *Journal of Anthropological Research,* introduced by Nagengast and Turner (1997), and the special issue of *North–South Coalition* (1988*).*

References

Alston, P. (ed.) (1992), *The United Nations and Human Rights: A Critical Appraisal*, Oxford: Oxford University Press.

Berenstein, A. (1981), 'Economic and Social Rights: Their Inclusion in the European Convention of Human Rights. Problems of Formulation and Interpretation', *Human Rights Law Journal*, 2: 257–80.

Cranston, M. (1964), *What Are Human Rights?*, New York: Basic Books.

Dembour, M.-B. (1996a), 'Human Rights Talk and Anthropological Ambivalence: The Particular Contexts of Universal Claims', in O. Harris (ed.), *Inside and Outside the Law*, London: Routledge, pp. 9–24.

—— (1996b), 'From Female Circumcision to Genital Mutilation Back to Circumcision: The French Lesson', paper given at the 4th EASA Conference held in Barcelona in July 1996, ms.

—— (1999), 'The Conscious Death of a Two-Year-Old: Beautiful and Unbearable', *Omega: Journal of Death and Dying.*

Donnelly, J. (1989), *Universal Human Rights in Theory and Practice*, Ithaca: Cornell University Press.

Donnelly, J. and R.E. Howard. (1988), 'Assessing Human Rights Performance: A Theoretical Framework', *Human Rights Quarterly*, 10: 215–48.

Garibaldi, P. (1976), 'General Limitations on Human Rights: The Principle of Legality', *Harvard International Law*, 281.

Gibbard, A. (1989), 'Utilitarianism and Human Rights', in E.F. Paul, F.D. Miller Jr and J. Paul (eds), *Human Rights*, Oxford: Blackwell, pp. 92–102.

Glendon, M.A. (1991), *Rights Talk: The Impoverishment of Political Discourse*, New York: The Free Press.

Golding, Martin P. (1984), 'The Primacy of Welfare Rights', in E.F. Paul, F.D. Miller, Jr and J. Paul (eds), *Human Rights*, Oxford: Blackwell, pp. 119–36.

Hatch, E. (1997), 'The Good Side of Relativism', *Journal of Anthropological Research*, 53: 371–81.

Henkin, L. (1981), 'Economic and Social Rights as "Rights": A U.S. Perspective', *Human Rights Law Journal*, 2: 223–36.

Laslett, P. (ed.), (1970), John Locke's *Two Treatises of Government*. Cambridge: Cambridge University Press.

Lefeuvre-Déotte, M. (1997), *L'Excision en Procès: Un Différend Culturel?*, Paris: L'Harmattan.

Marx, Karl (1975), *Early Writings*, edited by D. McLellan, Oxford: Oxford University Press.

Mellor, P.A. and C. Shilling (1993), 'Modernity, Self-Identity and the Sequestration of Death', *Sociology*, 27: 411–31.

Meron, T. (1986), 'On a Hierarchy of International Human Rights,' *American Journal of International Law*, 80.

Milne, A.J.M. (1980), 'The Idea of Human Rights: A Critical Inquiry', in F.E. Dowrick (ed.), *Human Rights: Problems, Perspectives and Texts*, Farnborough: Saxon House, pp. 23–40.

Nagengast, C. and T. Turner (1997), 'Introduction: Universal Human Rights versus Cultural Relativity', *Journal of Anthropological Research*, 53(3): 269–72.

North/South Coalition (1988), 'Human Rights: Universal or Culture Specific', *Information Bulletin* 1, Oslo, 173 pp.

Panikkar, R. (1982), 'Is the Notion of Human Rights a Western Concept?', *Diogenes*, 120: 75–102.

Parekh, B. (1973), *Bentham's Political Thought*, London: Croom Helm.

Peces-Barba, G. (1981), 'Reflections on Economic, Social and Cultural Rights', *Human Rights Law Journal*, 2: 281–94.

Pennock, J.R. (1981), 'Rights, Natural Rights, and Human Rights – A General View', in J.R. Pennock and J.W. Chapman (eds), *Human Rights*, Nomos XXIII, New York: New York University Press, pp. 1–28.

Pollis, A. and P. Schwab (1979), 'Human Rights: A Western Construct with Limited Applicability', in A. Pollis and P. Schwab (eds), *Human Rights: Cultural and Ideological Perspectives*, New York: Praeger, pp. 1–18.

Rendel, M. (1997), *Whose Human Rights?*, Stroke on Trent: Trentham Nooks.

Renteln, A.D. (1988), 'Relativism and the Search for Human Rights', *American Anthropologist*, 90: 56–72.

Scheper-Hughes, N. (1996), 'Theft of Life: The Globalization of Organ Stealing Rumours', *Anthropology Today*, 12: 3–11.

Stammers, N. (1993), 'Human Rights and Power', *Political Studies*, 41: 70–82.

Szabo, I. (1982), 'Historical Foundations of Human Rights', in K. Vasak and P. Alston (eds), *The International Dimensions of Human Rights*, Paris: Unesco (first edition), reprinted by Greenwood Press, Vol. 1: 11–40.

Van Boven, T. (1982), 'Distinguishing Criteria of Human Rights', in K. Vasak and P. Alston (eds), *The International Dimensions of Human Rights*, Vol. 1.

Villey, M. (1983), *Le Droit et les droits de l'homme,* Paris: Presses Universitaires de France.

Winter, B. (1994), 'Women, the Law, and Cultural Relativism in France: The Case of Excision', *Signs*, 19: 939–74.

Framing Care: Alternative Visions in Dialogue

This section includes two chapters which critically examine ways in which ideas about care are researched, debated and presented for public consumption. Part 1 began with the voices of experience at the receiving end of care, and Part 2 looked at broad-spectrum issues of debate around patient rights and the top/down control of caring practice. The chapters in Part 3 illustrate how a holistic understanding of research around medical advances in care must not privilege some disciplines over others, or medical experts over the experiences of recipients.

Lambert has extended the boundaries of care to look at health care for the 'well' (like Russell in the last section). In particular, she has studied attitudes about screening for raised blood cholesterol and the role that such technology might have in assessing coronary heart disease risk. Interesting ideas about different moralities of intervention are illustrated in the words of her informants who have been involved at the receiving end of this preventive health-care process. She argues that these 'subjectivities' need to be considered when one attempts to make sense of the scientific and economic debates around the pros and cons of screening. Lambert reveals how different interest groups benefit differently from supporting or cutting off these tests for cardiovascular disease. Economies of care grapple with 'scientific' constructions of 'risk' and 'benefit', as well as the urgencies of patients' individual expectations about the preventive care that they are due.

The 'medical science' of care has tended to be as conceptually isolated from the economics and politics of care in the public imagination as it has been from the 'grounded' voices of the patients it purports to serve. The chapters by Lambert and McKechnie both question these constructed hierarchies and boundaries of knowledge. While both chapters are grounded in detailed interview-based investigations of subject attitudes (on screening in the first example and on sexual behaviour in the second), they then step back to reflect on the ways in which the research process as a whole is shaped. McKechnie's chapter shows that, while human immunodeficiency virus (HIV) and acquired immunodeficiency syndrome (AIDS) have been studied with a genuine benevolent urgency by representatives of every academic discipline under the sun, the understanding and cooperation between them, and with various activists and other interest groups intimately involved in the issues, remain limited. Reflection on her own role straddling disciplinary boundaries (trained in anthropology and practising with sociological tools and paradigms) helps her to look analytically at evidence of the distrust and communication failure that have developed in the world of HIV/AIDS research. Both chapters in this section suggest that only by revealing the different agendas, convictions and interests that contribute to any particular focus on care may we pave a way forward for more holistic, communicatively rich and sensitive advances.

5

Caring for the Well: Perspectives on Disease Prevention

Helen Lambert

In this chapter I consider the implications of extending the concept of 'care' to cover the healthy and their protection from future sickness, with a particular focus on the issue of screening. I try to explore the differing meanings and referents of 'care' among the interest groups that are concerned with one particular area of disease prevention and health promotion – raised blood cholesterol and its role as a risk factor for coronary heart disease (CHD). In medicine and public health, disease prevention is conventionally divided into three types, of which only primary prevention refers to the prevention of disease in healthy individuals and populations (Lambert and McPherson 1993). Secondary prevention concerns measures to avoid the further development of disease in individuals who already have signs or symptoms of a disease, while tertiary prevention refers to treatment and improvement in the quality of life of those with disease (ibid.:144). Ethical concerns have conventionally focused on the implications of 'care' within the secondary and tertiary realms. This reflects the fact that, until recently, 'health care' has been associated with therapeutic management of the sick. As the term itself is intended to denote, however, contemporary health care increasingly focuses on protection of the healthy from sickness. With the gradual broadening of medicine to encompass monitoring and protection of the health status of ostensibly healthy as well as that of sick individuals, 'health care' becomes homologous with 'prevention' in its broadest sense. The ways in which this extension of the boundaries of 'care' are negotiated by a range of actors with contesting understandings of what it means to care are the central focus of this chapter.

My material is drawn primarily from a study on patients' understanding of medical science in relation to a group of hereditary conditions known as 'familial hyperlipidaemias'.[1] These conditions, which together are estimated to affect approximately 1 in 300 of the British population, influence the levels of lipids – including cholesterol – in the blood. The most widely known and best understood of these hyperlipidaemias is familial hypercholesterolaemia (FH), which has a prevalence of 1 in 500 of the UK population. This results in high (approximately twice the average) levels of blood cholesterol and substantially increased risks for CHD. The disease is caused by a dominantly inherited single-gene defect, such that a child of a parent who has FH in its heterozygous form has a 50% chance of inheriting the same defect.[2] This type of familial hyperlipidaemia produces characteristic symptoms in some patients, such as deposits of cholesterol which build up around the tendons (tendon xanthomata) and eyes (xanthelasmata), but these do not necessarily occur and, if they do, they are often not readily noticed. Thus most of those who come to be identified as having this or another form of familial hyperlipidaemia are diagnosed by blood cholesterol testing (Table 5.1).

Table 5.1 Routes to diagnosis of familial hyperlipidaemia.

Blood test subsequent to relative's diagnosis	19
Blood test subsequent to relative's death	2
Medical check-up requested due to family history	4
Presentation to GP of signs of raised blood cholesterol	3
Blood test after developing symptoms of CVD, including:	14
Angina	6
Myocardial infarction (heart attack)	3
Stroke or transient ischaemic attacks	3
Angina and coronary bypass surgery	2
By chance, including:	10
Medical check-up for feeling unwell	3
General preventive check-up	3
Work-related medical check-up	1
Unrelated medical encounter	3
Total	52

GP, general practitioner; CVD, cardiovascular disease.

Among our sample, over one-third had been diagnosed by a blood test following the diagnosis of a relative, while another fifth had been diagnosed by chance. Only a quarter had already developed signs of cardiovascular disease (CVD). Those who are diagnosed prior to the development of any signs of heart disease or other noticeable symptoms, in other words who consider themselves to be well, have to accept that they have inherited a potentially life-threatening condition essentially as an act of faith. This is, however, sometimes initiated or sustained by a sense of personal risk resulting from the deaths of close relatives. During the data-collection phase of the research, we were particularly interested in how such people made meaning out of a condition which is in itself largely asymptomatic, and indeed many of those interviewed spontaneously remarked upon this feature as an important dimension of their understanding (Lambert and Rose 1996).

Although this chapter concerns one particular debate and the ethical implications of differing positions on 'health care' taken within it, the case I consider offers but one example of a general question about the morality of intervention that is raised by the development of screening for preclinical, or asymptomatic, disorders. In the health field today, preventive health care is a theme of increasing importance; 1976 saw the publication of *Prevention and Health: Everybody's Business* (Department of Health and Social Security 1976), the first UK Government White Paper on disease prevention, while in 1992 *The Health of the Nation* (Department of Health 1992) set out the first national targets for disease prevention and health promotion in the UK. The rise of preventive strategies based on individual behavioural change depends in part upon the growth of epidemiological knowledge, derived from population-based techniques of medical surveillance (Armstrong 1994; Kuh and Davey Smith 1997). This identifies potentially modifiable 'risk factors' that are taken to denote susceptibility to future ill health at an individual level. Screening as a particular type of disease prevention strategy additionally depends on the production of increasingly refined biochemical techniques and associated medical technologies, that enable detection of such individual 'risk factors' or predisposing signs prior to any clinical evidence of ill health. Analyses of the 'technological imperative' in medicine suggest that the rapid 'routinization' of new technologies is associated with a moral bias towards their use (Koenig 1988). In both curative and preventive medicine, this bias results in the continual incorporation of new diagnostic technologies into the definition of what constitute – in both professional and popular conceptualizations – minimum standards of 'adequate care'. In the area of preventive screening, this tendency, paradoxically, both encourages and is encouraged by the rise of 'healthism', which places responsibility for health on the individual in the form of a moral duty (Foucault 1980; Crawford 1984). Developments in molecular biology enable identification of subclinical biochemical changes and advances in molecular genetics that produce the ability to screen for genetic predispositions to disease. At the same time, epidemiological techniques that can identify elevated risks at the level of populations, combine with societal imperatives to promote the detection of abnormalities in ostensibly healthy populations. Questions are thereby raised as to what 'care' means, when the forms of scientific research involved necessarily conflict with subjective perceptions of health status.

Biomedicine has been seen in general terms as an instrument of social control (Zola 1972; Foucault 1973, 1980; Mishler *et al.* 1981), in which the development of medical knowledge has historically facilitated ever-closer surveillance and regulation of individual bodies by the state. Feminist analyses have documented the ways in which female reproductive processes have been progressively brought under medical control, while sociologists and historians have discussed the medicalization of a range of what were previously considered to be social or political problems, from teenage pregnancy to child development (Illich 1977; Mishler *et al.* 1981; Wright 1988). Seen from a social constructionist or political economic perspective, preventive screening of ostensibly 'healthy' individuals using new medical technologies can be viewed as a particular example of medical surveillance, relating to a shift in the focus of twentieth-century medicine from the older binary division between the 'normal' and the 'pathological' to a concern with those 'at risk' along a continuum of relative healthiness (Ryle 1947; Armstrong 1994). From such a viewpoint, screening contributes to the erosion of individual autonomy and responsibility for care.

In contrast, within medicine, public health and health promotion, screening techniques that provide individuals with new medical information about their personal health status are seen as enhancing individual agency. This is achieved by enabling individuals to act in ways that will preserve or improve their own health. This view, however, takes little account of the ways in which individuals make sense of what information they receive, although some medical researchers have expressed concerns as to the possible negative psychological and social effects of screening (Skrabanek 1994; Stewart-Brown and Farmer 1997). More broadly, by focusing on the question of the extent to which individuals do or do not take up and act upon medical knowledge, this knowledge itself is implicitly taken to be unified and unequivocal. In reality, it is diverse and negotiable (Irwin and Wynne 1996: 7). The ways in which differing group interests shape what is considered to be relevant information, how it is to be delivered and who is to receive 'care' as a result of the diagnoses – and sicknesses – thereby produced, are an important focus of this chapter. The particular perspectives of different actors importantly influence what they consider to constitute 'care'. Here, instrumental concerns mesh with social and moral values in a manner that cannot easily be disaggregated.

Cholesterol Controversies

Widespread publicity about the dangers of cholesterol as increasing one's risk of CHD, and public health education campaigns directed at the need for everyone to reduce the levels of saturated fat in their diets, have been interspersed in the past decade with stories in the popular media about the dangers of lowering cholesterol. Certain studies have caused public alarm by demonstrating a link between low blood cholesterol levels and the development of cancer. In the early 1990s, analyses of the results of clinical trials of cholesterol-lowering therapy caused a stir by demonstrating an association with increased mortality from violent death (Muldoon *et al.* 1990). The value of lowering cholesterol levels in order to prevent the development and progression of CHD has since become part of medical orthodoxy (Oliver *et al.* 1995). However, the possibility that dietary and other strategies to reduce cholesterol may have unforeseen effects on behaviour (Wardle 1995) demonstrates the uncertainties inherent in assessing the implications of attempts to modify specific, medically identified sources of risk.

Differences tend to arise not only among experts but between expert and popular views of what constitutes 'acceptable' risk. Apart from these 'scare' stories, there have been continuing differences of opinion within medicine as to the benefits of a low-fat diet (Connor *et al.* 1997). Frequent shifts in nutritional advice (including the promotion of the 'healthy' properties of vegetable-oil-based margarine, advocacy of olive oil, particular types of fish and 'the Mediterranean diet', and the reclaiming of butter as a 'healthy' fat) have contributed to public scepticism about the putative risks associated with high blood cholesterol levels and the accuracy of information concerning dietary modification (Frankel *et al.* 1991). These forms of scepticism derive not only from the intrinsically provisional character of scientific knowledge, but also from the ways in which such knowledge is reported by the media and from mistrust in the institutional sources of authority and technical expertise among the general public (Nelkin 1989; Wynne 1996).

Over the same period, a succession of papers in major medical journals have debated the merits of various public health strategies for cholesterol reduction and, in particular, the relative advantages of the 'population' and the 'high risk' strategies. The first of these approaches refers to educating and motivating the public to lower the overall (average) level of blood cholesterol in the population by dietary change as a means of reducing the population prevalence of CVD. The second identifies individuals at particularly high risk of CVD through screening, which includes cholesterol testing. The use of both strategies in tandem has become part of established health policy in the UK, since health professionals (apart from a few dietary nihilists) generally agree that population-level dietary change should be encouraged for the improvement of health, while more targeted interventions are warranted to prevent the onset of CVD in those at higher risk. The area of disagreement which is of particular relevance to this chapter concerns whether screening for raised cholesterol levels should be extended to cover the whole population, as has occurred in the USA.[3]

Contested Meanings

Within particular fields of expertise and interest, the debate about cholesterol screening takes on different meanings. Within the medical profession, for example, lipid specialists tend (predictably) to favour universal lipid testing. In contrast, cardiologists, the traditionally dominant medical specialists in the field of heart disease, have focused primarily on surgical therapeutic intervention rather than on prevention. General practitioners (GPs) are more divided on this issue, with the impetus to adopt cholesterol testing as a new tool in health care management being tempered by concerns about limited resources and the potentially enormous – and economically burdensome – patient load that would be created by mass screening for raised cholesterol. As well as enabling identification of individuals at above-average risk of developing CVD, clinicians in favour of screening argue that screening itself is a powerful motivational device for dietary and lifestyle change (a position that is discussed in more detail below). Public-health specialists and epidemiologists, in contrast, tend to argue that it is more important to create a favourable climate that encourages such a change at the level of the population, for example by means of a healthy food policy and easy access to sports facilities. Other groups with differing positions include the manufacturers of medical instruments, who have an interest in promoting screening, the pharmaceutical companies, who develop, manufacture and sell lipid-lowering drugs, and their actual or potential patients. The varying perspectives of these groups are based on differing institutional concerns and instrumental interests, such as the enhancement of career possibilities to be gained through the promotion of a particular medical specialization, or the economic gains to be made by the sale of certain types of drugs. They are also based on the attribution of different meanings to available scientific evidence. I now turn to my case study to illustrate these differing positions and understandings in more depth.

An Association of Interest: the Case of the Family Heart Association

A particular focus of our study was the activities and membership of a patients' support organization, the Family Heart Association (FHA), most of whose members are concentrated in central and southern England. Research included in-depth interviews with a total of 52 people with some form of familial hyperlipidaemia, of whom one-third were drawn from the lipid clinic of a large teaching hospital in the north of England while the others were members of the FHA. The study also involved limited participant observation in selected settings, including out-patient clinics and meetings hosted or sponsored by the FHA, and interviews with medical professionals involved in this field. An initial intention of the study had been to focus on the organization itself as a group of lay persons acquiring, negotiating and disseminating medical information. By the time the field research started, however, the FHA was undergoing a process of transformation from its origins as a small, largely volunteer-run patient support group with a very small budget. By the end of 1990, when the study finished, the FHA had become a fully-fledged charity with seven full-time professional staff, managed by a steering committee composed of lay members and medical advisers.

Although it had for several years been able to run an operation larger than would be expected on the basis of its fairly small membership, the transformation was completed when in 1990 the last unpaid volunteer ceased to have a role in the basic organization and everyday running of the association. It is intriguing to note in this context that, whereas initially it was founded, staffed and run almost exclusively by women, by the time the first professional (male) director was appointed, only two women remained on the eight-person voluntary steering committee.

The FHA was initially established as the Familial Hypercholester-olaemia Association in 1984 by a small group of clinicians with interests in lipids, together with two women patients who had been diagnosed as having FH and who welcomed their consultants' idea of a patient support group. It was originally conceived by its founder members and medical advisers as both a 'self-help' or 'support' group for patients, providing information and support for those diagnosed as having a particular genetic disorder (FH), and a pressure group for increasing awareness of the condition within the medical profession, especially among GPs. The Association soon acquired several instant cholesterol-testing machines free from the manufacturers, which they then loaned out to GPs in order to encourage screening for blood cholesterol levels. This awareness-raising aspect of their work continued to be emphasized, but the dimension of lay participation (often regarded as a defining feature of 'self-help' groups) was limited to a few local meetings convened by individual members and the Association's annual general meeting, which is usually attended by around 40 people. Efforts in the mid-1980s to initiate a nationwide network of local support groups, run by members designated as 'area contacts' largely foundered. The Association has remained a rather centralized organization, with little direct contact between members except among those who sit on the steering committee (most of whom themselves have familial hyperlipidaemia). Telephone contact with a volunteer and subsequently with a professional nurse-dietitian has always been provided as part of the FHA's services to members. The main channel for exchanges of information with and among the members was and continues to be the regular newsletter; there is no other established forum through which members/patients can offer mutual support.

The FHA's rapid expansion over the first five years or so of its existence was less a result of increasing membership (which by 1990 was still probably under 1000), individual donations or local-level fund-raising than of substantial financial, advisory and technical support and sponsorship of specific campaigns from pharmaceutical companies that manufacture cholesterol-lowering drugs. The policy of the FHA also shifted over this time from an initial concern exclusively with the single condition of FH to an aim of supporting those with and spreading awareness about all hereditary hyperlipidaemias. This was signalled by its change of name in 1987 to the Family Heart Association, and its subsequent embracing of more general strategies of diagnosing inherited hyperlipidaemias through cholesterol testing and comprehensive heart-disease risk assessment. Since 1990, it has undergone a number of changes in staffing and some periods of financial uncertainty. These have resulted in several changes and, for a period, to the reinvolvement of one of the founder members (who had ceased to take an active role as the Association professionalized) in managing the FHA. Today the FHA maintains its particular concern with the constituency of those having familial hyper-lipidaemia while embracing the wider population through an emphasis on family heart health. It advertises its constituency and aims as follows:

> The Family Heart Association is a patient information charity working to help prevent premature coronary heart disease. The FHA specialises in blood lipid disorders, including inherited high cholesterol (FH and FCH), and dietary and other lifestyle aspects of the management of these conditions. The FHA is committed to the early detection in the community of families with genetic lipid disorders and those prone to premature angina and heart attack for other reasons, and participates in the post-registration training of nurses. (Family Heart Association 1997)

The relatively non-participatory character of the Association may derive partially from the very nature of the condition itself, which, as described earlier, lacks any overt or debilitating symptoms. As one of the committee members put it, 'It's not like local psoriasis groups where they all go round and scratch together, there's nothing to focus on.' Indeed, many of those interviewed for our study expressed their difficulty in explaining to others the nature of their condition, fearing being seen simply as 'faddy' or as overly concerned with an aspect of health status (blood cholesterol) which is not regarded by the general public as life-threatening (see Lambert and Rose 1996: 72, 77–8). Within the organization itself, tensions surrounding what constitutes appropriate policy for the FHA with respect to the promotion of cholesterol testing related precisely to the substantial overlap that exists between endogenously produced (inherited) and 'lifestyle-induced' high cholesterol levels – that is, between the identification and management of a particular component of overall risk for CHD in the bulk of the population, and its close association with premature mortality in the subgroup which is the particular constituency of the FHA. These tensions reflect in a profound fashion the ethical dilemmas posed by the different implications of 'caring', where what is appropriate for the few may not be congruent with what is beneficial for the many.

While it is difficult to define self-help, 'everyone seems to be for it just as everybody is against sin' (Williams 1989: 135). In the medical sphere, such groups are seen to represent patients' interests and most studies have focused on the psychological and social support benefits of membership in such groups (Trojan 1989). The FHA was established specifically in cooperation with, and with initial impetus from, a section of the medical profession with interests in that medical field (see von Gizycki 1987: 77). This nexus of interest that allies doctors and patients may be fairly characteristic of voluntary organizations concerned with specific medical conditions, since they need, perforce, to rely at least to some extent on support from medical professionals and thus may have limited power to position themselves in opposition to medical authority (Williams 1989: 153). Given that one of the two primary objectives of the organization has been to promote awareness of familial hyperlipidaemia within the medical profession itself, close ties into medical practice are essential. Additionally, the representation of medical science within the Association is such that promotion of medical knowledge and expertise is seen as inherently congruent with the promotion of patients' interests, as demonstrated in more detail below.

Identifying the Afflicted: Medical Information as White Knight

The other main aim of the FHA is the dissemination of information about FH, in order both to provide advice and support to people with FH and, by promoting awareness of the condition, to increase the chances that those with FH get diagnosed in the first place. Long-standing members held strong views about the importance of this task:

We've got to make the public aware, we've got to make everyone aware. Because people are dying, they're dying every day! And they needn't. I mean it's so simple to get treatment now . . . It can save their lives. It's immoral that people aren't getting this information!

And as far as I'm concerned, when you've got information, you've got prevention, so that's how I feel about it anyway.

The members and staff of the FHA saw the establishment of generally available cholesterol screening as a vital means for detecting familial hyperlipidaemia within the general population. Most of those I talked to regarded widespread testing as an unequivocal good; some considered it more strongly as a moral imperative. These patients viewed their own diagnosis as life-saving and pointed to the numbers of undiagnosed people who are unaware, due to the asymptomatic nature of the disorder, that they are at risk of sudden death from – in the words of the FHA's publicity brochures – a 'silent killer'. Those who were actively involved in the FHA as founding members, committee members or local representatives went further; having been diagnosed in time to save their own lives and health, they regarded it as an ethical obligation to extend such benefit to others:

I don't think I'm interested in the medical side of it. All I know is that we've got to help people out there, and this is what I'm interested in . . . So I'm, I'm . . . trying to care for . . . people.

if you stick with people with FH, you're responding to the situation. If you go and find those people [by screening], you're being very positive and you're helping them. (FH19 Cm6)

unless you go for the general public, they're not going to know and you're not going to find them, so the only way you're going to get a family is for mum and dad to pop up at one of the screening clinics . . . you get the adult then you get the child, which is what I want. (FH26 Cm7)

From their perspective, 'care' here means being concerned for others with a similar condition by helping to identify them. Theirs was a more or less explicitly proselytizing attitude, expressed most clearly by a former chairman of the Association:

I feel that people who have . . . helped themselves and do understand . . . and have gained the knowledge through the FH[A] can . . . *go* out and preach and convert other people, and so it will have this . . . um . . . knock-on effect all throughout. (FH6 Cm2 – original verbal emphasis)

This kind of 'caring' in effect seeks to pick out of the undifferentiated mass of those who have raised blood cholesterol only those who have a genetic predisposition to it. That the rest would be left to fend for themselves, despite also being at substantially increased risk, is a consequence that was rarely seen among those interviewed as a matter of explicit concern. The response of many FHA activists to the question of how others were to be 'cared for' was that their Association is particularly concerned for affected children and for future generations, as suggested by the former chairman:

That's . . . that's a difficult one because I . . . I er *am* of the opinion that we should help *everybody* . . . in trouble, specially . . . people that do need it erm . . . but I can see that . . . the . . . FH has a . . . true role to play, and that is *finding* these people, because . . . the others could be caused for other . . . reasons . . . having reproduced children, those children could have it without knowing about it, so if we could . . . just isolate them take our particular case and find out if the people have got it . . . then find out if their children have got it, because it's the *children* we're after, and, you know . . . this should be our main role, finding, trying to save the children, and the children's children, and so on . . . indefinitely. (original verbal emphasis)

Implicitly such children were contrasted, as blameless innocents, with those who have 'self-inflicted' raised cholesterol arising from non-hereditary causes (such as a diet high in saturated fats). Much of the FHA's early publicity pictured families and young children portrayed as being, in the words of one newspaper headline, 'Just a heartbeat away from death' and strategies for heightening attention to familial hyperlipidaemia have included an emphasis on the potentially fatal nature of the condition. A prominent lipid specialist included in his talks on the topic several slides of a man with his stereotypically 'happy family' of a wife and two children, after showing which he reveals that the man depicted died in his early forties. Clearly the preoccupation among many FHA members with 'saving others' is often a direct consequence of the shocking nature of unexpected death in a member of close kin, but the emphasis on premature mortality among the apparently healthy also acts as an effective vehicle for eliciting both public empathy and anxiety.

I think there are other organizations can cope with other people, I think we're specifically there to help people with the inherited factor. If they already knew about it, fair enough . . . then in time we can broaden our remit, but I think until we've got that message across to the one family in three hundred or whatever that's carrying this faulty gene I don't think you can dilute our activities. (FH13 Cm3)

This kind of selectivity was facilitated by the role of the dominant single-gene defect FH as a conceptual model for all familial hyperlipidaemias and by an accompanying emphasis on the hereditary and (implicitly) immutable nature of FH. Although FH undoubtedly confers heightened risk for CHD, the familial hyperlipidaemias as a group are in fact genetically highly heterogeneous and their clinical expression in individuals is rather variable, with widely differing implications for levels of individual risk and appropriate therapy (see Lambert and Rose 1996: 67).

The Political Economy of Cholesterol Lowering

The area of disease prevention in which the FHA is situated became a major issue in contemporary health politics, due to the gathering weight of epidemiological and clinical evidence relating blood cholesterol levels to risks for CHD, the development of major new drugs to lower cholesterol and a growing emphasis on health promotion as longevity has increased. The growth of the FHA has been related to and concurrent with these developments and – perhaps inevitably – it has increasingly taken on the character of a lobbying organization that campaigns for the widespread availability of cholesterol tests in the UK. In 1990 it established a 'walk-in' screening service at its offices in Oxford and its dietitian and nurse initiated an employee screening service for private companies and firms. It also began to offer an accreditation scheme for instant cholesterol testing centres in chemist's shops and private health checks during this period. Today it gives its logo to supermarket packaged meals that contain FHA-approved healthy low-fat foods in return for financial support.

The FHA receives medical advice and public support from various established members of the medical profession who specialize in lipid disorders. Several of the clinicians involved with the FHA from its early years almost simultaneously established the British Hyperlipidaemia Association, a professional body that encourages awareness of lipid disorders within the medical profession and promotes the establishment of specialist lipid clinics in hospitals across the country. It has always maintained close links with the FHA and its 1989 conference was sponsored by the Association, which in turn funded the conference through a grant from a major pharmaceutical company that makes an important cholesterol-lowering drug. Clearly lipid specialists see the FHA as having a useful role in the establishment and growth of their own medical speciality, which has had to contend with the traditional dominance of cardiologists (in FHA folklore a group almost entirely oblivious to the importance of lipids in the development of CHD) in the field of heart disease.

The FHA's 'free-market' activities, their acceptance of funding from the drugs industry and their sometimes vocal support for widespread cholesterol testing have not endeared the FHA to other charitable organizations in this field, such as the Coronary Prevention Group, which emphasizes the multifactorial and socially patterned nature of most heart disease. Some epidemiologists, pointing to the fact that CHD resulting from hereditary hyperlipidaemias comprises only a tiny fraction of the burden of this disease in the UK, have strongly contested the FHA's stance on cholesterol screening. Public health professionals and policy-makers are more interested in the potential of health education and health promotion to encourage shifts in diet and lifestyle in the population at large. Such shifts would reduce the incidence of CHD in the population overall, even though some individuals – in particular those with a genetic predisposition to hyperlipidaemia and thus CHD – would not reduce their own risk significantly by changing their diets. None the less, to encourage a favourable ethos for the 'healthy heart lifestyle', it is necessary for the whole population to participate.

Some public health activists and epidemiologists who were aware of the FHA during the research period viewed the organization as tainted by the acceptance of drug companies' money and saw it as little more than a publicly acceptable mouthpiece for the pharmaceutical industry. The enormous costs of universal cholesterol screening for an underfunded health service and the relative cost-ineffectiveness of mass screening provide cause for concern among policy-makers. Further, widespread testing can itself have negative health consequences, such as unnecessary anxiety and false reassurance, given the difficulties of providing appropriate and available counselling and the problematic issues of the standardization and unreliability of tests. Given these concerns, widespread testing is seen by some as both individually harmful and economically exploitative, since it could not be backed up by appropriate care. Opponents of mass screening are additionally concerned with the possible implications of establishing, through screening, that a significant proportion of the British population would fall within the group to be considered for drug treatment according to present guidelines. That the FHA does not appear to acknowledge this is imputed to the influence of the drug companies, and the Association's espousal of the case for universal screening is regarded by those concerned with general population health as ethically dubious.

What comprises an ethical position is, for those familiar with familial hyperlipidaemia, radically different from the view held by such public health specialists. From the perspective of patients who see themselves as having been saved from premature and unexpected death by the intervention of specialist diagnosis and the availability of cholesterol-lowering drugs, or of lipid clinicians who encounter numerous cases of heart-attack victims or angina sufferers whose heart disease could have been prevented by timely diagnosis and therapeutic intervention, the case for widespread cholesterol testing is unassailable. Asked about their views on this matter, most active FHA members viewed the drugs and their manufacturers in a positive light, strongly identifying their own interests not only with the medical knowledge that enables life-saving diagnosis but with the research for drug development undertaken by commercial companies. An extreme example is a woman who was diagnosed with FH following urgent coronary bypass surgery aged 35. She expressed her relief at the new enzyme-inhibiting drugs that controlled her cholesterol levels effectively for the first time and her gratitude to its manufacturers:

> And I also at the time phoned the manufacturers [Merck Sharp & Dome] and spoke to a very very nice man there, one of the doctors in the research

department, who was extremely helpful and sent me all sorts of information on the drug, because I wanted to read up about it . . . and he was so kind and he said you know do let me know how it goes, and I honestly touch wood haven't looked back, it's been a godsend.

Obviously her personal experience had substantially shaped her attitude to the drug company sources of FHA funding:

where [financial support] comes from I think at the end of the day is neither here nor there, the fact that they [FHA] need money is the main priority in my book anyway, and if the drug companies which I am sure can afford it will support them, then I think they should do everything to get what they can, you know because it's very worthwhile. I mean having said that I think the people who do work at the drug companies are the ones who really save lives at the end of the day, and I have a great admiration for these people who sit in labs and test things because they are the ones that are helping, just as much if not more than the organizations and the charities and the associations that are sort of built up around them, but you can't have one without the other . . . And the fact that they're all pulling together is what we need really . . . I mean by the fact that the drug companies are sponsoring associations is going to give them publicity anyway and they are the ones that are producing these wonder drugs that are doing everything they can to sort of keep people alive longer, it can't be a bad thing, it's all got to grow up together. (FH33 AC7)

Another member shared a similar view:

obviously there are companies now, the company who make Questran are obviously making a fortune out of it, but it just happens to be a very good drug at the moment, so everyone [benefits]. Yes everyone makes money out of illness and people die and there are always going to be those companies who will make money, that's the way it is, well if they give some of that money back to people like the FHA to help making people more aware, then I think that's quite good. (FH28 AC1)

These members in effect considered the research work done by drug companies and the usefulness of the drugs they produce to be implicit evidence for their essentially ethical nature. The positive purposes to which their funding is put by the FHA as a beneficiary of company sponsorship further justified the acceptance of such donations. This kind of rationale was shared by FHA committee members:

Nearly all the research that's been done in the past throughout the world has been substantially funded by drug companies so it's not unique in that. And we're not talking about those who produce heroin, we're talking about those who produce ethical drugs which are effective in curing conditions so I don't see any great problem . . . (FH18 Cm5)

I think you have to accept in any medical area, you can make millions – are made by drug companies. I mean you look at the profits of the drug companies, they're . . . But they *do* put a lot of money into research and when all's said and done, you do *need* a drug. I mean I need a drug to control my cholesterol level. (FH19 Cm6 – original verbal emphasis)

Other members acknowledged the economic interests of drug companies but view the association as having built-in checks for exploitation. Some considered the committee of the FHA to act as such a constraint, as expressed by several former and current committee members:

No I don't think it's a worrying thing . . . as long as they don't expect the FHA to do too much in the way of publicising that particular drug for them . . . now that drug companies are on the lookout for ways of exploiting the likes of the FHA. I think we've got to be very careful as to who we make deals with so that it doesn't go the wrong way, and I think it's useful that . . . the Director and the rest of the administration running the FHA still to a certain extent have to answer to the committee of patients with FH that started it. (FH34 AC8)

What I see is that you have to be careful with it [pharmaceutical money]. You have to accept the responsibility of it. That is actually on the committee to take on the responsibility. (FH19 Cm6)

I think the committee we've got now is very aware about prickliness of everything, I mean it is our duty as a charity to be aware and safeguard other people's feelings, you see we go through some of the big . . . medical drug, pharmaceutical companies, and we are not in the pockets of a new drug and we mustn't be seen to be in the pockets of anybody, we are our own committee, our own charity . . . so we must always be aware of that . . . we don't mind being used but so long as we know how we're being used and in what direction it is, this is where the committee is so valuable. (FH6 Cm2)

Other members located institutional checks to overprescribing or misuse of drugs within the health care system itself. Some, pointing out that the FHA's role is exclusively to facilitate diagnosis of those with FH and provide them with information and support, regarded responsibility for the possible implications of widespread diagnosis as beyond their remit:

You're into the political field there, it's very political, because obviously the cost of the drugs is astronomical, you know if you suddenly find 1 in 300 of the population, stick them onto some drug or another, that could be a bit naughty but, no as I say that's political. (FH26 Cm7)

Another committee member presumed that the drug-licensing authorities provide sufficient control over the promotional activities of pharmaceutical companies:

you tell them the facts and they will make up their own minds. The claims made for a drug must be verified before it's put on the market. I'd assume there was an authority that controls what can be said about drugs. (FH19 Cm6)

A more common argument used by activists was that well-informed doctors insist on dietary control except where familial hyperlipidaemia is clearly diagnosed, thus obviating the danger of inappropriate prescribing.

the FHA have nothing to do with the drugs people are taking, that's prescribed by the doctors and the specialists, so that [receiving pharmaceutical company funding] cannot affect treatment that people are getting. They can make members aware of a certain drug but they can't and we can't prescribe it for ourselves, so I don't think in that way is affecting it. (FH28 AC2)

I don't think they just dish out the drugs willy nilly, I think you know they always give the diet a run first. (FH27 AC1)

There is a problem over the funding, from drug and . . . companies and so on but it's a problem of perception, it's not a problem of the fund influencing our policy, which they don't. Now, we know that diet is the first line of attack on these conditions. We would not sponsor any drug as such against any other . . . [The FHA] certainly doesn't support the sale of the drug but they know of course that with public knowledge there are more people being treated, some are going to need drug treatment, so their drug along with other people's will be sold more, that's why they give the support. But it doesn't affect our policy . . . My own opinion is that the funding we have is entirely ethical. (FH18 Cm5)

This position is the same as that adopted as the official policy by the lipid clinicians' professional association (SCRIP 1992). Other work on the relationship between pharmaceutical companies and the medical profession has, none the less, amply demonstrated the influence that the former has over the latter's prescribing practices (e.g. Anon. 1983; Lexchin 1987, 1988; Chetley 1990: 51–68; Abraham 1995). It is difficult to find other ways to account for the huge sums of money spent by drug companies on entertainment of physicians, medical education, advertisements in medical journals and drug marketing representatives who visit every GP.

Situating Ethics in Health Policy

The preceding set of observations are not in the least intended to imply that lipid clinicians do not believe that they are acting in the best interests of patients. The stance of the FHA itself, to some degree the doctors, and even perhaps the pharmaceutical companies, in this respect illustrates what Bourdieu (1977: 195), following Althusser, has termed *méconnaissance* or misrecognition. This is, roughly, a phenomenon common to capitalist societies wherein forms of economic and social self-advancement are seen by the actors as socially beneficial, even altruistic. The FHA certainly sees the development of private screening services, its official endorsement of 'healthy' consumer products and services (such as breakfast cereal and commercial testing facilities) and pharmaceutical company sponsorship as just so many means towards the end of detecting and treating familial hyperlipidaemia and thereby preventing repeated tragedies of early deaths within affected families. Counter-arguments, such as the potential dangers of overtreatment with cholesterol-lowering drugs in the population generally, are regarded as insignificant relative to the need to prevent future suffering. The FHA and those clinicians working in the field of hyperlipidaemia see themselves as offering care through detection and subsequent prevention to a subsection of the population whose life-threatening condition is otherwise cruelly ignored.

Their position is in important respects supported by epidemiological evidence. Those on the 'public health' side of the debate admit (in the face of unassailable evidence of increased premature CHD mortality among those with FH) that a subgroup of those with raised cholesterol will be unable to reduce their risk adequately by dietary changes alone. Individual cholesterol screening of those 'high-risk' individuals who have a strong family history of CHD or other apparent risk factors (for example, smoking, obesity or angina) is considered by them to be the most appropriate way of identifying these individuals, and current health-care policy supports this approach. However, given both the variability in clinical expressions of FH and the differential effects on men and women – which means that an individual's family history may not look particularly bad when the genetic disorder has passed through female ancestors – persons who have inherited hyperlipidaemia may not fall into the category of those at 'high risk' in the first place and so would not be identified for screening using this approach. Because of this, the FHA is correct in asserting that universal screening constitutes a more effective means of unequivocally identifying all those who are genetically susceptible. However, the implication that refusal to implement universal screening verges on the unethical, since those at heightened risk may remain undetected, only makes sense when seen from this perspective. It cannot readily be shared by public health and policy experts, who are primarily concerned for the 'care' of the majority population. From their point of view, severe resource constraints within the health service and the potentially detrimental psychological and social effects of screening healthy individuals clearly favour a policy of cholesterol screening that is restricted to 'high-risk' individuals.

Thus a key tension for the FHA is that their primary aim of detecting people with FH through screening takes them unavoidably into general issues of public health policy, in which the welfare of the majority of the population must be considered. Precisely because of their specific concern with the familial hyperlipidaemias, they are unable to represent adequately the interests of that majority who would be affected by policy changes concerning cholesterol screening, and their claims are consequently seen by some in this field as illegitimate. This difficulty is recognized by FHA employees and has led to a more prominent emphasis being placed on a different rationale for the promotion of general lipid screening. In 1989 the then director of the FHA participated in a King's Fund Consensus Conference on Cholesterol Testing, at which he strongly argued the case for widespread testing, although the Conference did not ultimately recommend universal testing. Following the publication of these recommendations, the FHA issued a press release, which stated that, despite this, 'The FHA is alligning [*sic*] itself with those doctors who see a simple test as a powerful motivator.' There is little evidence either to support or refute this contention, but it reflects a widely accepted position in health education, which holds that provision of information about health status in itself constitutes a form of health care, because, once informed adequately about risks to health, individuals will act to reduce them. The press release went on to state that the FHA will 'support research to demonstrate in this country what is already known elsewhere – namely that when people know their "cholesterol number" they take steps, through diet and lifestyle to improve general health.' This is a reference to the much more widespread campaign in the USA which encourages all individuals to undergo blood cholesterol checks.

Conclusion

This case study has given a small taste of some of the contentious issues that arise for health policy and health care once attention becomes focused on the preventive arena. Various interest groups stand to benefit in different ways from encouraging or blocking preventive health care for CHD. These, of course, include ordinary people, the future patients, who, in the view of advocates for screening, will not become patients if they are cared for preventively. It would be simplistic to imply that economic interest in the field of prevention is necessarily suspect. The development and widespread utilization of medically useful tests and therapeutic interventions largely depend on their commercial viability to manufacturers. The broader social and ethical implications of preclinical screening, however, demand general attention. Ethical guidelines are built into policy considerations for evaluating screening programmes, but these do not obviate the need to consider more broadly the potential implications of medical and epidemiological findings for medicating or medicalizing healthy populations as part of 'health care'. More fundamentally, what 'care' means and to whom it should be directed inevitably differ depending on the subjectivities of those involved. The moral imperative that drives most FHA members to argue for the introduction of universal cholesterol screening coincides with the economic interests of commercial manufacturers, but is no less inherently ethical than the stance of those public health experts who are implacably opposed to such a policy. In the nexus of contested interests which the FHA represents, subjective emotions surrounding matters of illness and death cannot be disentangled from more instrumental concerns.

Notes

1. The research project 'Genetic Disorder: Self-help, Knowledge and Dissemination' was initiated by Prof. Hilary Rose at the University of Bradford. The project ran from 1988 to 1990 as part of a research programme in the Public Understanding of Science, funded by the Economic and Social Research Council of the UK, whose support is gratefully acknowledged.
2. Individuals who have the homozygous form (inherited from two heterozygous parents) are very rare – approximately 1 in a million – and usually die in their teens or early twenties from fatal heart attacks.

3. There is insufficient space within this chapter to document the details of this debate or refer to the enormous international medical literature devoted to the topic of cholesterol-lowering. It is possible here only to sketch out the broad parameters of the debate in the shape it has taken within the UK as it relates to the case study under consideration.

References

Abraham J. (1995), *Science, Politics and the Pharmaceutical Industry*, London: UCL Press.

Anon. (1983), 'Doctors and the Drugs Industry', *British Medical Journal*, 286: 579–80.

Armstrong, D. (1994), 'Medical Surveillance of Normal Populations', in G. Lawrence (ed.), *Technologies of Modern Medicine*, London: Science Museum, pp. 73–80.

Bourdieu, P. (1977), *Outline of a Theory of Practice*, Cambridge: Cambridge University Press.

Chetley, A. (1990), *A Healthy Business? World Health and the Pharmaceutical Industry*, London, New Jersey: Zed Books.

Connor, W.E., S.L. Connor, M.B. Katan, S.M. Grundy and W.C. Willett (1997), 'Should a Low-fat, High-carbohydrate Diet be Recommended for Everyone? and Beyond Low-fat Diets' [Clinical Debate], *New England Journal of Medicine*, 337(8): 562–7.

Crawford, R. (1984), 'A Cultural Account of 'Health': Control, Release, and the Social Body', in J.B. McKinlay (ed.), *Issues in the Political Economy of Health Care*, New York, London: Tavistock, pp. 60–103.

Department of Health (1992), *The Health of the Nation*, London: HMSO.

Department of Health and Social Security (1976), *Prevention and Health: Everybody's Business*, London: HMSO.

Family Heart Association (1997), 'About the Family Heart Association: What We Are and What We Do . . .' *The Family Heart Digest*, 57, March, Maidenhead: Family Heart Association.

Foucault, M. (1973), *The Birth of the Clinic: An Archaeology of Medical Perception*, London and New York: Routledge.

Foucault, M. (1980), *Power/Knowledge: Selected Interviews and Other Writings*, New York: Pantheon.

Frankel, S., C. Davison and G. Davey Smith (1991), 'Lay Epidemiology and the Rationality of Responses to Health Education', *British Journal of General Practice*, 41: 428–30.

Illich, I. (1977), *Medical Nemesis: The Expropriation of Health*, New York: Bantam Books.

Irwin, A. and B. Wynne (1996), 'Introduction', in A. Irwin and B. Wynne (eds), *Misunderstanding Science? The Public Reconstruction of Science and Technology*, Cambridge: Cambridge University Press, pp. 1–17.

Koenig, B. (1988), 'The Technological Imperative in Medical Practice: The Social Creation of a "Routine" Treatment', in M. Lock and D. Gordon (eds), *Biomedicine Examined*, Dordrecht: Kluwer, pp. 465–96.

Kuh, D. and G. Davey Smith (1997), 'The Life Course and Adult Chronic Disease: an historical perspective with particular reference to coronary heart disease', in D. Kuh and Y. Ben-Shlomo (eds), *A Life Course Approach to Chronic Disease Epidemiology*, Oxford: Oxford University Press, pp. 15–41.

Lambert, H. and K. McPherson (1993), 'Disease Prevention and Health Promotion', in B. Davey and J. Popay (eds), *Dilemmas in Health Care*, Milton Keynes: Health and Disease Series, Book 7, Open University Press, pp. 143–64.

Lambert, H. and H. Rose (1996), 'Disembodied Knowledge? Making Sense of Medical Science', in A. Irwin and B. Wynne (eds), *Misunderstanding Science? The Public Reconstruction of Science and Technology*, Cambridge: Cambridge University Press, pp. 65–83.

Lexchin, J. (1987), 'Advertisement Scrutiny', *Lancet* 1: 1323–4.

Lexchin, J. (1988), 'The Medical Profession and the Pharmaceutical Industry: An Unhealthy Alliance', *International Journal of Health Services,* 18(4): 603–17.

Mishler, E.G., L.R.A. Singham, S.T. Hauser, R. Liem, S.D. Osherson, and N.E. Waxler (1981), *Social Contexts of Health, Illness, and Patient Care*, Cambridge: Cambridge University Press.

Muldoon M.F., S.B. Manuck, and K.A. Matthews (1990), 'Lowering Cholesterol Concentrations and Mortality: a Quantitative Review of Primary Prevention Trials', *British Medical Journal,* 301: 309–14.

Nelkin, D. (1989), 'Communicating Technological Risk: The Social Construction of Risk Perception', *Annual Review of Public Health*, 10: 95–113.

Oliver, M., P. Poole-Wilson, J. Shepard, and M.J. Tikkanen (1995), 'Lower Patients' Cholesterol Now', *British Medical Journal,* 310: 1280–1.

Ryle, J. (1947), 'The Meaning of Normal', *Lancet*, 6436–40.

SCRIP (1992), No. 1696, 28 February, p. 23.

Skrabanek, P. (1994), *The Death of Humane Medicine and the Rise of Coercive Healthism*, London: Social Affairs Unit.

Stewart-Brown, S. and A. Farmer (1997), 'Screening Could Seriously Damage Your Health', *British Medical Journal*, 314: 533–4.

Trojan, A. (1989), 'Benefits of Self-help Groups: A Survey of 232 Members from 65 Disease-Related Groups', *Social Science and Medicine*, 29(2): 225–32.

von Gizycki, R. (1987), 'Cooperation between Medical Researchers and a Self-help Movement: The Case of the German Retinitis Pigmentosa Society', in S. Blume, G. Bunders, L. Leydesdorff, and R. Witley (eds), *The Social Direction of the Public Sciences,* Sociology of the Sciences Yearbook, Vol. XI, D. Reidel, pp. 75–88.

Wardle, J. (1995), 'Cholesterol and Psychological Well-being', *Journal of Psychosomatic Research*, 39(5): 549–62.

Williams, G. (1989), 'Hope for the Humblest? The Role of Self-help in Chronic Illness: the Case of Ankylosing Spondylitis', *Sociology of Health and Illness*, 11(2): 135–59.

Wright, P.W.G. (1988), 'Babyhood: The Social Construction of Infant Care as a Medical Problem in England in the Years around 1900', in M. Lock and D.R. Gordon (eds), *Biomedicine Examined*, Dordrecht: Kluwer Academic, pp. 299–329.

Wynne, B. (1996), 'Misunderstood Misunderstandings: Social Identities and Public Uptake of Science', in A. Irwin and B. Wynne (eds), *Misunderstanding Science? The Public Reconstruction of Science and Technology*, Cambridge: Cambridge University Press, pp. 19–46.

Zola, I. (1972), 'Medicine as an Institution of Social Control', *Sociological Review*, 20: 487–504.

6

Identifying Boundaries in Care: Human Immunodeficiency Virus and Men Who Have Sex with Men

Rosemary McKechnie

Care and Research

The issues raised in this chapter stem from experience as an anthropologist working on a large-scale survey of changes in sexual behaviour in response to human immunodeficiency virus (HIV)/acquired immune deficiency syndrome (Aids). The aim here is to look critically at how boundaries are constructed around care, delimiting the role of social and cultural research on health and illness. The concept of care is integral to sociological and anthropological concern with health and illness. Specific aspects of care have been dealt with from many different perspectives (see Oleson 1989). Yet, while care has been theorized and investigated across a spectrum of levels, from self-care through to theoretical critiques of the way medical knowledge and institutions frame care, there has been little reflexive consideration given to the relationship between research itself and care. Care is what happens out there – it is external. Research is generally conceptualized as operating at a different level, observing, analysing and theorizing the social relationships involved in care, and then feeding new knowledge back into the context of care (either as critique, or as an aid to improving care). I shall argue that this conceptual boundary or gap is potentially dangerous, and that reflexive unpacking of the social and cultural forces that maintain it is an exercise that research should take seriously.

The responsibility of researchers to those they research and the nature of the relationship between the two parties have, of course, been a central concern of all disciplines involved in research. This concern is reflected in ethical guidelines and debates about their interpretation and implementation to ensure that research is developed, carried out and disseminated in ways that are mindful of the consequences that they have for those who are the subjects of research. I would like to focus here on one particular problematic aspect of ethical guidelines and codes: the principal of beneficence (Marshall 1991: 214). This principle addresses the obligations of researchers to: (1) do no harm; and (2) maximize the benefits and minimize potential harm to those they research. Determining whether the benefits of research outweigh potential risks, including long-term social and cultural consequences, is not straightforward (see Cassell 1978).

First, research often focuses on the interface between groups, researchers then have to balance a more complex equation allocating beneficence between competing interests. Second, research populations are always diverse, they encompass different needs, viewpoints and interests. Again, the apportioning of risk and benefit may be complex, particularly since it is likely that some members of any group will be in a stronger position to voice their views and have their interests served than others.[1] I shall return to these points later. Third, the organization of research is complex. Individual researchers, or even research groups, are unlikely to be in a position to determine alone how research is conceptualized, developed and carried out. This can only be determined in dialogue with others (other researchers, other disciplines, funders, ethical committees, academic reviewers, etc.). Just as among the populations subject to research, this dialogue will be subject to the social and cultural relations that enable some voices to carry more authority than others. Similarly, individuals involved in research are unlikely to be in a position to determine by themselves the way research data are used. As Marshall points out, researchers are subject to competing claims from policy-makers, funding bodies, employers and the research community, among others (1991: 222). Cassell and Wax argue cogently that ethical analyses which examine only the relationship between researcher and researched, as if it occurs in a social vacuum, are misconceiving the nature of research (1980: 264).

These points are of particular importance in considering the relationship between researcher and researched in the area of health and medicine. There is something of a perceived division of labour in sociological and anthropological research in this area. Some research sets specific health issues within the wider context of the social relations shaping medical knowledges and institutions. Impetus for this kind of research has come from several directions in sociological enquiry. One is the micro-sociological focus on doctor/patient relations, which developed in the sixties, much of which was critical of the power of medical professionals.

Another is the developing body of work that draws on wider sociological theory to conceptualize a broad range of health-related issues, from the experience of illness to institutional shifts (Gabe *et al.* 1991: 5). However, at the same time, much research that is carried out in medical settings is problem-led. While funding for medical sociology research units has steadily decreased, association with social medicine and epidemiology has provided research funding and employment. This has not been without consequences. Scambler (1987) remarks on the increasing number of medical sociologists doing research that is policy-led and accepting of medical diagnostic categories. Gabe *et al.* argue that 'those working as sociologists in medicine have had to surrender much of the responsibility for selecting topics for investigation to physicians and civil servants' (1991: 5). The area dealt with in this chapter, research on HIV/Aids, comes in for particular criticism from them: 'For example, the large scale funding of research in AIDS, whilst providing new opportunites for medical sociology, illustrates the danger of a return to research being defined primarily by policy makers' (ibid.). Stacey notes the paradox that the sociology of health and illness has a clearer identity than ever before, and yet most research is located outside sociology departments, as researchers work closely with practitioners and people in other disciplines (1991: 27). She emphasizes the need to retain links to the parent discipline in order to maintain the wider focus necessary to a rigorous reflexive sociological analysis of health-policy issues.

Within anthropology, similar processes have taken place. Disciplinary imperatives require that anthropologists set any issue within a cultural context. The scope of this contextualization, however, is a moot point. Some, from a Marxist position, have argued that it should include a critical perspective on the political economy of social systems, which creates health issues and structures medical visions and practices (Taussig 1980; Singer 1990). Scheper-Hughes (1990) examines the distinction between a 'critically' and a 'clinically' applied anthropology. She is concerned that failure to engage with irreconcilable differences between anthropological knowledge and biomedical knowledge is leading to a reification of sickness and suffering, as it is understood by anthropologists, but also a reification and diminution of medical anthropology itself. The 'rich' data of anthropologists are carefully packaged for easy consumption, neutralizing any critical content. The fear that biomedicine can englobe social and cultural perspectives in its powerful vision, reducing other disciplinary approaches to the position of 'handmaiden', is an important undercurrent in interdisciplinary relations.

Frankenberg (1987: 123), for example, argues that the focus of sociological interest on certain aspects of dying has a conservative function. Rather than demystifying oppressive or uncomfortable aspects of life, it has helped demystify death-denying practices within the hospital, and contributed to a useful social technology that helps ensure a smooth passage to 'the other side'. In discussing this, Walter notes that this encapsulates the difference between a 'humane' and a 'radical' sociology, and, while he does not criticize the achievement of the former, he notes that it is 'curious' for an approach to limit itself in this way (1993: 272). This use of the word 'curious' is, I think, interesting. Such expressions do not often find their way into academic descriptions. Yet the misunderstandings and lack of communication between disciplines and between orientations towards similar subjects of enquiry have all the material and semantic characteristics of any meeting of category systems (see Ardener 1982). While some academic debates rage, many disciplinary differences remain 'muted'; they are taken for granted and worked around. The misunderstandings and mismatches that generate stereotypical views of 'disciplinary others' are reified in everyday interactions, as worlds collide in the contemporary research machine. Interdisciplinary research gives rise to genuine puzzlement at the way other people work, think and express themselves: their mania for detail in one area, and sloppiness in another. It also gives rise to moral evaluations of the theoretical and practical projects of others. Misunderstandings between perspectives are not of a superficial nature, not merely a matter of theory or method.

The division of labour in the medical context means that there are many salient ways of conceptualizing the physical and social body. This is a source of potential conflict, or potential dialogue and exchange. Perhaps it is surprising that there is so little of either. I think it is worth considering how the boundaries that order the diversity of approaches brought to bear on care are maintained. Part of the answer must lie in the way the division of labour itself creates separate arenas and discourses within which knowledge is generated and disseminated. This knowledge can be hierarchically ordered in relation to biomedicine, shaping what is considered to be the most useful or effective kind of knowledge at any one time.[2] The political context of research structures research perspectives, shaping the role they can play. The social and cultural structure of the research separates it from direct concern with care in medical settings. Research on health and illness seldom attempts to reflexively explore the way that political, institutional and disciplinary contexts shape the execution and communication of work. I am not advocating a critical gaze on how power relations limit the agency of some perspectives to define their research fields and be heard, or an attack on the hegemony of the biomedical world-view. Rather, I am suggesting that more understanding of the way others conceptualize the field of research, and more open articulation of this, might change relations between researchers, and between researchers and funders or policy-makers. Rather than bemoaning the narrowness of others' vision, or their moral inadequacies, creating the basis of more open communication by translating between moral and intellectual universes might be useful. This would entail taking seriously how everyday and mundane social relations play their part in re-creating boundaries in the meetings between the many cultures of research and making visible the way the groups involved construct the others they interact with. I am suggesting that researchers are engaged in modes of defining and understanding difference which could be said to be, in many respects, stereotypical (McDonald 1993: 220). We might take seriously the way groups re-create differences not within, but over ethnic boundaries. Looking at the similar processes among academics and bureaucrats may appear trivial and inappropriate. From an anthropological perspective, however, this seems like an important process shaping the interaction between key groups of people. Hastrup notes on the anthropological condition, 'Through our perception of separate worlds, we sense the inadequacy of local categories. In our devising of new categories, different realities may be discovered' (1989: 228). The following account of some of my own experiences is an attempt to edge towards bringing a silenced (and therefore invisible) area of social relations into language.

Not Another Naïve Anthropologist

The questions I address here are viewed primarily from the disciplinary home of anthropology. This is a description of how I experienced being involved in a project which was sociological and quantitative in design. The empirical work that I draw on comes from carrying out interviews on a large-scale survey of men who have sex with men. It is based on reflections on both the interviews themselves, and on participating in a kind of research that was very different from my disciplinary training. I am writing as a stranger in the world of those I was involved in researching and the world of research I came to work in. I entered the world of survey research as a novice; it was not just the methodology that was unfamiliar, the whole practical and conceptual orientation towards the world to be studied was different. Ostensibly my task was to participate in research that would map the (predefined) salient features of the world of men who have sex with men, and to analyse them. However, in the beginning, my first task was to understand what I was supposed to be doing – to understand how sociological research in medicine viewed the world it described and explained. This disarray was more complete than I had imagined and something that I felt I had to dissemble: my understanding of my engagement was 'muted'. As Ardener (1975) points out, while 'world-views' are total (in that they englobe everything from the point of the definer), they are not equal in the ways in which they are voiced and heard. Structural factors in any context will give priority to some (dominant) views, and silence the communication of others. As the survey progressed through its planned stages, I did not unconsciously move into this research world and stop being a stranger. Rather, I became increasingly fascinated by the ways in which one world was creating the object of its gaze.

This is not an ethnographic description of how the sociologists working on the project went about their work. Rather, I am drawing on my own experience to explore the 'lack of fit' between the particular world-views involved. My participation as the project progressed threw up as many questions about the practice of anthropological research as about large-scale sociological research and the relationship between different research fields. As Hastrup has suggested, situated anthropological research is not about the other but the relationship between the other and the researcher – 'participation in fieldwork today implies the observation of participation itself' (1995: 19). After all, I was spending many days with others trying to map out categories of human sexual behaviour. On the one hand, I did not really believe that 'behaviour', as such, existed set apart from contextualized conceptual categorizations of the world. On the other hand, I was convinced that the epidemiological framing of such survey research did provide a powerful machinery for mapping links between transmission pathways of disease over human relations, and thought it possible that surveys might generate some patterning of perceptions of risk and sexual conduct. Dilemmas of this kind are endemic in the HIV/Aids research field (see Gagnon 1992).

HIV/Aids: One Research Field?

This was a field of research which, after some delay,[3] blossomed with the magnitude of the epidemic it tracked. It brought together extremely disparate disciplines and generated a dynamic research context, where methodological innovations engaged with the problems of dealing with a new disease. There was a shared sense of urgency that scientific and social knowledge were needed to understand the virus, how it was transmitted, which sectors of the population were involved, etc. This involved a massive research drive, which needed to explore populations in a way that had never before been attempted on such a wide scale. Social sciences and epidemiology were deployed in the absence of scientific certainty to provide a mapping of disease prevalence and isolate transmission pathways. Finding out about sexual behaviours and, in the absence of a cure, discovering ways of communicating methods of protecting against the disease drew in sociologists and anthropologists. Research related to HIV provided an enormous impetus to medical anthropology in particular, as cultural boundaries were perceived as barriers both to knowledge about behaviour and to communication about how to change it (Herdt 1992). The social surveillance of populations needed to invade the body (to evaluate sero-status, immunological deficiencies, contributory physiological factors) and to invade the privacy of individuals and groups to map sexual conduct and preferences.

This was an area where a sense of commitment pulled researchers with very different views together and also pushed them apart, as competition for research funds and their different positions on the many debates thrown up by HIV/Aids separated them (Weeks 1989; Watney 1990; Gagnon 1992). The HIV/Aids debates brought science together with some of its most articulate critics. For many researchers, it became a personal as well as an academic matter: the boundaries between activism and academia became indistinct. The quest to limit the harm caused by the virus was perceived by many as requiring a special kind of commitment. The extension of social surveillance involved in this massive research effort left many uneasy, particularly those who had previously adopted a critical position *vis-à-vis* medical science (Treichler 1992). But the medical professional may also be gay, and may be an activist, and the endemic ambivalence of HIV-related research could be experienced at a very personal level. Researchers were often involved in researching people who were like themselves and experienced an uncomfortable double vision, experiencing subjectively the imperatives of the models they worked with.

The epidemiological distribution of the virus in Western populations only served to intensify worries about whether the information produced by research is so tainted by ideology that its potential for affirming oppressive social and cultural practices could do more harm than good. Human immunodeficiency virus threw into sharp relief divisions in the societies it appeared in. A high prevalence of HIV was found among intravenous (IV) drug-users and the gay community in Europe and in the USA. In addition, the US black and Hispanic populations were disproportionately affected (Kane and Mason 1992; Quimby 1992). In the developing world, some of the poorest nations were hardest hit (Frankenberg 1989). Existing boundaries of discrimination, moral marginalization and structural poverty were reified by the stigma of association with a mainly sexually transmitted disease, repeating the ignominious social responses to previous sexually transmitted disease epidemics (Weeks 1989).

Social fractures were made visible by HIV. It gave rise to disconcertingly public divisions within the research world. The politics of research, usually a muted issue, was suddenly laid bare in interdisciplinary wrangles. These took place within science and medicine,[4] and between disciplines.[5] These divisions were exacerbated by a new phenomenon: the politics of identity and sexuality had created a sophisticated activist grouping among gay men, capable of questioning the status and practices of medical knowledge. Feminists also noted the differential treatments of women by biomedicine, and black and Hispanic activists noted the discrimination within the health services which left their communities vulnerable. This contestation rendered visible a whole host of new ethical questions (see Nelkin *et al.* 1991). Inequalities in health care were exposed, legal rights were questioned (could individuals be tried for knowingly infecting others?) and the integrity of the insurance industry was criticized. Dominant professional groups, which had taken for granted their ability and their status to define the world, found their knowledges and their positions as experts challenged.

The 'Other' Interviews: The Meaning of Unruly Narratives

I joined the longitudinal study of the changing sexual behaviour of 'men who have sex with men' in relation to HIV/Aids in the second phase of interviewing. The main focus of the study was sexual behaviour and perceptions of risk, but the interview also included sections on experiences and attitudes towards condoms, testing for HIV and, for men who were HIV-positive, experiences of health care.[6] The closed questionnaire used in the interview was carefully designed to elicit details of sexual behaviour with a number of (male and female) partners within different time frames (the last month, year and five years). The questionnaire comprised 90 pages of closed questions, taking different forms (check-lists, Likert scales, questions with a number of predefined optional responses). The questionnaire imposed a rigid organizational framework on participants' responses. While carrying out the research interviews, however, I became fascinated by the ways that the men I talked to continually escaped from the framework of the questionnaire. They moved back and forward in time and over partners, they digressed into anecdotes and explanations where none were required by the questionnaire, they discussed their feelings about partners, and specific events.

I had imagined that the difficulty involved in structured interviewing would have been eliciting enough information, particularly given the topics covered. However, I discovered that often the problem was rather to channel the flow of narratives, bring them back to the time frame, event and partner specified in the questionnaire. I carried out roughly 150 interviews and recorded 40 of these. I told the men that they should feel free to add any information they felt was relevant which the questionnaire did not cover. The taped interviews were not noticeably different in length or content from those which were not taped.

I would like to explore in more detail here the strong narrative trains that these interviews produced. There has been a strong interest in narrative research within social science research in medical areas. This stemmed originally from a growing awareness of the dissonance between biomedical conceptualizations of health and illness[7] and those of patients. Hydén (1997) points out that patients' views and actions were linked to biomedical conceptions by means of terms like 'illness behaviour', or 'lay perspective'. Only when a distinction was made between illness and disease was there a possibility of treating people's narrative accounts of their experiences as integral to the course of the illness. This meant that the focus could shift from illness to suffering and its transformation in different social contexts, so that 'the foundation was laid for conceiving of the patients' speech as a voice strong enough to stand up against the voice of medicine' (ibid.: 48–9).[8]

Bury (1982) developed the idea that biographical narratives could give insight into the significance of the disruption caused by chronic illness, viewed as altering the relationship between the patient's body, self and surrounding world. Two important aspects of this have been developed by Bury, in the ways he looks at the links between the practical organization of everyday life and self-understanding. Critical to self-understanding is the individual's view of others – uncertainty is closely connected to doubts about the responses of others – individuals cannot be sure that their own perceptions and definitions will be shared by others (Bury 1991: 454). Bury notes that meaning and context in chronic illness cannot easily be separated, different conditions carry with them different connotations and imagery. These differences may have a profound influence on how individuals regard themselves and how they think others see them (ibid.: 453).

Narrative research carried out with people who have HIV/Aids has emphasized the importance of social context. Viney and Bousfield (1991) noted that the social consequences of HIV were given prominent importance in the narratives of men they interviewed. Individual experience was articulated by collectivizing the illness experience and questioning the social implications of the illness. Carricaburu and Pierret (1995) looked at how being HIV-positive gave rise to biographical work, which drew on the social context, creating new biographies: 'There is a collective dimension to HIV infection that shapes the individual's experience. Interpretations of AIDS are rife. Everyone is familiar with public discourses about AIDS' (ibid.: 71). The biographical work of the French gay men interviewed by Carricaburu and Pierret was associated with self-directed changes in their lives. Men emphasized the importance of self-care, and a renewed focus on personal life and relationships. All adopted strong restraints and self-restraint, changing sexual behaviours. Other studies working on narrative constructions of illness have emphasized other aspects of narratives that should be taken into account – for example, the practical material context that the narrator lives within,[9] and the individual's agency to create personal meaning.[10] Maintaining a focus on the practical, social and individual aspects of people's narratives requires both a close and distant focus on their lives, setting them in socioeconomic and cultural context, but also listening to the way that they as individuals are grappling with their situation. Hydén (1997) suggests that, in addition, more attention be paid to the context within which narratives are spoken, and to whom. Rather than regarding the narrative as a window on the world behind the narrative, it is perhaps best to view it as a situated communication, tied to a particular meeting of two worlds. The way that the medical world shapes that context has to be taken into account. Hydén (1997) argues that medical contexts may give rise to conflict between the 'voice of medicine' and the 'voice of the lifeworld' (following Mishler 1984).

The material I am about to discuss may appear to embody this distinction. The way the interviews I carried out were framed is in many ways completely at odds with the methodological approach adopted in narrative research, which aims to allow people to give voice to their own personal account in their own words. Rather, they exemplified a situation where the 'unruly narratives' of the interview subjects challenged and escaped the medical and sociological framing of their experience. These narratives often acquired a life of their own, disappearing and then re-emerging in the course of the interview, developing a particular coherency that linked the divergent topic areas together in a way which was meaningful and personally relevant to the individual. The systematic way that sex and relationships were broken down into artificially created parts in order to establish valid and reliable facts relevant to the frame of research was reconstituted by individuals in terms of reflections on their own biographical experiences and the experiences of others, their knowledges, their desires, hopes and fears.

It is this very conflict that I would like to examine in the following section. As an anthropologist engaging with a group of people that had no clearly defined social or cultural boundaries, I found it difficult to envisage how I could frame the research material. There was no context to set them in; all they had in common was that they might have sex associated with risk of HIV infection, and the way they were visualized by research (see Kane and Mason 1992). However, I could think anthropologically about the meeting between these two worlds. I viewed the interview as a dialogue between two (at least) conceptual frameworks. Where men chose to express and develop their responses to the interview, they were actively working with the way the survey conceptualized their lives, bodies and histories. Although I cannot develop the themes of this dialogue at length here, and I shall only focus on the part of the questionnaire concerned with sex and relationships, I hope to provide material for thinking about the engagement of research with the people it studies. First I shall look at the framing of sex and relationships that has occurred in relation to HIV.

Slaughtering the Event: Framing Sex and Relationships

Research concerning sex and sexuality was, until recently, the province of rational, scientific enquiry.[11] In the 1970s and 1980s radical critiques began to emerge which began to deconstruct social concepts of sexuality and sex, showing how they were historically contingent. These also criticized the embedded assumptions about the value-free nature of scientific research on sex (see Weeks 1985). However, new debates about sexuality and sex were overshadowed by the HIV epidemic and the need for instrumental knowledge about sex (Gagnon and Parker 1995). The aims and interests of different agencies involved in generating knowledge about sex were not always compatible.[12] However, there were some broad agreements about the need: to establish the risks associated with particular sexual activities; to write appropriate health education literature; to enable people to negotiate to protect themselves from risk; and to foster new and positive sexual conduct and identity.

The difficulties involved in researching sex generated innovatory techniques.[13] It is, I think, important to note that research with different populations gave rise to different kinds of focus. Research with gay men has been particularly concerned with ways of creating language to describe and contextualize sexual experiences.[14] Research among women has focused rather on the social relations that shape sexual encounters and women's knowledge of their bodies, in terms of the constraints imposed on women in negotiating safer sex (Holland *et al.* 1991; Schoepf 1992; Heize 1995). These differences reflected the prior research interests and identities of the researchers concerned. The divisions they produced, bringing together the identification of populations and problems with theoretical perspectives and methodologies, could soon be reified as people developed expertise and arenas for dissemination of their results, and their successes were rewarded by the channelling of funding towards recognized research groups.

The frame adopted by the survey I worked on attempted neither to access individuals' own semantic definitions of sex, nor to exhaustively categorize sexual acts. Mapping the incidence of risky sex within a population, sometimes in relation to the knowledge of what constituted 'risk', had been carried out by a number of studies. Here the aim was to extend this by setting sexual encounters in some context, to try and elicit the salient factors which framed encounters where men had risky/safer sex. The previous stage had already indicated that the status of a partner was a very important factor in relation to the kind of sex men had. While knowledge was generally high, and many men had changed the kind of sex they had with casual partners, unprotected penetrative sex was still occurring within established relationships. This survey looked at perceptions of partners, evaluations of the risk involved, trust, and how communications took place. Setting sex in context, no matter how cursory this context might appear to an anthropologist, was taking a stance against the predominantly individualistic psychological approaches that had been associated with survey research.[15]

The framing of population groups in relation to risk has come under heavy criticism. Anthropologists have been particularly scathing about the way both culture and risk behaviours have been reified by overly simplistic epidemiological models. These assume the group ascribes to a single set of cultural values and practices (see Glick-Schiller *et al.* 1994 on gay men), ignores the structural factors that make individuals and groups vulnerable and excludes relationships that cut across the boundaries of a group (partners of IV drug users or prostitutes, for example (Kane and Mason 1992)). 'Men who have sex with men' was a deliberately fictive group to avoid the association of findings with an existing social group, mindful of the diversity the men who participated in terms of their sexuality and their social and their cultural backgrounds.

Unruly Narratives: Work in Progress?

Many of the gay men and younger men interviewed were familiar with the language used in the survey, and with the implicit distinction made between safer and risky sex. They were well informed and already practised at thinking about their sexual encounters in this way. For them, retrieving from memory the last time they had unprotected penetrative sex (if this was relevant) was easy, because this was already marked as a significant kind of activity for them. For others, the language was foreign; even using language at all to describe sex was difficult. This was not just a 'translation' problem, say between 'fucking' and 'anal penetrative sex' (although exploring that difference could be a chapter in itself). They were unfamiliar with the practice of conceptualizing sexual experiences in semantically discrete categories. They had to retrospectively dismember the flow of events, using new and unfamiliar terms, a task they needed help with. It is usually assumed that, in working with language to communicate experience, people can stretch categories to fit experience. However, since the categories here were predefined, experience had to be tailored to fit this dominant categorical framework. Fitting experience into categories defined by others seemed to engender reflexivity, to render the taken-for-granted self-conscious. If this is a violence of sorts, it was not taken passively by all who were interviewed.

Men did quibble with the categories. Some were annoyed at how little of their sexual experience was captured. For example, the drama of a richly orchestrated S and M extravaganza, which gave pages of narrative description, was reduced to two ticks on a grid – a cause for humour and chagrin. A few gay men were scathing about this – they wanted to see some attempt to engage with the richness of sexual activity, which could be used to create more appropriate and inviting educational material. Safer sex need not be boring, but the interview schedule was, in their view.

The schematic nature of the survey approach laid bare patterns of sexual behaviour for men. Before their eyes the same boxes were ticked on page after page, collapsing years of sexual experience into a tiny repetitive matrix of marks. This patterning could be shocking – some were aghast that their sex lives could appear so limited. This was exacerbated by some of the questions relating to the context that sex took place in – one question asking whether the sex was planned or not had the option 'routine within the relationship'. Most men strongly resisted the categorization of sex as 'routine'. The number and timing of sexual encounters often gave rise to self-reflection. This could be of the 'so many' or, equally, the 'so few' ('has it really been two years?') kind. Setting sex into the time frame of the survey imposed a new standardized viewpoint on the self and the past, one that did not sit well with self-identification or experiential time. The cut and dried sex of the survey was wrestled into life in many interviews. Remembering sex could not be done without remembering much else. Some of the framing memories that were articulated were orientated towards the physical self, in visceral memories of past lives, of missed sexual behaviours. Sex was also tied to the sexual partner, their desires and bodies. Questions were included about partners in a second section, which looked at two sexual encounters in more detail, but detailed descriptions of these partners had usually made an appearance earlier in men's narratives. Often partners not touched on by the interview made an appearance too – men or women who had been important in their lives. Experiences with them were carried into future relationships. It was important for men to convey what their partner was like, not just what he liked. Some narratives painted very strong affective images of relationships. One man tried to convey the contentment of a relationship when asked about his feelings for a past partner. He started by describing how he had to drive long distances at that time, and there was one particular place in the country he would stop off where he would eat his packed lunch and have a smoke. He was describing happiness and contentment, and, if eating a packed lunch seems far from the passions, anxieties and eroticism of sex, that was the point. He was resetting an agenda, refocusing on his relationship and its personal meaning.

Relationships are difficult to describe rationally. The interview asked detailed questions about the last time unprotected penetrative anal sex took place. Since this often happened within regular important relationships, then the last time was often at the end of a relationship. The emotional complexity of this last sexual encounter often defied categorization. Categories suited for casual relationships, or those in a steady state, failed to capture those points where life is unsteady.

> My feelings at that point in time? What was happening on that particular occasion was we were splitting up . . . Tremendous mixed feelings . . . I was . . . I was . . . I think the best thing I could say is that I was deeply loving him . . . I was hoping it would still work out and continue indefinitely.

The emotional tumult at the end of relationships, or the beginnings, or during crises, is difficult to master conceptually, to break down into component parts. Yet these are likely to be the times when commitments, decisions, changes are made. Again, the task of finding language for experience not usually determined in this way is problematic.

A salient issue in many interviews was that of inequality and dominance within relationships: were men able to express their wishes, were they able to act on them, or were they coerced by others? These issues often came up early in narratives, before they were asked in the schedule, because they were often crucial to men's understanding of what had happened in a sexual encounter. For example, when asked, 'How did you communicate what you wanted [in one particular encounter] one man replied:

> We more or less just understood . . . there is something you haven't touched on though . . . at the time I was taking anal sex under a lot of pressure because the bloke I was with, if I didn't do it he thought I was getting it elsewhere . . . so I was under a lot of pressure . . . but then of course as it went on I got used to it . . . and I didn't bother . . . like you get used to it don't you.

And later in the interview, in answer to the question 'Who would you say was the dominant partner in the encounter?':

> he had a lot of hold over me because he could have thrown me out or anything and all that crap . . . well he'd had me thrown out quite a lot of times and I've had the police and stuff . . . but that's how he kept the pressure up . . . he was a bastard.

Several men discussed an episode concerning risky sex in relation to a temporary period of vulnerability, of uncertainty, or depression: after a long monogamous relationship had ended, or after losing a job. In some narratives, factors such as material dependency, age, education and confidence in sexuality or as a sexual actor figured strongly in men's descriptions of relationships. These issues have been looked at in a social and relational context in research concerning women; however, studies concerning men have tended to look at these factors only in relation to individual agency. Questions concerning how power can become sexualized in particular social and relational situations have not been pursued.

The idea that personal efficacy could be considered as an individual, ahistorical characteristic was, to put it mildly, questioned by the narrative material. The ways men thought about sex and acted in sexual encounters changed over time, in relation to the social contexts they moved through, in relation to their biographical history, in relation to the information and ideas about HIV, and in relation to social representations about sex and about sexual identity (see Carricaburu and Pierret 1995). The narratives prompted by the interviews resulted from reflection on the self in the past, in the present and projected into the future. They were often contradictory, often ambivalent and often questioning rather than assertive. They might be viewed as 'work in progress', the work of individuals placed under particular pressure to be reflexive, both by the wider context and more immediately by the interview. The vitality of some of these narratives showed people who were in a variety of ways actively drawing on social, cultural and individual resources to impose some sense on problems that were novel, making them familiar.

I would like to pursue this in relation to one section in the schedule which focused on one sexual encounter to explore the way men made decisions about what kind of sex they would have. This section gave rise to narratives that displayed deeply conflicting elements. 'Trust' is a key term in relation to discourses about risk and sex. 'Safer sex' is premised on awareness and acceptance of risk and, in turn, on the production of trust (Scott and Freeman 1995: 162). The orthodoxy that has developed within the context of HIV and Aids information is rather ambivalent. Talk/ communication is emphasized as a route to risk reduction (as sexual histories are exchanged, safer sex can be negotiated in appropriate ways), and yet knowledge of a partner can never be complete (ibid.). The production of 'trust' can be a high-risk activity (ibid.).

Trust was certainly complex in many relationships. Trusting another who is close means trusting someone despite knowing them well enough to be aware that they are fallible. This man asserted his complete confidence in his partner early in the interview and emphatically stated that he trusted him implicitly. Yet, later in the interview in the section on experiences of health care, he started to talk about him again: 'He lies about little things, covering his tracks . . . I think they're worse . . . I know he'd never . . . I mean in my heart I don't think he'd ever be unfaithful to me.' The way men talked about 'trust' as integral to their decisions and negotiations of sex showed considerable ambivalence. This is perhaps exemplified by two diverging responses to the same question. One man, who always had safer sex with his main partner, had already said he knew a lot about his partner's previous sexual history and had evaluated this as not at all risky. When asked how risky it would be to have unprotected sex with him, he replied: 'I guess I should say not very risky, if I believe him . . . emmm . . . but that's not my reaction . . . I'd never take that risk . . . but . . . uhhh . . . I guess it's not very risky.' Another repondent gave a very different, though still ambivalent, answer to the same question. He did have unprotected, penetrative anal sex with his partner. Again, he had already spoken of how they had exchanged information about their sexual past, and that his partner's past was not at all risky:

> Well, not very. I was his first . . . well . . . I suppose . . . say 'don't know' . . . it's more accurate, less of an assumption . . . I can't actually say that I would be 100% sure he hadn't . . . but I would be 99.9 because we talked about it a lot . . . I mean he'd had heterosexual penetrative sex using condoms, partly due to the fact that he was using them as a contraceptive and partly because he'd known about the risk of other things . . . not HIV . . . He'd also had sex with other men but that was masturbatory.

The uncertainty of both of these passages was reflected in the hesitation with which they spoke. This was clearly a difficult area to bring into words. In the first case, although he did trust his partner, he found it difficult to say that sex with him would not be risky (although in the end he did). He was not just saying that intellectually he knew it could not be considered safe, he was saying that he felt that it was not safe, 'that he would never take that risk'. In the second case, although his trust in his partner had been acted upon, he was aware that this could not be justified rationally, he still chose 'don't know' as the proper category to describe his knowledge about his partner. Both of these men said they 'totally trusted' their partner in a later question.

This deep ambivalence does exemplify the processes described by Beck (1992), whereby public policy and expert systems have moved towards identifying the individual as ultimately responsible for the assessment and avoidance of risk (Scott and Freeman 1995: 163): '[Experts] dump their conflicts and contradictions at the feet of the individual and leave him or her with the well intentioned invitation to judge all of this critically on the basis of his or her own notions' (Beck 1992: 137, in Scott and Freeman 1995: 162). As Scott and Freeman point out, neither Giddens's nor Beck's approach to risk is particularly well suited for considering processes of risk management in personal and sexual relations (Scott and Freeman 1995: 164). Their ideas about personal reflexivity as a means of recon-structing the self (see Giddens 1991), and as creating a critical perspective on the institutions and expert knowledge which produce risk, do not give much insight into the very personal engagement of these men. These theories are predicated on a very generalized model of society and of the individual which does not engage with the social context, with power in relationships or with kinds of reflexivity that are not predicated on rational intellectual choices (McKechnie and Welsh 1994). The 'trust' that men spoke of was not the 'solution to a specific problem' (Scott and Freeman 1995: 162) of safer-sex discourses. Trust was an emotionally rich term: men tied external discourses of control of the body into their own hopes, desires and knowledge about another. What they meant by trust was only knowable within the context of their own biographical history, set in its relational and social context. I would suggest that the deep ambivalence of this area could usefully be explored by qualitative research, which could frame such concepts as 'trust' in 'experience-near' terms.

I think it would be inadequate to think of these narratives as simply 'rich material' which could give depth to some of the concepts the survey was developing. I also think it would be wrong to see their narratives as simply contesting the sociological frame of the survey. I would suggest that their narratives could be viewed as in dialogue with the survey. In a shifting situation, they were working in life with many of the same concepts worked with in abstract by the survey. As well as offering data to be analysed by these abstract concepts, their views and experiences might well offer a contribution to the conceptual framework of research itself.

Taking seriously the experiences of people might change more than the concepts that are used to frame negotiations of safer sex. This would mean taking seriously the impact of the changes wrought by the way HIV has entered into different social contexts. Constructing and disseminating languages to talk about sex and models of interpersonal behaviour do more than provide a technology for self-protection. Since 'sexual behaviour' is so tied to individuals' self-identification and their intimate emotional and relational life, keystones of the socio-cultural context they live in, one might expect the unintended consequences of changing sexual behaviour to be profound.

This is clearly an area that would be interesting to study, and it might well be of benefit to those who were its focus. However, it is also possible to imagine harm resulting from such research. This would be invasive in a way that even research on sex is not. If material were to be framed unreflexively in a public health perspective, then the reification of 'culture', of boundaries around overdetermined sets of social characteristics, would be disastrous. Even if this were not to happen, creating language and concepts that render conscious 'taken-for-granted' areas of life would be a risky business in itself. Taking apart relationships and emotions, creating (more) expert discourses, would have many consequences. One might predict that, since this material would be borne into the symbolic battlefield of HIV-related research, there would be contestation concerning how to frame and use it. Research that was reflexive about the way it produces knowledge, and for whom, would be necessary. Communication between disciplines and perspectives and between research and policy-makers would be of key importance.

The dialogue that emerged from the narratives I taped touched on many important areas. Many of the narratives were about caring – caring about the self, about a partner, for friends and lovers who were ill. This kind of material would have much to offer social science research in relation to those who are HIV-positive, have Aids or care for someone who is ill with HIV-related illnesses. Many of these areas are not attracting either policy-makers or funding. I think there is a strong case to be made for such dialogues to continue. More convincing arguments have to be made for the hardness of 'soft' facts and better efforts made to translate between research and policy worlds.[16]

Theoretical and Methodological Engagement: Different Strokes for Different Folks?

The points I have made above might be read in different ways. They could be read as a critique of quantitative methods, of the approach taken by the survey, in favour of a qualitative approach, which could get closer to the experience of those grappling with the impact of HIV on their lives. However, this is not the case. My respect for the rigorous approach of those I worked with increased as I came to understand the aims the survey set and the methods used to achieve these aims.[17] I was also impressed by their careful qualification of the data in presentation. The material was always lucidly presented and clearly demarcated what it could be used to explain and where further research was needed. Indeed, the research was presented in such a way as to emphasize the dynamic context, and to suggest that social, cultural and emotional processes would need to be addressed in future research (Fitzpatrick *et al.* 1989).

On the other hand, I might be viewed as making a case for the pragmatic and eclectic application of appropriate methods to suit a research problematic – methods being horses for courses. However, I do think that the theoretical specificity and methodological training that develop within disciplinary specialities are valuable. I would argue, however, that an approach which is clearly situated and reflexive about the kind of knowledge it is producing is appropriate. This kind of research would be involved in care. A fuller and more thoughtful engagement between disciplines and perspectives is called for, as there are real discussions, not to say arguments, to be conducted between them. So far, in relation to HIV, qualitative research has often been packaged, as Scheper-Hughes (1990) describes, bracketed from its explanatory vision and used as rich data within the framework of biomedical and larger-scale sociologial frameworks. Some aspects of research are heard, others apparently disappear into an abyss of misunderstanding between experts.

Unless the chain of relations involved in constructing 'problem-based' research is reflexively questioned, it will continue to reframe constituent knowledges as they pass through different frames (of biomedicine, epidemiology, policy-making, funding, researchers, subjects) and then back again. This is reminiscent of Will Hay's comedy routine: as 'Going to advance, send reinforcements' was whispered down the line in the trenches, the message transformed into 'Going to a dance, send three and fourpence.' It is depressing to think of the health and illness equivalent of 'Going to a dance, send three and fourpence' carrying on indefinitely.

The division of labour within social science allows very different perspectives to develop alternative strategies for a positive contribution to caring practice. The divide between 'humane' and 'radical' research undermines communication. While critical viewpoints are necessary, divisions can easily be morally reified. Cassell and Wax (1980) point to the dangers of creating a moral 'other' of different perspectives. In any case, taking the moral high ground is no longer straightforward. As Bury (1997) points out, in relation to disability issues, the critical perspectives that were once levelled by social science at medicine are now being levelled at social science itself by activist groups claiming that their experiential and political viewpoint should be shaping research aims. Bury points out that these claims, although sometimes persuasive, should be examined carefully, particularly in terms of the representativeness of activists claiming to speak for a larger diverse population. He also points out that activists themselves are framing their demands in relationship to concepts such as 'individual empowerment', which are central to the dominant ideologies of late modernity (ibid.). All research has an impact on the world it objectifies. Contestation over moral high ground (and academic status) certainly raises questions that should be addressed, but they should not be a substitute for self-critical reflection, nor should they be allowed to block potentially fruitful avenues of dialogue. Neither should they obscure the diversity of active ways that people are working with ideas of health and illness themselves. Breaking through the boundaries that keep these voices from articulating their concerns, experiences and needs and finding ways of engaging in our different ways with the material, social and physical factors that shape health care and communication are important. Being aware of how our research cultures and institutions shape our approaches and our social relations as researchers might start to break down some of the barriers that keep researchers from seeing their own participation in care.

Notes

1. For a discussion of this point in relation to anthropological research, see Hastrup and Elsass (1990).
2. Although here I should be clear that I am not claiming this is a timeless, rigid hierarchy. The dominance of disciplinary knowledge both within and in relation to biomedicine is, of course, socially constructed. Armstrong (1995), for example, identifies what seems to be a recent shift from hospital to public health medicine as a key area of framing ideas about the body social and body physical.
3. As Shilts (1987) pointed out, the slow response of the medical and political establishment in the USA was linked to the first appearance of the disease in marginal groups.
4. Treichler (1992) describes how the claims and counter-claims of scientists and disciplines trying to establish their theories about HIV undermined the imagery of science as an objective community working together to establish facts. There has been a marked enhancement of the scientific status of the disciplines that succeeded in establishing their claims (virology and immunology).
5. The hierarchy of credibility and funding within the medical field created many dissatisfied researchers, who felt that they were working within the constraints of others' models (Glick-Schiller 1992; Kane and Mason 1992). There was also more outspoken frustration with disciplinary conflict than is usually voiced: Quimby noted: 'As people argue for academic turf, people in the trenches are being battered' (1992: 160).
6. See Fitzpatrick *et al.* (1989, 1990) and Dawson *et al.* (1991) for discussions of the findings of the first stage of research in relation to sexual behaviour, HIV test uptake and social support within the gay community. This study was funded by the Medical Research Council.
7. Comaroff characterizes the biomedical view succinctly:

In terms of formal medical aetiology, illness is explained predominantly as the result of the interaction of 'pathogens' and 'host' . . . These etiological models entail a specific image of man – and a tacit ideology. For they connote a view of disease as an asocial, amoral process, and a view of man as the decontextualised 'host' to a set of unmediated natural processes, which call for technical intervention. (1982: 59)

8. There is a parallel between the interest shown by social scientists in narrative and the development of what Armstrong (1979) has called 'biographical medicine'. He has described how, during the 1960s, the reinvigoration of general practice in Britain led to a questioning of the hegemonic position of hospital medicine. A new vision of the medical problematic emphasized the biographical elements of patients' problems.

9. Anderson *et al.*, in a study of the narratives of white and Chinese Canadian women coping with diabetes, suggest that 'The meaning and experience of illness is nested in a complex personal, socio-economic and political nexus' (1991: 101). Their study did find ethnically specific ways of managing illness, but they emphasized that material necessity and position on the labour-market were as important as cultural beliefs in shaping the way women worked with their illness (ibid.).

10. Chamberlayne and King (1997) were careful to set the narrative descriptions of women carers in East and West Germany within the context of both personal relations and the different social and welfare systems that constrained their caring relationships. They argue strongly that attention should be given to the individual agency of those creating narratives: 'lives are not just lived through different systems; systems are also played out individually in individual lives' (ibid.: 605).

11. The large-scale survey of sex pioneered by Kinsey and developed by Masters and Johnson constitutes the major social science approach to sex until the 1970s (Weeks 1985; Hawkes 1996: 50–71).

12. See, for example, Watney (1990) on friction between activist groups and health researchers.

13. See, for example, the use of diaries (Coxon 1988), network analysis and participation observation (Boulton 1992).

14. This kind of research was appropriated from medical and epidemiological surveys, which at the beginning of the epidemic tended to reify moralistic stereotypical categories of deviant and dangerous sexual practices (see Horton and Aggleton 1989; Boulton 1992).

15. As Bloor (1995) points out, research paradigms of risk and populations

range from the social psychological 'health beliefs model', in which health beliefs are measured in relation to individuals' self-perceived agency, to the 'culture of risk' approach developed by Mary Douglas (see Douglas and Calvez 1990), which argues that the different ways individuals act towards risk are shaped by the structure of the social group they are part of. Douglas formalizes this in the group/grid model of cultural context.

16. As Kirsten Hastrup (1993) contends, the dislocating traumatic experiences of famine deserve as much attention as data on disaster, which can be easily made into quantifiable fact. This experience is as 'hard' as any calorie count.

17. The study did show that there were some important patterns in sexual practices across a wide demographic spectrum in relation to HIV, and identified some important issues in terms of the care which men received (Fitzpatrick *et al.* 1990; Dawson *et al.* 1991). In addition, the study identified some important fallacies in more biomedically conceptualized research on risk and sexual behaviour, signalling the importance of relationships in shaping the kinds of sex which people had.

References

Anderson, J., C. Blue, and A. Lau (1991), 'Women's Perspectives on Chronic Illness: Ethnicity, Ideology and Restructuring of Life', *Social Science and Medicine*, 33(2): 101–13.

Ardener, E. (1975), 'The Problem Revisited', in S. Ardener (ed.), *Perceiving Women,* London: Dent.

—— (1982), 'Social Anthropology, Language and Reality', in D. Parkin (ed.), *Semantic Anthropology*, London: Academic Press.

Armstrong, D. (1979), 'The Emancipation of Biographical Medicine', *Social Science and Medicine*, 13A: 1–8.

—— (1995), 'The Rise of Surveillance Medicine', *The Sociology of Health and Illness*, 17(3): 393–404.

Beck, U. (1992), *Risk Society*, London: Sage.

Bloor, M. (1995), 'A User's Guide to Contrasting Theories of HIV-related Risk Behaviour', in J. Gabe (ed.), *Medicine Health and Risk: Sociological Approaches,* Oxford: Blackwell.

Boulton, R. (1992) 'Mapping Terra Incognita: Sex Research for AIDS Prevention – An Urgent Agenda for the 1990s', in G. Herdt and S. Lindebaum (eds), *The Time of AIDS: Social Analysis, Theory and Methods*, Newbury Park: Sage.

Bury, M. (1982), 'Chronic Illness as Biographical Disruption', *Sociology of Health and Illness*, 14(2): 167–82.

158 | **Rosemary McKechnie**

——— (1991), 'The Sociology of Chronic Illness: a Review of Research and Prospects', *Sociology of Health and Illness*, 13(3): 407–39.
——— (1997), *Health and Illness in a Changing Society,* London and New York: Routledge.
Carricaburu, D. and J. Pierret (1995), 'From Biographical Disruption to Biographical Reinforcement: the Case of HIV-positive Men', *Sociology of Health and Illness*, 17(1): 65–88.
Cassell, J. (1978), 'Risk and Benefit to Subjects of Fieldwork', *The American Sociologist*, 13(2): 134–43.
Cassell, J. and M. Wax (1980), 'Towards a Moral Science of Human Beings', *Social Problems*, 27(3): 259–64.
Chamberlayne, P. and A. King (1997) 'The Biographical Challenge of Caring', *Sociology of Health and Illness*, 19(5): 601–21.
Comaroff, J. (1982), 'Medicine: Symbol and Ideology', in P. Wright and A. Treacher (eds), *The Problem of Medical Knowledge: Examining the Social Construction of Medicine*, Edinburgh: Edinburgh University Press.
Coxon, T. (1988), 'Something Sensational . . . the Sexual Diary as a Tool for Mapping Detailed Sexual Behaviour', *Sociological Review*, 36: 353–67 .
Dawson, J., R. Fitzpatrick, J. McLean, G. Hart, and M. Boulton (1991), 'Gay Men's Views and Experiences of the HIV Test', in P. Aggleton, G. Hart and P. Davies (eds), *AIDS: Responses, Interventions and Care*, London, New York, Philadelphia: The Falmer Press.
Douglas, M. and M. Calvez (1990), 'The Self as Risk Taker: a Cultural Theory of Contagion in Relation to AIDS', *Sociological Review*, 38: 445–64.
Fitzpatrick, R., M. Boulton and G. Hart (1989), 'Gay Men's Sexual Behaviour in Response to AIDS – Insights and Problems', in P. Aggleton, G. Hart and P. Davies (eds), *AIDS: Social Representations, Social Practices*, Lewes, Philadelphia: The Falmer Press.
Fitzpatrick, R., J. McLean, M. Boulton, G. Hart and J. Dawson (1990), 'Variations in Sexual Behaviour in Gay Men', in P. Aggleton, P. Davies and G. Hart (eds), *AIDS: Individual, Cultural and Policy Dimensions*, London, New York, Philadelphia: The Falmer Press.
Frankenberg, R. (1987), 'Life Cycle, Trajectory or Pilgrimage?', in A. Bryman *et al.* (eds) *Rethinking the Life-Cycle,* London: Macmillan.
——— (1989), 'One Epidemic or Three? Cultural, Social and Historical Aspects of the AIDS Pandemic', in P. Aggleton, G. Hart and P. Davies (eds), *AIDS: Social Representations, Social Practices*, Lewes, Philadelphia: The Falmer Press.
Gabe J., M. Calnan, and M. Bury (1991), 'Introduction', in J. Gabe, M. Calnan and M. Bury (eds), *The Sociology of the Health Service*, London: Routledge.
Gagnon, J.H. (1992), 'Epidemics and Researchers: AIDS and the Practice of Social Studies', in G. Herdt and S. Lindenbaum (eds), *The Time of Aids: Social Analysis, Theory and Method*, Newbury Park, London, New Delhi: Sage.
Gagnon, J.H. and R.G. Parker (1995), 'Conceiving Sexuality', in J.H. Gagnon

and R.G. Parker (eds), *Conceiving Sexuality: Approaches to Sex Research in a Postmodern World,* London, New York: Routledge, pp. 3–19.

Giddens, A. (1991), *Modernity and Self-Identity: Self and Society in the Late Modern Age,* Cambridge: Polity Press.

Glick-Schiller, N. (1992), 'What's Wrong with this Picture? The Hegemonic Construction of Culture in AIDS research in the US', in *Medical Anthropology Quarterly,* 6(3): 237–54.

Glick-Schiller, N., S. Crystal, and D. Lewellyn (1994), 'Risky Business: the Cultural Construction of AIDS Risk Groups', *Social Science and Medicine,* 38: 1337–46.

Hastrup, K. (1989), 'The Prophetic Condition', in M. Chapman (ed.), *Edwin Ardner: The Voice of Prophecy,* Oxford: Blackwell.

—— (1993), 'Hunger and the Hardness of Facts', *Man,* 28: 727–39.

—— (1995), *A Passage to Anthropology: Between Experience and Theory,* London: Routledge.

Hastrup K.and P. Elsass (1990), 'Anthropological Advocacy: A Contradiction in Terms?', *Current Anthropology,* 31: 301–11.

Hawkes, G. (1996), *A Sociology of Sex and Sexuality,* Buckingham and Bristol, USA: Open University Press.

Heize, L.L. (1995), 'Violence, Sexuality and Women's Lives', in R.G. Parker and J.H. Gagnon (eds), *Conceiving Sexuality: Approaches to Sex Research in a Postmodern World,* London: Routledge.

Herdt, G. (1992), 'Introduction', in G. Herdt and S. Lindenbaum (eds), *The Time of AIDS: Social Analysis, Theory and Method,* Newbury Park, London, New Delhi: Sage Publications.

Holland, J., C. Ramazanoglu, S. Scott, S. Sharpe, and R. Thomson (1991), 'Between Embarassment and Trust: Young Women and the Diversity of Condom Use', in P. Aggleton, G. Hart and P. Davies (eds), *AIDS: Responses, Interventions and Care,* London: Falmer Press.

Horton, M. and P. Aggleton (1989), 'Perverts, Inverts and Experts: The Cultural Construction of an AIDS Research Paradigm', in P. Aggleton, G. Hart and P. Davies (eds), *AIDS: Social Representations, Social Practices,* London: Falmer Press.

Hydén, L.-C. (1997), 'Illness and Narrative', *Sociology of Health and Illness,* 19(1): 48–69.

Kane, S. and T. Mason (1992), '"IV Drug Users" and "Sex Partners": The Limits of Epidemiological Categories and the Ethnography of Risk', in G. Herdt and S. Lindenbaum (eds), *The Time of AIDS: Social Analysis, Theory and Method,* Newbury Park, London, New Delhi: Sage Publications, pp. 199–225.

McDonald, M. (1993), 'The Construction of Difference: An Anthropological Approach to Stereotypes', in S. MacDonald (ed.), *Inside European Identities,* Oxford: Berg.

McKechnie, R. and I. Welsh (1994), 'Between the Devil and the Deep Green Sea: Defining Risk Societies and Global Threats', in J. Weeks (ed.), *The Greater*

Evil and the Lesser Good: The Theory and Practice of Democracy, London: Rivers Oram.

Marshall, P.A. (1991), 'Research Ethics in Applied Medical Anthropology', in C.E. Hill (ed.), *Training Manual in Applied Anthropology*, Washington DC: Special Publication of the American Anthropological Association No. 27.

Mishler, E.G. (1984), *The Discourse of Medicine. Dialectics of Medical Interviews*, Norwood, NJ: Ablex Publishing Company.

Nelkin, D., D.P. Willis and S.V. Parris (1991), 'A Disease of Society: Cultural and Institutional Response to AIDS', in D. Nelkin, D.P. Willis and S.V. Parris (eds), *A Disease of Society: Cultural and Institutional Responses to AIDS*, Cambridge: Cambridge University Press.

Olesen, V.L. (1989), 'Caregiving, Ethical and Informal: Emerging Challenges in the Sociology of Health and Illness', *Journal of Health and Social Behaviour*, 30: 1–10.

Quimby, E. (1992), 'Anthropological Witnessing for African Americans: Power, Responsibility, and Choice in the Age of AIDS', in G. Herdt and S. Lindenbaum (eds), *The Time of AIDS: Social Analysis, Theory and Method*, Newbury Park, London, New Delhi: Sage Publications.

Scambler, G. (1987), *Sociological Theory and Medical Sociology*, London: Tavistock Publications.

Scheper-Hughes, N. (1990), 'Three Propositions for a Critically Applied Medical Anthropology', *Social Science and Medicine*, 30(2): 189–97.

Schoepf, B.G. (1992), 'Women at Risk: Case Studies from Zaire', in G. Herdt and S. Lindenbaum (eds), *The Time of AIDS: Social Analysis, Theory and Method*, London, Beverley Hills: Sage.

Scott, S. and R. Freeman (1995), 'Prevention as a Problem of Modernity: the Example of HIV and AIDS', in J. Gabe (ed.), *Medicine Health and Risk: Sociological Approaches*, Oxford: Blackwell.

Shilts, R. (1987), *And the Band Played On*. New York: St Martins.

Singer, M. (1990), 'Reinventing Medical Anthropology: Towards a Critical Realignment', *Social Science and Medicine*, 30(2): 179–87.

Stacey, M. (1991), 'Medical Sociology and Health Policy: an Historical Overview', in J. Gabe, M. Calnan and M. Bury (eds), *The Sociology of the Health Service*, London: Routledge.

Taussig, M. (1980), 'Reification and the Consciousness of the Patient', *Social Science and Medicine*, 14b: 3–13.

Treichler, P. (1992), 'AIDS, HIV and the Cultural Construction of Reality', in G. Herdt and S. Lindenbaum (eds), *The Time of AIDS: Social Analysis, Theory and Method*, Newbury Park, London, New Delhi: Sage Publications.

Viney, L.L. and Bousfield, L. (1991), 'Narrative Analysis: a Method of Psycho-social Research for AIDS Affected People', *Social Science and Medicine*, 32: 756–65.

Walter, T. (1993), 'Sociologists Never Die: British Sociology and Death', in D. Clark (ed.), *The Sociology of Death*, Oxford: Blackwell.

Watney, S. (1990), 'Safer Sex as Community Practice', in P. Aggleton, P. Davies and G. Hart (eds), *AIDS: Individual, Cultural and Policy Dimensions*, London, New York, Philadelphia: The Falmer Press.

Weeks, J. (1985), *Sexuality and its Discontents: Meanings, Myths and Modern Sexualities*, London: Routledge & Kegan Paul.

—— (1989), 'AIDS: the Intellectual Agenda', in P. Aggleton, G. Hart and P. Davies (eds), *AIDS: Social Representations, Social Practices*, London: The Falmer Press.

Nursing Care: Theory and Practice

It is appropriate that the book should end with a section on care within the context of nursing. Many of the wider themes touched on in the preceding chapters have particular relevance to the caring relationships which nursing exemplifies. Both of the chapters in this section deal in different ways with the way that nursing, in attempting to attain independence in its development and some parity of status with other medical professionals, has had to engage squarely with the concept of care. The status of nursing is centrally tied to the status of caring. Vangie Bergum is engaging with the concept of care as a protagonist. In her chapter she outlines her ideas concerning the need for care to involve a relational ethic, and she explores the potential for carers to take on a wider role as both mediator and advocate for patients in stressful medical situations. Her aim is to show that, rather than thinking about 'ethics' as an abstract set of rules, it is possible to adopt a questioning moral position which eschews formalism for contingency. She argues that it is only possible to realize ethics in enactment.

Jan Savage takes a more distanced approach to the debates about nursing theory, but her chapter is based on finely tuned ethnographic work in hospital wards, observing care in practice. She is able to explore just how theoretical debates can transform the nature and experience of care-giving and receiving. She draws on two studies, both concerned with the way 'care' is conceptualized, carried out and experienced in very different contexts: one being the domestic context of the family, the other a hospital ward where new nursing theory is being practised. She looks at the way nurses draw on familiar knowledge of care, which comes from within the domestic context, to re-create the ideals of new theories. In doing so, she is able to reflect on the most basic level of care-giving, in its bodily enactment, and show how this is linked to abstract ideas. From the basis of her observation, she is also able to ask searching questions about both theoretical constructions and the 'taken-for-granted' experience of care that women and men carry within themselves.

7

Ethics as Question

Vangie Bergum

Introduction

Ethics is about questioning: questioning ourselves, questioning our relationships with others and questioning our place, as humans, in the larger environment. The claim made in this chapter is that the nature of ethics, specifically health care ethics, is fundamentally a matter of the questioning, which requires openness, deliberation, self-reflection, uncertainty and contemplation. Ethical issues encourage the logic of question and answer; that is, ethical concerns require ongoing dialogue between interested and involved people, rather than the sureness hoped for in the self-sufficient propositional logic of scientific theory, which can then be applied to clinical practice. Moral decision-making is necessarily dynamic and relational, based on flexibility, contingency and context, rather than on formalized dogmatic, rigid, abstract pre-stated conventions. Zygmunt Bauman states rightly that a 'foolproof – universal and unshakably founded – ethical code will never be found' (1993:10). Moving away from ethical certainty and non-ambivalence does not make the moral or ethical life easier, Bauman warns, but it may make life more moral.

In this chapter, I propose that addressing ethical issues and concerns in health care (responding to questions such as 'how should you or I be treated?' or 'all things considered, what ought to be done?') must take place in an atmosphere of dialogue. Only by exploring, through dialogue, the situation experienced by the people both providing care (nurses, doctors, chaplains, other professionals, personal care staff, family, etc.) and receiving care (patients, clients, residents, consumers and their families, etc.) can clarity or rightness of ethical action become evident. At times, ethical dialogue means finding the question for the answer we already have, and at times, the dialogue is primarily internal, within the self. Most times the dialogue is verbal, and yet at some times the dialogue must be silent.

To explore the value of dialogue in ethical decision-making and action, I shall first outline the kinds of truths described by Ken Wilber (1996). Different knowledge and notions of 'truth' need to be considered in order to generate the constructive dialogue that ethics needs: the truth of correspondence theory and functional fit, the truthfulness of subjective experience and the justness of intersubjective truth. Accepting the possibility of many truths acknowledges the fact that there are different paths toward the development of knowledge and truth: science and technology (empirical research), self-expression (descriptive research) and intersubjective meaning (interpretive research). All forms of knowledge contain truth, and ethical dialogue must consider the logic of observational as well as interpretive research in order to come to understand truth and ethical rightness in its wholeness. Following a discussion of knowledge and truth and the various ways to find truth, I shall identify four activities helpful in generating and sustaining dialogue in order to discover and contemplate ethical truth in health care: connecting, quickening, interviewing and acting.

Searching for Truth

If the nature of ethics has to do with questions like 'how should you and I be treated?', the kind of enquiry generally given primacy in health-care decision-making in ethics needs rethinking. In health care, as in many field of modern knowledge development, natural science research is the preferred model – a model that searches for the truth – about disease, about risk and about cause and effect. But, from the point of view of ethics (where truth is not absolute, where life cannot be controlled and where human life is recognize as multifarious with complex dimensions), other forms of knowledge and truth are needed as well. Scientific knowledge has led us toward solving 'the riddle', as the surgeon Sherwin Nuland (1994) describes, but does little to assist with making ethical decisions about the best way to be treated at the beginning of life or the end of life.

Knowledge gained through the traditional scientific method (the modern agenda) has been particularly useful to differentiate between myth, magic, religion and science, but, when moral decisions of the culture are 'handed over to science and technical solutions', says Wilber, we are caught in a 'monological, surface, gaze' (1996: 267). Science and the scientific method are useful in distinguishing between subjective truths (aesthetics, arts, beauty) but the overemphasis on finding the 'it' (objective truth) of science is not sufficient for understanding the depths of humanness and what being human means. If fact, with the dominance of knowledge developed through the scientific method, we have become narrow and reduced in our thinking, so that we have come to live in a flat land where 'we do not recognize degrees of consciousness, depth, value and worth. Everybody simply has the same depth, namely, zero' (Wilber 1996: 128).

Some nurse philosophers are concerned that acknowledging that there are different views through which to understand the world and its people will lead to plunging nursing enquiry (and presumably all enquiry) 'into a welter of personal predilections, preferences, and prejudices' (Kikuchi and Simmons 1996: 16). They are concerned that the increased interest in attending to the truth of patients' experience leads to accepting truth as a matter of taste. What these nurse philosophers miss, in striving for a rigid logic of truth, is the recognition that life is complex and many-layered and that knowledge must reflect the complexity, intricacy and particularity of human life in order to uncover the possibility of the truth for ethical action.

Earlier I explored three increasingly complex and comprehensive levels of knowledge that are needed for ethical care: descriptive, abstract and inherent (Bergum 1994). Descriptive knowledge, the truth of personal experience (e.g. description of signs and symptoms), is not sufficient for ethical health care. It needs the knowledge gained by the abstract generalizable knowledge of empirical science (exploring the cause of the signs and symptoms). Yet objective science is not comprehensive enough either, because, of necessity, it focuses on fragmented, narrow and clinical knowledge. What is needed, in present health-care situations, is attention to the complexity of scientific knowledge, integrated with personal experience and exploration – inherent knowledge. Inherent knowledge includes experiential and cultural awareness, as well as objective observation, and as such is more comprehensive and complex. Interpretation is needed to generate ethical knowledge and 'such interpretation is not simply an affair of our conscious, and rational, mind but also of the deep memories that are buried within us, of feelings and intuitions that are only partly under our immediate control' (Niebuhr 1963: 63).

In this chapter, I shall build on my earlier thinking by exploring different kinds of truth (truth as correspondence, and as truthfulness and justness), and show why both these need to be considered in the question/answer discourse that ethical understanding requires. I am urging consideration of a hermeneutic understanding of human life, not just an empirical scientific one, in order to respond to the daily ethical decisions that must be made in health care.

Truth as Correspondence

The modernist agenda of more and more scientific knowledge that is generalizable and universal has improved the life and health of people. The scientific method, with its attention to isolating and fragmenting units in order to develop specific knowledge of the functioning of objects under study, is effective in giving clinical answers to particular problems and providing cures and effective therapy for many diseases. The scientific method, used by medicine and some fields of psychology, etc., is most easily carried out when the focus is limited to one aspect of life – for example, physical, social, mental, spiritual, legal or even moral aspects of knowledge. The nature of science is fragmented and reductionist, where no amount of connecting (for example, with systems theory or team meetings) will bring about holism. Without a determined integration of knowledge and recognition of different truths (of the inner meanings, as well as outer facts), holistic care is not achieved. The ecomap or genogram (used to see the relationships between family members and the community in which they live) remains simplistic and shallow without the conversation about what that map means (what is shown and what is not shown). The danger of 'care maps', produced in great abundance in Canadian health care agencies to control fiscal and physical outcomes and regiment protocol for medical care, is that they focus only on readily measurable parameters. If we are governed by the logic of the care map, deviation from the expected projection of recovery means failure. It is possible, in considering a care map, that a person may recover from an operation, for example, but is still not well. Ethical care needs the interpretive knowledge and truth of the inner experience of the person living in a particular culture, as well as the knowledge of the view provided by scientific objective truth.

Truth as Truthfulness and Justness

Experiential knowledge, as lived knowledge, is value-laden, absorbing the cultural and religious beliefs and practice of the everyday life of home and family. Personal experiential knowledge, when shared with health professionals, gives the possibility of understanding about how individuals live out their experience of health and illness, how they fit the disease, the health activity or the illness episode into their life, and how they make sense of all that is happening to them. Because of the excitement and immediate results that solving the riddle of illness provide (explanation of cause and effect, of diagnosis, of treatment and of prognosis of disease), the less dramatic research into the experience of illness is given secondary importance – it is seen as soft data. In recovering attention to human experience, through description and interpretation, the focus is not only on the individual's experience (as private and subjective) but on understanding shared human experience: truth is found in meaningful accounts that are historically situated. Although such research does not claim to discover universal, replicable, objective knowledge, it does strive to uncover the depths of truth about inner experience and the truthfulness needed for human flourishing. Personal experience (thoughts, feelings, perceptions, pain) cannot be known to anyone else without conversation and dialogue: intersubjective sharing rather than objective sharing is necessary. 'If you are alive to depth at all, you will come to know that depth in yourself and in others through truthfulness and sincerity and trustworthiness' (Wilber 1996: 111).

All interpretation is contextual, however. The importance of this idea needs reinforcement. Feminist philosophers, such as Susan Sherwin (1992), remind us that it is necessary to be attentive to the contextual knowledge in which understanding is grounded. This is true of both experiential and scientific knowledge. People experience life in a certain way because of the context (think of the fear that women experience walking alone at night, or the uncomfortableness that men experience in openly showing emotion in the face of deep grief). Even in the development of scientific knowledge, the context in which it takes place is being recognized as significant (for example, where women with breast cancer want to be involved in the direction and decisions of research).

Some scientists (for example, Maturana and Varela 1992) challenge the notion that objective knowledge is even possible, as one is always part of the situation one is observing and one observes in a certain way because of who the observer is. There is no outside from which the observer can stand and look in. The feminist agenda makes the context explicit. Interpretation of knowledge must always take into account the reality of life – for example, that women (and other groups) have experienced oppression from the white, male, dominant culture. Development of knowledge, from this perspective, would raise ethical questions about attitudes about uteruses and breasts in assessing the frequency of hysterectomies or radical mastectomies (are uteruses and breasts useless appendages?). Even women's health experience, such as childbirth, under control of the medical model of objective truth, misses the larger view that mothers, to be healthy, need a society that supports mothering and the children in their care (Bergum 1997). Sensitivity to the background contexts is imperative in understanding the meanings of human experience. The more contexts we attend to, the richer will be our interpretations, and the greater the possibility for mutual understanding, 'rightness' and cultural fit.

Finding Truth Through Dialogue

Discourse brings new knowledge, inherent knowledge, knowledge needed for ethical questions posed by the situation for this patient, this family and this health provider. Knowledge for ethical care is developed within the situation, between the nurse and patient, doctor and patient, doctor and nurse, etc. It is not merely attending to lived experience, the substance of experiential knowledge, or the application of scientific knowledge, coupled with the insight of contextual knowledge. Inherent, relational knowledge comes out of human relationship, out of dialogue, out of the back-and-forth conversation of true discourse (Habermas 1987). Knowledge developed through relationship may assist in re-engaging the person in his/her life following the experience of trauma, disaster, tragedy or other complex human experiences. Inherent or relational knowledge is incidental, situational and personal, for both the partners in the relationship, the care-giver and the patient, the patient and the family, or the other providers. Inherent knowledge is unique to each situation, although guided by tradition (principles and theories), past experience (professional, cultural and personal) and scientific knowledge ('the riddle'). Truths of health and illness are not merely subjective judgements but arise from a coherence of experiences – from both personal experience and experiences of the world which are 'not reducible to the person' (Tapp 1996: 16).

Connecting: Autonomy in Relation

The first questions of ethics are 'who am I?' and 'who are you?'.

The question of 'who am I?' is not a selfish one; rather it is one of self-knowledge. The question 'who am I?' is a question of humility, of self in relation to others – not in a self-effacing way but in a self-understanding way. Who am I as a woman or man? Who am I as a child or parent? Who am I as a nurse or doctor? Who am I as a patient or consumer? In each of these questions of self-understanding is the recognition of the other person, the man or woman, the parent or child, the nurse or doctor, or the patient or consumer. In knowing who we are, we know who we are not. And in knowing more about who we are, we know of other possibilities there are for our lives. What is masculine about my feminine self? How can being a child help us to be a parent? How do I nurse beside the doctor or the physical therapist or other health-care worker? What is the difference between being a patient and being a consumer?

Understanding of the self in this way offers an enlarged picture of the principle of autonomy, a picture of the autonomous person as one in connection to others rather than separate from others. Autonomous persons come to know themselves through relations with others – just as a child comes to know him- or herself from interaction with the mother or father or just as a woman comes to know herself as a mother through interaction with her child (Bergum 1997). Nurses and doctors come to know themselves through interaction with patients and each other. Autonomy, as relational, is one in which the distinction between people is less defined, less definite and less distant. Decision-making is a sharing, a discourse where it is not possible for one person to be the sole decision-maker and the other to lack choice. Parents, the obvious example, know that any decision they make is never completely independent; rather, each decision must take into consideration partners and children. Patients know that they, too, make decisions with their physicians – both having responsibility and commitment. The vision of people as separate decision-makers, according to Robert Burt (1979), is a result of the emphasis on abstract, universal, scientific knowledge, which disregards the bonds of mutual recognition that underlie everyone's sense of individuality. The vision of people in connection with others strives to keep a mutually satisfying ongoing dialogue between people.

The assertions either of a rigidly individualistic posture (that 'I' alone will choose the course for my 'self') or of a rigid paternalistic stance (that 'I' alone will choose the course for your 'self') equally threaten to destroy the possibility that either party will come to a coherent sense of self and other which rests on mutual perceptions of reciprocal self-assertions. Either stance can readily lock both parties into an interaction that demands the physical obliteration of one of them so that the other can escape from the relentless assault on his self-coherence that the interaction itself presents (Burt 1979: 42). Overemphasis on rights (individual, racial, religious) can lead to intolerance and, perhaps more significantly, to lack of responsibility for and connection with others – a life where everyone fends for the self. Self-in-relation is a notion that considers the complexity of who we are: persons with inner and outer meaning, both independent and dependent, with both individual rights and interdependent responsibilities, and with both intellectual abilities and emotional ties – at the same time.

The question of 'who am I, as a nurse?' helps me ponder what it means to be a nurse, what it means to be someone who nurses – who supports another person, who nourishes the other to grow and heal. What authority do I have to call myself a nurse and how am I able to profess (as a professional) that I am willing and able to nurse? In the increasingly technological world of medical care, the question of self-knowledge is even more challenging. At a national bioethics conference, research was presented exploring the experience of nurses, residents and staff physicians in end-of-life treatment of patients (Simmonds 1996). The researcher highlighted excerpts from interviews with these professionals, who were similarly upset about the over-treatment that the patients in intensive-care units (ICUs) received. In referring to over-treatment, the researcher meant the extensive technological interventions common to the ICU, not the treatment of the patient with too much attention, too much respect or too much unconditional regard. Rather, the technological over-treatment in the last stages of life was treatment few of the professionals wanted for themselves. In thinking about treatment in this technological interventionist way, there is grave danger of losing one of the meanings that the word treatment has – the manner in which one acts toward another. When treatment means only technological therapy or remedies that may effect a cure, the question of 'how should you and I be treated?' loses its meaning. The research project described above points to the hazard of the technological attitude, which is becoming more pervasive (Taylor 1991), one which Gadow warns is a situation where 'professionals, too, disappear as production is technologized' (1994: 306). Nurses and doctors (even) become mere objects themselves, managed and controlled, as the means to accomplish technological ends. Nurses and doctors lose themselves (as agents, or ends in themselves) by the treatment in effect of cure only. Here, the question of 'who am I?' no longer matters.

In contemplating the question of self, 'who am I?', within the nature of ethics as question, one abruptly confronts the question of 'who are you?'. If I am a nurse, then who are you in relation to me as a nurse: a woman giving birth to her first baby, a man dying of leukaemia or a young child having surgery? The ethical question of 'who are you?' is not merely to find out the medical or social history or a detailed account of the signs and symptoms (all of which are important), but to explore the ways and means of how I, the nurse, and you, the patient, can make connections: 'What is it like for you, Nel, to have a baby, you who have waited so long?' or 'How about for you, Celine, you who are only fifteen?', 'What is it like for you, Willi, to have leukaemia?' or 'for you, Christa, to have your leg amputated when only twelve years old?' Ethics as question not only looks to understand you, the you with a disease or health problem, but the you that connects with me even for a short time, during this procedure, this birth, this chemotherapy treatment or this surgery. As a nurse, as I know myself, I can connect with you, as I know you, so that we may explore, together, how to involve you in making your own decisions about what kinds of treatment you want when you are ill or how you want to be treated when you are dying. It may even have to do with you learning more about you, and me learning more about me. The need to understand the self and to understand the other includes the need to pay attention to the connecting 'and'. We need to understand self and other. We need to understand the connection.

Quickening: Moral Awakening

Ethics as question moves past the lengthy discussion in the literature and in the classroom about whether the health-care provider should use an ethic of justice (Rawls 1971), referring to the focus on the four common principles of respect for autonomy, beneficence, non-maleficence and distributive justice (Beauchamp and Childress 1989), or to an ethic of care that focuses on the caring relationship between health care provider and recipient (Gilligan 1982; Noddings 1984). Ethics as question, in its attention to questions like 'how do you, and I, want to be treated?' or 'what should we do now?' or 'given what we know, what is the best thing to do?', moves past these competitions. Instead of comparing one approach against the other, one could think about what helps to stimulate discussions about each situation we are in. Stimulating discussion could happen through explorations of traditions (casuistry), principles, rules and moral reasoning (ethical theory), or impulses that move us to consideration of others (moral quickening).

The almost forgotten idea of quickening offers a way to think about our ethical commitment to others. Barbara Duden (1993) describes how the word quickening, meaning the first inner movement of the baby felt by the woman, has been almost eliminated from common usage, because medical science places greater value on objective knowledge displayed on the ultrasound monitor than on the woman's detailed description of movement of the child within. Step by step, we have looked to technology to give precise facts about the foetus (sex, structural abnormalities, growth parameters). Not only does the foetal monitor give information about the foetus but it also gives information about the nature and frequency of contractions. With such particular technical knowledge available to the professionals, the woman no longer has to give any information about how and when she experiences contractions and the movement of the baby toward birth. Yet the knowledge gained by women through the experience of quickening gives knowledge that lays the foundation of the lifelong relationship of mother and child. The mother experiences the child in a way that no one else can, and her knowledge opens herself to her child through her body – she feels in her body the reality of the new life of another being. Through the experience of quickening, she touches her child. Such knowledge, which describes the moral move from self to other, cannot be found in technological measures. The knowledge that gives women authority to announce the coming of the baby is easily over-shadowed by the technological knowledge.

Quickening is not confined to pregnancy. Jessica's father (that is how he referred to himself in a local radio commentary) described the change that had occurred for him with the birth of his child.

> I used to be a normal egocentric down-to-earth guy. Now . . . I am less certain of the order of things, less certain that the world revolves around my concerns. What really matters are things I only play a small part in. I have accepted that I'm not the centre of things, even within my own world. I know my place. (Gillespie 1996: 2)

This father experiences the moral impulse which moves him from a self-centred vision of the world to one in which others are important as well. Other life experiences are equally de-centring of self – falling in love, looking into the eye of the enemy, near-death experiences, being dazed by the beauty of the mountains, or the strength and majesty of wild animals – an emotional, spiritual, bodily experience. Referring to the work of Emmanuel Levinas (see 1979), Soren Kierkagaard and others, Bauman (1993) places the experience that triggers the primordial experience of the moral impulse in the erotic caress. What is interesting about the notion of a moral impulse is not where it is first experienced but what happens to the affected person.

Bauman (ibid.) suggests that, in modernity's active promotion of the self, the individual, and its intense attention to individual rights and needs, there is danger of losing the self, the moral self. Rather, he claims, awakening to being for the other is actually an awakening of the self. The moral impulse, as awakening to being for the other person, has a dual nature, an experience that moves one to being for the other person as well as one which engenders the potentiality of one's deeper self as a moral self (Bergum, 1997). With such attention to our moral selves, we have the ability to respond to ethical questions that confront providers in daily practice, in situations of social dialogue and in personal life. Quickening as a moral impulse affects the body as well as the mind; it opens one to knowledge of the 'Other' through the experience of the body and, as such, moves beyond the rationality of moral reasoning.

Interviewing: Mutuality in Communion

Much of health care depends on the communicative ability of both the health care providers and the recipients of care. Although it often seems that the health-care professional is the interviewer and the patient is the interviewee, the reverse also happens. In our environment of second opinions, patients often look for a doctor or nurse who has an approach to care that matches their own. So not only does the provider interview the recipient but so too does the recipient interview the provider (especially true in a non-emergency situation).

But another look at the word interview offers a different perspective. The original meaning of the word interview, rooted in the Old French word *entrevue* from *entrevu* (past participle of *s 'entrevoir*), means to see each other. Seeing each other suggests the opportunity of seeing the views of each other, sharing the different viewpoints, as a way of coming to an understanding of the situation as it is for the recipient of health care as well as the provider of health care.

Sharing of viewpoints, an inter-view, suggests perspectives from particular vantage points or fields of vision. In order for dialogue between people to occur there needs to be an openness to see those points of view and to respect them as important to the dialogue. We have begun to recognize the importance of points of view, especially of the health-care team – the pharmacist, the nurse, the speech therapist, the dietitian, the physician, the patient's daughter, the husband, the employer or the patient herself. Yet this seemingly holistic enterprise can still be limited if each point of view is confined to fragmented objective science. Truly seeing each other must mean considering the complexity, and even mystery, of human life – people who are subjects, conscious, with morals, virtues, values and interiors. To truly see each other, one must enter the messy knowledge of interpretation and empathetic mutual understanding in order to move beyond the infinitely easier empirical and monological studies of scientific truth (Wilber 1994: 128-9).

This notion of inter-view attends the many others involved in the dialogue and their differing points of view, which must be considered in coming to decisions. It means reconsideration that all beliefs about an illness have truths – some better or worse but all legitimate. Diane Tapp reminds us that we need to accept the legitimacy of the points of view of others, not only because of a shared humanity, but because 'their ideas, beliefs, behaviours and explanations of experiences . . . have arisen through the course of their existence and reflect the ways that they have conserved their existence' (1996: 10). If we can accept the legitimacy that others have different points of view (their truth), we must figure out ways to offer different points of view (our truth) without negating them.

The notion of inter-view encourages a context where thoughtful exchange might occur by 'offering ideas as invitations to reflection' (ibid.: 20), where people can listen, question, clarify and arrive at a response that is best for them. The concern of the care-giver for the patient's best interests has, for so long, been expressed as the need to convince him/her about a particular action or compliance to particular knowledge and advice, whereas, in an inter-view, the nurse might be able to ask questions and offer ideas which persuade the patient and family to entertain other possibilities for addressing the problems and dilemmas they are encountering (Tapp 1997). Within the inter-view experience, the health professional is also asked to be questioning and open to new possibilities of understanding. The reciprocality of such an approach means that vulnerability or humility (Lebacqz 1992), as well as confidence, is inherent in dialogue.

Acting: Being There

Ethics as question opens one to action. Of course, one must be careful when thinking about action. Action means more than just doing something, such as active intervention (or treatment to effect a cure). Sometimes action means just being there: 'Don't just do something, stand there!' Be there. Be with the other. In nursing, as in all health-care professions, ethical questioning is a daily activity. Comparison is frequently made between little 'e' ethics (everyday practice, how we show respect, the consent process, etc.) and big 'E' ethics (euthanasia, reproductive technologies, the genome project, etc.). Yet by thinking of ethics as question the distinction loses its meaning, for at the root the question is the same: 'How should you and I be treated?'.

A recent Dutch film, *Death on Request* (Maarten Nederhorst, 1994) brings ethics as action clearly to light. In the film, Mr van Wendel de Joode (Kees), with rapidly progressive amyotrophic lateral sclerosis (ALS) requests that the family doctor, Dr Van Oijen, assist him to die when he decides that life is no longer bearable. The film shows the process of decision-making by Kees, Antoinette (the wife) and the doctor, to the point of Kees's death. The dialogue about euthanasia is raised throughout this drama between Kees and Antoinette, Kees and the doctors, with Antoinette and Dr Van Oijen, and with other professionals. The question of euthanasia is acted out in all the activities leading to the death, a death described as right, peaceful and beautiful by Kees's wife. The tragedy of the experience is present throughout. Logical thinking, touch, emotion, pain are all there. This film does not lead us through a theoretical discussion of euthanasia; rather, it shows the struggle to meet the needs of another human being faced with a tragic life experience. It shows that the ethics as question is the human struggle, for Kees, for Antoinette and for Dr Oijen. At the end of the film, the question of euthanasia remains – as it should. Ethics as question leads to the ongoing ethical dialogue of how to be more human (Grondin 1995).

Conclusions

If the notion of ethics as question has any validity, it means that ethical decision-making is uncertain and that decision-makers (both providers and receivers) are vulnerable. In this context, the attributes of uncertainty and vulnerability are not negative. Instead, these attributes offer the opening needed to attend, with both wisdom and compassion, to the wonder and hope of human life and the mystery of human and humane death. Openness to the question of ethics, of 'what we should do', increases the possibility of learning to live together in increasingly respectful and considerate ways. Ethical decision-making is an everyday activity in health care, which responds to the question 'what should be done in this situation?' by considering many facts, such as the extent and prognosis of the disease, the patient's wishes based on values and beliefs, the family's involvement and support, and the care-giver's experience and knowledge. This means that dialogue must include facts and figures (statistics, scientific knowledge and social systems), as well as the inner meanings (integrity, mutual understanding and cultural fit). The questioning that ethics requires never ends.

References

Bauman, Z. (1993), *Postmodern Ethics*, Oxford: Blackwell Publishers.
Beauchamp, T.L. and J.J. Childress (1989), *Principles of Biomedical Ethics*, 4th edn, New York: Oxford University Press.
Bergum, V. (1994), 'Knowledge for Ethical Care', *Nursing Ethics. An International Journal for Health Care Professionals*, 1(2): 72–9.

Bergum, V. (1997), *A Child on Her Mind,* Westport, Connecticut: Bergin & Garvey.

Burt, R. (1979), *Taking Care of Strangers: The Rule of Law in Doctor–Patient Relations*, New York: The Free Press.

Duden, B. (1993), *Disembodying Woman. Perspectives on Pregnancy and the Unborn*, trans. L. Hoinacki, Cambridge: Harvard University Press.

Gadow, S. (1994), 'Whose Body? Whose Story? The Question about Narrative in Women's Health Care', *Soundings*, 77(3–4): 295–307.

Gillespie, C. (1996). 'The Kid'. Commentary on CBC Radio Active, Canadian Broadcasting Corporation, 9 January.

Gilligan, C. (1982), *In a Different Voice*, Cambridge, Massachusetts: Harvard University Press.

Grondin, J. (1995), *Sources of Hermeneutics,* Albany: State University of New York Press.

Habermas, J. (1987), *Knowledge and Human Interests*, trans. J. Shapiro, Cambridge, UK: Polity Press.

Kikuchi, J. and H. Simmons (1996), 'The Whole Truth and Progress in Nursing Knowledge Development', in J. Kikuchi, H. Simmons and D. Romyn (eds), *Truth in Nursing Inquiry,* Thousand Oaks: Sage Publications, pp. 5–18.

Lebacqz, K. (1992), 'Humility in Health Care', *The Journal of Medicine and Philosophy*, 17: 291–307.

Levinas, E. (1979), *Totality and Infinity,* Boston: Martinus Nijhoff Publishers.

Maturana, H.R. and F.J. Varela (1992), *The Tree of Knowledge, The Biological Roots of Human Understanding,* Boston: Shambhala.

Niebuhr, H.R. (1963), *The Responsible Self. An Essay in Christian Moral Responsibility,* San Francisco: Harper.

Noddings, N. (1984), *Caring. A Feminine Approach to Ethics and Moral Education*, Berkeley, California: University of California Press.

Nuland, S. (1994), *How We Die. Reflections of Life's Final Chapter*, New York: Alfred A. Knopf.

Rawls, J. (1971), *A Theory of Justice,* Cambridge, Massachusetts: Harvard University Press.

Sherwin, S. (1992), *No Longer Patient: Feminist Ethics and Health Care*, Philadelphia: Temple University Press.

Simmonds, A. (1996), 'Reflections on life and death in a technological society: experiences of doctors and nurses with dying patients in intensive care', unpublished Doctor of Ministry Thesis, Toronto School of Theology and Emmanuel College of Victoria University.

Tapp, D. (1996), 'The "soundness" of scholarly work in hermeneutic research', unpublished paper, University of Calgary.

Tapp, D. (1997), 'Exploring therapeutic conversations between nurses and families experiencing ischemic heart disease', unpublished doctoral dissertation. University of Calgary.

Taylor, C. (1991), *The Malaise of Modernity*, Concord, Ontario: House of Anansi Press.

Wilber, K. (1996), *The Brief History of Everything*, Boston: Shambhala.

8

Relative Strangers: Caring for Patients as the Expression of Nurses' Moral/Political Voice

Jan Savage

Introduction

Anthropologists are concerned with moral universes, their basic task being to understand the perceptions and intentions of individual actors within specific social worlds (Overing 1985).[1] This chapter uses an anthropological approach to consider the social world of a group of British hospital nurses, in order to glimpse the moral imperatives that underpin their practice and thus contribute to debates about the morality of care. In particular, the chapter focuses on a fundamental, multifaceted problem in nursing arising from perceptions of personhood, the construction of difference and the often inevitable intimacy of the nurse–patient relationship.

Nursing as paid employment is located in the public domain[2] but is, at the same time, concerned with emotions and the body, aspects of life in Western culture that have been classified as private and consigned to the domestic sphere (Lawler 1991). Theoretically at least, nurses are expected to develop a 'professional closeness' with relative strangers (patients), in which they are to set aside their own interests, concerns and needs and focus exclusively on those of the patient (Peplau 1969). This ostensible bias[3] in the nurse–patient relationship is suggestive of an 'ethic of care' first outlined by Gilligan (1982), a moral orientation of care and responsibility, of relatedness and responsiveness to others.

The problem this chapter focuses on is twofold. First, modern nursing carries an assumption of relatedness:[4] patients are initially 'distant others', who are to be cared for as if they are 'close'. This poses the question of whether and, if so, how nurses bring about this transformation. Secondly, a significant number of nursing theorists have drawn on an ethic of care, such as that described by Gilligan, to argue for nurses' 'moral voice' and thus promote the status of nursing (Wilkes and Wallis 1998). Yet this ethic of care is gendered in that it is strongly identified with characteristics attributed to women rather than men, characteristics that have been used historically to confine women to the domestic domain. There would therefore seem to be something inherently problematic about the espousal of an 'ethic of care,' a gendered moral voice, by an occupation such as nursing, which, through its association with women, caring and the domestic domain, remains subordinate to others. In other words, there is a tension between nurses' aspirations for professional autonomy and their ideal of care, which suggests that their moral voice cannot be divorced from a political one.

To explore this dilemma, this chapter considers the 'ethic of care' underpinning nursing practice in a specific unit, which I shall refer to as Jones Ward. This ethic of care, identified through ethnographic study, evolved within a particular physical, moral and political space, in which patients were often extended the kind of care generally associated with the domestic domain (Savage 1995). I aim to show that the expression of caring on Jones Ward was shaped by at least two factors. One of these was the nurses' moral stance, which was informed by the ideology of 'new nursing' (see below), and concerned with recasting those who were 'other', or encountered in the context of the public sphere, into those who shared private space and became, in many ways, 'same' or close. The second influential factor was the nurses' political agenda, which sought to challenge the traditional status of nursing.

Central to my argument is the claim that the ethic of care on Jones Ward became embodied in the actual practice of nurses, and was made flesh through nurses' adoption of the comportment and gestures associated with women in the domestic domain. Such a link between ethics and embodiment has been postulated by Diprose (1994). Drawing on the derivation of the term 'ethics' from the Greek word *ethos*, meaning character and dwelling, or habitat, Diprose suggests that a habitual way of life, ethos or set of habits determines an individual's character, with these habits constituted by the repetition of bodily acts shaped by the habitat that the individual occupies. Thus even if we grant that ethics is about moral principles and moral judgement, it is also about location, position and place. It is about being positioned by, and taking a position in relation to, others (ibid.: 18).

Through a particular set of embodied practices, nurses were very often able to define the nature of the ward's symbolic space and whether it was taken to represent a public or private sphere.[5] In doing so, they were able to suggest a quasi-kinship between themselves and patients. However, I shall argue that these references to the domestic domain were surface representations of deeper, moral principles that informed nursing care, namely the principles of closeness, openness and sameness, which might be differently represented in other contexts.[6] These moral principles can be glimpsed in part through nurses' use of the body and the orientational metaphors they employed in describing their work. To support this contention I shall draw on an earlier study (Savage 1991) which uncovered the significance of sameness, openness and closeness for the recognition of relatedness in relationships, including those characterized as ones of 'blood' or 'flesh and blood'. However, before going on to describe the two studies, the chapter will start by looking in a little more detail at caring and an ethics of care, the historical links between nursing, femininity and the domestic sphere, and the ideology of 'new nursing'.

Caring and an 'Ethic of Care'

Caring, as Davies has noted, is a concept that is hard to define or measure, although she suggests that it 'involves the creation of a sustained relationship with the other' (1995: 141). Caring has been characterized as a commonplace activity, but, at the same time, as an art (Kitson 1993), a moral ideal (Watson 1985) and a humanistic interaction that is best realized when it is least noticed (Brykcžnška 1997). Despite the ambiguity of `care', however, many theorists agree that a distinction can be drawn between caring about someone and caring for someone (Dunlop 1994; Chipman 1991). In general, to care about someone suggests an attachment or an emotional relationship but implies little about carrying out practical activities or devoting time to them. In contrast, caring for someone implies providing for that person's needs without necessarily suggesting anything about affection or affinity (Ungerson 1983).

In the sociological literature, this distinction between 'caring about' and 'caring for' has often been linked to an assumed dichotomy between informal and formal spheres of care; caring about is associated with unpaid care, emotion and the private realm, while caring for is linked with paid work, affective neutrality and the public domain. According to Ungerson (1990), because of these associations, care within the domestic domain is assumed to be superior. While the line between public and private or domestic varies historically and cross-culturally, the domestic sphere and the emotionality associated with it are generally deemed to be the province of women.

Throughout this century, many feminists and others arguing for the greater involvement of women in the public domain have assumed that women are inherently more moral than men,[7] or, drawing upon the argument first launched by Gilligan (1982), that men and women have different ethical voices.[8] Carol Gilligan's work can be seen both within the tradition of thinking which proposes a distinctive, gendered world-view (Davies 1995), and in the context of Hegel's understanding of identity as relational and a product of social interaction (Diprose 1994). Gilligan's 'ethic of care' represents a challenge to traditional moral theories and an 'ethic of justice', in which moral development was gauged on the basis of an individual's ability to solve moral dilemmas using universal ethical principles and a contract model of social exchange (Diprose 1994). Gilligan was concerned that, according to the theory of moral development propounded by her tutor, and later colleague, Lawrence Kohlberg (1971), women would be categorized as morally immature because they tend to reject the concept of individual rights in favour of responsibility and care. According to Gilligan, women's abilities to consider context, the minutiae of relationships and the viewpoint of the other are essential prerequisites for moral maturity. Gilligan does not straightforwardly claim that this different moral voice can only be uttered by women,[9] although her work has often been interpreted as such in the feminist literature (Tronto 1994), with references to a `women's morality' that is vaguely concerned with the sustenance of life, the community, `family' and children (see French 1985).

Attempts to use the concept of a women's morality as a political tool to improve women's standing in the public sphere have met with little success. According to Tronto (1994), this is largely because claims for a 'women's morality' have been made without adequate reference to the political context in which caring takes place. More specifically, a 'women's morality' has been theorized only with reference to existing moral boundaries. According to Tronto, all theories construct moral boundaries by making some questions central and thus others more marginal. Tronto argues that current moral boundaries separate politics from morality, public from private, same from other, but ignore the way that constraints of power within our lives affect our moral judgements. Critiquing Gilligan's work, she suggests that: 'We need to be able to consider what our relationship with other people who are close and distant should be, but we also need to be attentive to viewing others' circumstances in a whole context' (Tronto 1994: 14).

Nursing, Femininity and the Domestic Sphere

This debate is of huge relevance, if not poignancy, for those practising nursing. There has been considerable interest within the female-dominated occupation of nursing in feminist models of caring that have been informed by the work of Gilligan or by the notion of a gendered morality.[10] The suggestion that nurses might have a 'different voice' has had a strong appeal for an occupational group that has struggled for recognition and independence. However, Tronto's comments as to the failure of a 'women's morality' as an effective political tool are pertinent here, particularly in reminding us to think of the political context in which nursing care takes place. Nursing is a domain in which the boundaries between the moral and the political (Tattam and Thompson 1993) and between the public and the private (Lawler 1991; Savage 1997) are constantly renegotiated. For example, British nursing takes place in a society which views it as 'women's work', that is, as tasks that are normally carried out without pay by women in the private sphere. This might mean that those cared for by nurses might expect the kind of morally informed care that women provide within 'the family'. However, the association of nursing with women and the domestic sphere and the fact that caring is not the exclusive province of nurses have dogged the attempts of nurses to achieve decent pay or professional standing (Hugman 1991; Swanson 1991; Davies 1995).

All this suggests a permeability between public and private, an inter-penetration that is evident in the way that caring relationships in the domestic domain are often taken as prototypes to inform the nurse–patient relationship (Davies 1995). As Dalley (1988:22) argues, 'the ideology underpinning domestic relations becomes a major organising principle upon which social relations outside the domestic group are based', with the construct of 'the family' providing a standard against which other social relations are measured and judged.

Perhaps it is not surprising, then, that analogies between home and hospital are recurrent themes within the social sciences. Gamarnikow (1978: 97), for example, suggests that the subordination of nursing to medicine has structured the nurse/doctor/patient relationship, 'which comes to take on the ideological resonances of the power relations between men, women and children within the patriarchal family' (see also McCurdy 1982; Oakley 1984; Turner 1995). Traditionally, the good nurse has been equated with the good woman and the good mother (Gamarnikow 1978).

Nurse theorists have made similar links, suggesting that nursing knowledge takes the form of 'motherhood knowledge' (for example, Colliere 1986: 105) or that the therapeutic effect of nursing lies in the possibility that 'the relationship between mother and child is in many ways reflected in the relationship between nurse and client' (Sundeen *et al.* 1985: 156).

This analogy between nurse and mother is becoming increasingly problematic, based as it is on a view of nurses as devoted, self-sacrificing and self-effacing women, who love, comfort and pity their patients (Gamarnikow 1978). Equating the good nurse with the good woman/ mother fails to take into account the fact that almost 10% of the nursing workforce is constituted by men. In addition, recent developments in nursing are grounded in the axiom of partnership between the nurse and patient. This role does not sit well with an image of nurse as mother, whether this is characterized by unconditional nurture, maternal benevolence or matriarchal authority.

Indeed, the study of nurse–patient interaction that I shall describe found that nurses appeared to play down any maternal image, despite an emphasis on the emotional content of their relationships with patients. However, it was interesting that, in clarifying their relationships with patients, they still appeared to draw upon the model of the family or the domestic sphere to create an appropriate context in which to provide care. Significantly, though, their interaction was modelled less on genealogical relationships than on those more broadly characterized by 'closeness', a phenomenon viewed as the foundation for a therapeutic relationship by many involved in the movement for reform that is exemplified by 'new nursing'.

Closeness and New Nursing

The past ten to fifteen years have been marked by a significant change in the way that many British nurses both conceptualize and organize care. Previously, nurses organized their work by dividing up the care of patients into tasks, which would be carried out by a range of different nurses; junior staff would bring a bedpan or tidy the patient's locker, while more senior nurses would dress patients' wounds or give medications. Such discontinuity served to hinder the development of an affective relationship between nurses and patients (Menzies 1960). Within the framework of 'new nursing' (Salvage 1990), however, nurses are encouraged to offer a form of care that is both instrumental and emotionally expressive (Pearson 1988). Although much of the impetus for this new approach undoubtedly arose from nurses' desires to improve the patient's experience of care, 'new nursing' and the styles of practice that attend this ideological approach are not entirely divorced from the needs of many nurses to attain the status of professionals and to free nursing from the shadow of medicine. Thus 'new nursing' can be seen as part of a longer struggle for professional identity, status and power (Bowers 1989). Additionally, as Bowers notes, the initiative fits neatly with the aims of broader policies, such as the introduction of general management into the National Health Service (NHS), through, for example, disseminating and clarifying the areas of responsibility of individual members of staff. In other words, the ethic of care propounded by new-nursing protagonists as patient-centred is also entwined with the political agendas of nurses and perhaps, to a certain extent, their managers.

The traditional fragmentation of the nursing role has been seen as a way of preventing the development of a sustained nurse–patient relationship and one of a number of measures employed to reduce nurses' anxiety (Menzies 1960). The stress put on 'distance' may also have represented an attempt to deal with the ambiguities of nurse–patient interaction arising from the necessity of physical intimacy (Lawler 1991). This policy of detachment, which Menzies found to be inherent in traditional nursing, is markedly different from current expectations of the 'new nurse'. Within contemporary nursing, there is a general acceptance, at least at a theoretical level, that nursing requires some involvement with the patient, 'a sufficient projection of self into the private world of the other, to be able (at least partially) to understand *effectively* what the experience means for *them*' (Brykczñska 1992: 6, original emphasis). Within this trend, new nursing encourages nurses to achieve successful nursing outcomes through the establishment of emotionally 'close' relationships and through attempting to use this 'closeness' to therapeutic effect in a planned and systematic way (see, for example, Pearson 1988). There has, however, been little elaboration on the meaning of 'closeness' in the nursing literature; Peplau (1969) has explained it as 'being closer to the truth' of another's predicament, although it more often seems to imply emotional rather than existential involvement. Given the looseness of the concept and, significantly, Menzies's findings on how nurses used to protect themselves through distance, I set up a study to discover how nurses understood 'closeness' and to see if developing closeness with patients presented nurses with problems.

The Nursing Study

This study used an ethnographic approach, based on participant observation and in-depth interviews with hospital nurses and took place over a one-year period. The part of the study I describe took place on Jones Ward, which dealt specifically with patients who had chronic gastro-intestinal problems, most frequently of the pancreas and liver. The patients on Jones Ward were all male and generally middle-aged. Because of the chronic nature of their illness, they were generally long-stay or tended to be repeatedly readmitted to the ward, and nurses and patients often came to know each other very well. At the time of the study, the permanent nursing staff were all female, with the exception of one unqualified health-care assistant.[11]

One striking feature of life on Jones Ward was that, unlike many other wards, there was no rigid routine determining patients' everyday activities, such as when they should wake up, eat breakfast or take a bath. Again unusually, the ward telephone was available for use by patients for incoming calls, and tea and coffee could be made whenever patients wished. These and other measures gave the ward the appearance and feel of a domestic rather than a public space, so much so that patients frequently described the ward to me as 'a home from home'.

This process of 'domestication', in which the extraordinary situation of patients (and nurses) was made more ordinary,was further effected by the way that relationships between patients and nurses were transposed into those of 'the family'. Patients identified certain nurses as 'caring for me like a daughter' or 'like family'. Similarly, for nurses, good nursing care was that which was given 'as if' caring for a family member or 'one of my own'. Domestication was also furthered by nurses' use of the body and space. Nurses dismantled any specifically nursing space on the ward, sharing the patients' space as much as possible. For instance, they removed the nurses' station, gave the nurses' office over to other use and carried out all the activities that might have been performed in these areas (such as paperwork or teaching) at the patient's bedside. They also shared the patient's space through sitting in close proximity with patients, using a great deal of touch and mirroring the patient's position in space as far as possible – for example, sitting or kneeling by the side of patients who were in bed or in a chair. Nurses also made use of empty beds for teaching and so on, but, rather than sitting upright, they would be semi-reclining. Furthermore, they shared emotional space with patients in terms of bringing their private selves into their relationships with patients and discussing personal issues.

Given that these nurses were all female and were extending care by exploiting the potential offered by connectedness or attachment, their actions might be interpreted as the expression of a gendered morality. However, the nurses' recasting of physical, emotional and symbolic space on Jones Ward and the dismantling of boundaries between themselves and their patients arguably go beyond the articulation of a gendered ethic of care: they simultaneously represent the political strategy of nurses who were pressing for occupational closure.

First, at the level of moral principles, the collapse of space was integral to the development of 'closeness'. Sitting close to patients and becoming emotionally close to patients was viewed as a necessary element of a therapeutic relationship. There was also a way in which nurses' physical openness[12] may have indicated an emotional receptiveness to patients. This finding bears some similarity to the arguments put forward by protagonists of 'new nursing', who suggest that in the therapeutic relationship, 'the nurse who provides care and/or support conveys a *proximity* to the patient in a variety of ways. These include, for example, "presence" through close or frequent contact, remaining with and being attentive to the patient and conveying an understanding of the patient's experience' (Ersser 1991: 71).

Second, at a political level, these findings suggest that nursing praxis was shaped by nurses' own professionalization agenda, namely their demand for autonomous practice. Sharing space strengthened their identification with patients and thus demonstrated and endorsed their position *vis-à-vis* other hospital staff. According to nurses, they were the only group with unquestionable authority to enter the patient's space, while a hierarchy of access existed for others, such as relatives, doctors or professionals allied to medicine. Similarly, nurses saw themselves as the only members of the health-care team who physically aligned themselves with patients, either by sitting in close proximity or placing themselves at the same level as patients (what they referred to as 'getting down to the patient's level'). In doing so, nurses saw themselves not only encouraging a greater equality in their relationships with patients, but also emphasizing the difference in their approach, compared with other health-care professionals. Nurses would criticize the way that medical staff, for example, would stand over patients, and see this as a sign of doctors' remoteness from the patient's experience. Finally, nurses' emotional closeness similarly endorsed their claim to be the most authentic representative of the patient, the best placed to be the patient's voice. Stressing the informal and mundane aspects of nurse–patient interaction, nurses strengthened their association with patients by playing down the importance of being a nurse. As one nurse put it, 'I think patients see us as normal people; you know you're not just coming to work and being a nurse'. At the same time, adopting an informal posture with patients (lolling on beds; sitting with limbs sprawled), nurses constructed the space they inhabited with patients as domestic space. In this space, their actions could be interpreted as the caring gestures of women and intimating that the care they provided was 'care about', the superior kind of care associated with the private sphere. In other words, overall, nurses stressed their closeness to patients, their closeness to being the same as patients, which helped to differentiate them from other professional or occupational groups. It served the political purpose of endorsing their claims that nurses had a unique role and area of practice.

Nurses' actions on Jones Ward, such as their removal of nursing space and attempts to approach 'sameness' with patients, cannot be neatly disentangled and labelled as political or moral in nature. 'Closeness' emerges as a multilayered abstraction that plays a part across a range of nursing agendas relating to patient care and professional standing. What does seem striking, though, is that the principles of 'openness', 'closeness' and 'sameness' that appeared to inform nurses' praxis on Jones Ward were also strongly reminiscent of early research I had carried out concerning English kinship, and which it seems relevant to draw upon here.

The Kinship Study

'Closeness' is a term frequently used by anthropologists in debates about kinship, although, as in nursing, its meaning has been assumed. According to Schneider (1980), 'closeness', at least in the context of American kinship, is understood to refer to the degree to which individuals shared 'blood', but often the meaning of 'blood' is taken to be self-evident, denoting a fixed biological or genetic substance (see Fox 1967). However, in a study of Englishwomen's views on procreation (Savage 1991),[13] I found that a metaphysical 'closeness' was important in the recognition of relatedness and often more central than sharing the same genetic material in the definition of 'blood' relationships.

Linked to a complex view of how life came into being,[14] informants shared a number of perceptions which determined whether individuals were seen to be related to each other. 'Being related' rested partly on the recognition of shared 'blood' and, additionally, on certain, differently weighted 'principles', which could be interpreted in either physical or metaphysical terms. These were the principles of 'closeness', 'openness' and 'sameness'.

At the beginning of fieldwork, I did not specifically ask informants about 'closeness'; it was a notion that I took for granted myself. It was only when I found women in the study repeatedly using the term that I started to look at it more critically, although it always remained somewhat ambiguous. 'Closeness' might be facilitated by physically proximity, but more than anything it referred to shared understandings about private worlds and shared expectations of support. In short, 'closeness' was generally used to indicate a shared moral view. In this way 'closeness' might be understood in terms of being 'close to the same moral identity'. In addition, the development and continuation of 'closeness' were dependent on a physical and emotional openness between individuals.

The principles of 'closeness' and 'sameness' were exemplified by the example of informants' attitudes towards breast milk and the practice of surrogate feeding or wet-nursing. Many informants thought that, through the marked degree of physical proximity entailed, including the baby's ingestion of another's substance, the act of breast-feeding helped to confer common identity (or sameness) and, consequently, informants were disturbed by the possibility of surrogate feeding.[15] Among the women I talked to, a breast-feeding woman and her child were seen as supremely 'close' – so much so that the suckling child appeared to be regarded as an extension of the mother's self. This impression was supported by informants' views that personhood[16] was acquired gradually and only began to be attained once children gained a degree of independence from their carers (notably their mothers), extended their support network and began to 'stand on their own two feet'. Finally, the principle of 'openness' was double-natured; it was strongly associated with the openness of the procreative body and its processes of birth, breast-feeding and sexual intercourse, while emotional openness was viewed as a precondition for the development or maintenance of a 'close' relationship between those understood as related.

Although the principles of 'closeness', `sameness' and `openness' can be seen as providing the basis of a range of different moral relationships, they were most clearly marked in the discourse referring to 'blood' relations and to those of 'flesh and blood'. A 'blood' relationship was one in which common substance (such as shared genes) might be recognized but, more importantly, where common identity and common interests were acknowledged. Additionally, 'flesh and blood' appeared to refer to a core group of individuals who shared the greatest degree of 'sameness' and 'closeness'. From the informant's perspective, this group was usually comprised of grandparents, parents, offspring and siblings, who shared the closest approximation to 'sameness' in terms of substance, such as genetic material. Yet, more importantly, 'flesh and blood' referred to those involved in the collective and morally charged task of 'upbringing', the raising to personhood. For example, one informant told me that, as her father had left home when she was very young and her mother had become an alcoholic, she was really 'brought up' by the woman who lived next door and this was the only person she would describe as her 'flesh and blood'.

What this work suggests is that the moral attribute of 'uprightness', perceived as a feature of domestic life, is intimately connected with the ontological principles of 'sameness', 'closeness' and 'openness', which collectively constitute the basis of a specific ethic of care, a 'morality of kinship'. While making no claims for the universal nature of such a morality, the final section suggests that echoes of this 'morality of kinship' can be discerned when we consider the work of the nurses on Jones Ward.

By juxtaposing these two studies of kinship and nursing, I am suggesting that certain ontological principles found in the broader cultural field were drawn on by the nurses of Jones Ward in the development of an ethic of care. Expressed in the context of a space that had become construed as private or domestic, this ethic of care shaped the provision of compassionate, 'as if family', care for patients. To support my assertion of some correspondence between the ontological principles that appear in both studies, in the last part of this chapter I take the principle of 'closeness' and show how, rather like the 'flesh and blood' of women in the kinship study, nurses who were 'close' to patients helped to raise those who had 'fallen' ill and assist them towards greater independence.

The Raising of Patients

The kinship study suggested that personhood was a moral state of uprightness premised on autonomy and attained with the support of those who are 'close', those who help to raise the individual towards the state of personhood. The association between moral rectitude and physical uprightness has been remarked on elsewhere. For example, in a study of selfhood and the experience of being embodied, Levin (1985: 270) states that moral and physical uprightness are inseparable or ontologically intertwined, saying 'a morally upright life begins with, and is inseparable from, a balanced, upright posture'. Levin appears to talk in universal terms when he refers to the experience of being. Others have confined themselves to demonstrating a historical association of posture and morality within Western culture (Schmitt 1989; Vigarello 1989).

Informants in the kinship study indicated that becoming 'upright' is a continuing process referred to most clearly as 'upbringing'. Moreover, those who were perceived as 'blood' – and particularly those of the same 'flesh and blood' – and those who were regarded as 'close' appeared to play a particularly important role in individuals' 'uprightness' or 'standing'. For example, when asked to elaborate on 'closeness', informants claimed that those who are 'close' will 'never let you down'. Similarly, 'You can always fall back on your parents . . . your parents are always there' and 'they're always there to support'. These expressions give the sense of those who are 'close' as forming a protective ring around the individual, preventing him or her from keeling away from an upright stance.

The notion of 'closeness' was not independent of other notions of 'openness' and 'sameness', which similarly appeared to indicate something of the morality associated with relatedness, in which a complex of personal ethics shared some correspondence with a bodily idiom. By this I mean that the notion of 'openness', for example, was found to refer to a physical stance, a body open to 'close' others, such as the suckling child, and, at the same time, a psychological openness or receptivity that allows the exchange of intimate confessions. Similarly, 'sameness' suggested shared physical and metaphysical traits – a degree of shared biological substance, perhaps, but, more importantly, a shared set of values, the same moral perspective.

From this it can be argued that the positional metaphors used by informants, such as 'upbringing', indicated a code of ethics expressed in a bodily idiom and concerned with the development of the moral identity or personhood of those who are recognized as 'the same', or close to the same.

Turning to the other study, nurses on Jones Ward thought that their positioning *vis-à-vis* patients was highly important and all nurses were encouraged during interaction with patients to 'get down to the patient's level'. This phrase appeared to refer to both a physical and an existential level. In one sense, its use represented a deliberate attempt to disrupt the traditional power inequalities between patients and health-care workers. The decision to squat or kneel beside patients, rather than to tower over them, was consistent with nurses' attempts to empower patients (although, as suggested earlier, claiming to share the same space as patients had political advantages for nurses as well). At the same time, these forms of posture, the occupation of common space and the breach of the usual social rules governing proxemic behaviour gave a sense of family-type relationships.

Nurses' repeated reference to 'getting down to the same level' also began to suggest that their use of metaphor might indicate how nurses understood the concept of 'care', the way in which they operationalized this concept. Not only did 'getting down to the patient's level' refer to the need to adopt the same physical level as the patient, it also communicated the way in which nurses needed to position themselves with the patient in a metaphysical sense. Patients were seen to have `fallen ill' or to have 'been brought low' by their illness. Nurses' work involved a number of measures which were seen as therapeutic in a broad sense, which might help to raise patients from this state. These measures included the use of touch, 'being with' the patient, spending time talking and, especially, using humour; when practised appropriately, these strategies were seen to help 'lift' the patient.

Metaphor has been observed to demonstrate the intertwining of the physical and the non-physical. For example, the anthropologist Michael Jackson has referred to the way in which we fall or are 'thrown' when our environment is disrupted. For instance, when we 'fall ill' or 'fall in love', there is a simultaneous disorientation of mind and body:

> In this sense, uprightness of posture may be said to define a psychophysical relationship with the world, so that to lose this position, this 'standing', is simultaneously a bodily and intellectual loss of balance, a disturbance at the very centre and ground of our Being. Metaphors of falling and disequilibrium disclose this integral connection of the psychic and the physical; they do not express a concept *in terms of* a bodily image. (1989: 123)

According to Jackson, bodily praxis may induce or suggest ethical ideas. Applying this insight to the work of nurses on Jones Ward, it appears that these nurses developed an ethic of care in their work with quasi-strangers which, to some extent, mirrors that suggested by women in the kinship study. There, however, women were referring to the moral care of family members. In both instances the process of 'upbringing' is important. In each case, care is apparently premised on a similar notion of 'closeness', which refers to both a physical and an emotional proximity. And, again in both cases, the care involved in 'upbringing' and 'lifting' can be understood in terms of the development (or restoration) of independence that is both physical and moral. The integral connection between the physical and non-physical aspects of caring apparent in these research findings suggests that the study of nurses' bodily idiom offers a way of understanding their ethic of care.

Yet, at the same time, it should not be overlooked that nurses' bodily idiom was also gendered. It gained much of its meaning and persuasiveness from the context in which it occurred, a context which was to some extent constructed by nurses through their manipulation of the boundary between the private and the public for political purposes.

Conclusion

This chapter has been concerned with two interrelated areas. The first of these refers to the nature of nurses' moral voice. It was noted that the idea that nurses might have a 'different voice', or that nursing might be informed by a 'women's morality' had appealed to some sections of nurses as a political tool. The ethic of care apparent within practice on Jones Ward might, at first glance, be interpreted as a 'women's morality', associated as it is with an all-female group of nurses and orientated towards relatedness, responsiveness to others and the relations of connectedness characteristic of the domestic domain. This interpretation, however, fails to take account of the context in which nurses worked and the political aspects of their practice, which may be less informed by issues of gender. It was suggested earlier that nurses on Jones Ward strengthened their position in relation to other occupational groups by manipulating the symbolic space of the ward, and by exploiting the meanings associated with care in the domestic sphere. However, it was notable that nurses, although all women, laid no claim to a different voice as women, but rather as carers, with an implicit recognition that male nurses who shared their philosophy of care would be able to share this voice. Moreover, this different voice was not unambiguously moral in nature but was at times overtly political: it spoke of the rights of nurses to greater autonomy. Significantly, this claim to autonomy was not a separate issue from care, but, as shown by the range of practices promoting their special relationship and closeness with patients, it became an integral part of their everyday caring practice. Thus moral and political aspects of care were inextricable.

The second, but related area considered in this chapter refers to a fundamental dilemma within nursing, that is, how to offer care for distant others (relative strangers) with the compassion they would expect if they were close. Nurses on Jones Ward suggest one possibility; rather than manage the dilemma posed by patients viewed as 'Other', they transformed patients into a group whose members were viewed as 'close' or same, largely through manipulating the boundary between public and private. I am not suggesting that this is what all nurses do; how nurses manage this dilemma and how they manipulate boundaries is probably context-dependent. What I do want to show is the permeability of moral boundaries[17] and the leakage between categories, such as moral and political, public and private, same and other, suggesting that an analysis of caring practices demands some acknowledgement of this incontinence.

Acknowledgements

I would like to thank delegates attending the Medical Ethics: Extending the Boundaries of Care conference, at Oxford in 1994, who commented on an early version of this chapter. Financial support was gratefully received from the Economic and Social Research Council (ESRC) for the kinship study. My heartfelt thanks go to the participants in both the kinship study and the study on Jones Ward. Finally, many thanks to Gosia Brykczñska of the Royal College of Nursing (RCN) Institute, London, and Rosemary McKechnie as editor, for their helpful comments on the chapter during its preparation.

Notes

1. Howell (1997) has suggested that anthropologists have always studied social constructions of morality, with implicit references to moral codes, but the explicit investigation of indigenous moralities has been rare. Having said that, Howell suggests that there is some consensus among anthropologists on what is meant by morality: 'Today, most would agree that a scholarly pursuit of the moral system of any one social group must in some way take account of indigenous perceptions about the human being; about personhood, agency and sociality' (ibid.: 7).
2. A distinction between public and private domains provides a useful conceptual framework, particularly for exploring male and female roles across cultures. In this classificatory scheme, what is viewed as public space is generally associated with production and men, while what is understood as private or domestic is largely associated with reproduction and women. However, precisely what constitutes these spaces and whether or how they become gendered are culturally and historically specific. It has been strongly suggested, though, that women's status is generally lower where space is strongly differentiated in terms of public and private spheres (Rosaldo 1974).
3. Many nurses would argue that, in modern nursing at least, the nurse–patient relationship is characterized by a greater degree of reciprocity

than Peplau suggests (see, for example, Savage 1995).

4. For example, Bevan (1998: 735) claims that 'Not only does care enable, but it also demonstrates the nurse's relatedness to the patient through the art of nursing.'

5. The fragility of their construction of space was made evident in their relations with medical staff. For example, nurses' authority to determine the nature of the ward space was noticeably undermined by senior doctors, whose arrival on the ward usually served to recast it as public space (see Savage 1997).

6. For example, current research that I am carrying out on a ward where nurses care predominantly for people with human immunodeficiency virus (HIV) suggests that, instead of family relationships, the perception of shared youth (which has little reference to the age of nurse or patient but everything to do with attitude) provides an important way of intimating 'sameness' between nurses and those they care for.

7. One example of this kind of supposition is the identification of women and peace. The reasoning behind this claim has generally assumed that the character of women is shaped by their reproductive role: as Ruddick (1992: 298) has said, 'the conventional and symbolic association between women and peace has a real basis in maternal practice'. However, it is not simply women's involvement in childbirth or child-care that is seen to underscore their association with peace, but the experiences arising from this involvement, particularly experiences of continuity and connectedness, which give them a special voice with which to oppose war and the discontinuities it imposes (Soper 1992).

8. For other, more recent work in the area of gender and morality, see, for example, the volume edited by Larrabee (1993).

9. Gilligan states in her introduction how, over the previous ten years, 'I have been listening to people talking about morality and about themselves. Halfway through that time, I began to hear a distinction in these voices, two ways of speaking about moral problems, two modes of describing the relationship between other and self' (1982: 1). She suggests, though, that the `different voice' she identified is not characterized by gender: 'Its association with women is an empirical observation, and it is primarily through women's voices that I trace its development, but this associate is not absolute, and the contrasts between male and female voices are presented . . . to highlight a distinction between two modes of thought rather than to represent a generalization about either sex' (1982: 2). However, as Davies (1995) has noted, later in the same book Gilligan claims to provide a depiction of *women's* development.

10. See Wilkes and Wallis (1998), for example, for an overview of the development of feminist models of care within nursing.
11. For more details of this study and its findings, see Savage (1995, 1997).
12. Nurses' comportment was marked by expansive gestures, in which arms were not held close or across the body and legs were often open. The work of Young suggests that this is unusual for women, whose stance often suggests that they live in an enclosed space as a defence against forms of invasion, both subtle and crude, physical and non-physical. Thus 'women tend to project an existential barrier enclosed around them and discontinuous with the "over there" in order to keep the other at a distance' (1989: 67). In this study, nurses do not appear to be projecting such a barrier, at least between themselves and their patients.
13. This study was largely based on tape-recorded, in-depth interviews with 97 women, who described themselves as English and were attending an inner-city family planning clinic.
14. It was the view of most women in the study that male and female biological parents made an equal contribution towards the creation of a child. This contribution was understood in terms of genetic material, which was passed on from each parent and went to form the substance of the child. However, coexisting with this belief was a second, monogenetic model of procreation, in which a unique creative power was attributed to the male parent, who 'impregnated' the mother or 'fathered' a child. In other words, men were perceived to initiate and women to sustain pregnancy. Similar beliefs have been described elsewhere (see Warner 1985; Delaney 1986). Yet among these informants the female parent was portrayed as providing a highly valued, caring role, which was central to the moral task of 'raising' a child to full personhood. Thus informants' understandings of procreation incorporated notions of gender as well as biology and referred to ontological as well as ontogenetic development.
15. This view is not uncommon cross-culturally: for example, Schefold (1982) describes how, for the Khmir of north-western Tunisia, even a scorpion who drinks a mother's milk becomes the sibling of the child she suckles.
16. Personhood was largely understood by women in the study as a state acquired through the support of those who were 'close', but characterized by relative autonomy and independence, and associated with moral uprightness.
17. The nature or placing of these boundaries, Tronto (1994) suggests, cannot be separated from considerations of power.

References

Bevan, M. (1998), 'Nursing in the Dialysis Unit: Technological Enframing and a Declining Art, or an Imperative for Caring?', *Journal of Advanced Nursing*, 27: 730–6.

Bowers, L. (1989), 'The Significance of Primary Nursing', *Journal of Advanced Nursing*, 14: 13–19.

Brykczyñska, G. (1992), 'Caring – a Dying Art?', in M. Jolley and G. Brykczyñska (eds), *Nursing Care: The Challenge to Change*, London: Edward Arnold.

—— (1997), 'A Brief Overview of the Epistemology of Caring', in G. Brykczyñska (ed. with editorial advisor M. Jolley), *Caring: The Compassion and Wisdom of Nursing*, London: Arnold.

Chipman, Y. (1991), 'Caring: Its Meaning and Place in the Practice of Nursing', *Journal of Nurse Education*, 30(4): 171–5.

Colliere, M. (1986), 'Invisible Care and Invisible Women as Health Care Providers', *International Journal of Nursing Studies*, 23(2): 95–112.

Dalley, G. (1988), *Ideologies of Caring: Rethinking Community and Collectivism*, Basingstoke: Macmillan.

Davies, C. (1995), *Gender and the Professional Predicament in Nursing*, Buckingham: Open University Press.

Delaney, C. (1986), 'The Meaning of Paternity and the Virgin Birth Debate', *Man* (NS), 21: 494–513.

Diprose, R. (1994), *The Bodies of Women: Ethics, Embodiment and Sexual Difference*, London: Routledge.

Dunlop, M. (1994), 'Is a Science of Caring Possible?', in P. Benner (ed.), *Interpretative Phenomenology: Embodiment, Caring and Ethics in Health and Illness*, Thousand Oaks: Sage.

Ersser, S. (1991), 'A Search for the Therapeutic Dimensions of Nurse–Patient Interaction', in R. McMahon and A. Pearson (eds), *Nursing as Therapy*, London: Chapman Hall.

Fox, R. (1967), *Kinship and Marriage: An Anthropological Perspective*, Harmondsworth: Penguin.

French, M. (1985), *Beyond Power: On Women, Men and Morals*, New York: Summit Books.

Gamarnikow, E. (1978), 'Sexual Division of Labour: the Case of Nursing', in A. Kuhn and M. Wolpe (eds), *Feminism and Materialism: Women and Modes of Production*, London: Routledge and Kegan Paul.

Gilligan, C. (1982), *In a Different Voice: Psychological Theory and Women's Development*, Cambridge, Massachusetts: Harvard University Press.

Howell, S. (1997), *The Ethnography of Moralities*, London: Routledge.

Hugman, R. (1991), *Power in Caring Professions*, Basingstoke: Macmillan.

Jackson, M. (1989), 'Knowledge of the Body', in M. Jackson (ed.), *Paths Toward a Clearing: Radical Empiricism and Ethnographic Enquiry*, Bloomington: Indiana University Press.

Kitson, A. (ed.) (1993), *Nursing: Art and Science*, London: Chapman and Hall.

Kohlberg, L. (1971), 'From Is to Ought: How to Commit the Naturalistic Fallacy and Get Away With It in the Study of Moral Development', in T. Mischel (ed.), *Cognitive Development and Epistemology,* New York: Academic Press.

Larrabee, M.J. (ed.) (1993), *An Ethic of Care: Feminist and Interdisciplinary Perspectives,* New York: Routledge.

Lawler, J. (1991), *Behind the Screens: Nursing, Somology and the Problem of the Body,* Melbourne: Churchill Livingstone.

Levin, D. (1985), *The Body's Recollection of Being: Phenomenological Psychology and the Deconstruction of Nihilism,* London: Routledge and Kegan Paul.

McCurdy, J. (1982), 'Power *is* a Nursing Issue', in J. Muff (ed.), *Socialisation, Sexism and Stereotyping: Women's Issues in Nursing,* St Louis: C.V. Mosby.

Menzies, I. (1960), 'A Case Study of the Functioning of Social Systems as a Defence Against Anxiety: A Report on the Service of a General Hospital', *Human Relations,* 13: 95–121.

Oakley, A. (1984), 'The Importance of Being a Nurse', *Nursing Times,* 80(50): 24–7.

Overing, J. (1985), 'Introduction' in J. Overing (ed.), *Reason and Morality,* London: ASA Monographs 24, Tavistock Publications.

Pearson, A. (1988), 'Trends in Clinical Nursing', in *Primary Nursing: Nursing in the Burford and Oxford Nursing Development Units,* London: Chapman Hall.

Peplau, H. (1969), 'Professional Closeness', *Nursing Forum,* 8(4): 342–60.

Rosaldo, M. (1974), 'Women, Culture and Society: a Theoretical Overview', in M. Rosaldo and L. Lamphere (eds), *Women, Culture and Society,* Stanford: Stanford University Press.

Ruddick, S. (1992), 'Preservative Love and Military Destruction: Some Reflections of Mothering and Peace', in M. Humm (ed.), *Feminisms: A Reader,* New York: Harvester Wheatsheaf.

Salvage, J. (1990), 'The Theory and Practice of the "New Nursing"', *Nursing Times Occasional Paper,* 86(4): 42–5.

Savage, J. (1991), 'Flesh and blood: notions of relatedness among some urban English women', unpublished PhD Thesis, University of London.

—— (1995), *Nursing Intimacy: An Ethnographic Approach to Nurse–Patient Interaction,* Harrow: Scutari.

—— (1997), 'Gestures of Resistance: the Nurse's Body in Contested Space', *Nursing Inquiry,* 4: 237–45.

Schefold, R. (1982), 'The Efficacious Symbol', in P. Josselin de Jong and E. Schwimmer (eds), *Symbolic Anthropology in the Netherlands,* The Hague: Martinus Nijhoff.

Schmitt, J.-C. (1989), 'The Ethics of Gesture', in M. Fehr (ed.), *Fragments for a History of the Human Body,* New York: Zone.

Schneider, D. (1980), *American Kinship: A Cultural Account,* 2nd edn, Chicago: University of Chicago Press.

Soper, K. (1992), 'Contemplating a Nuclear Future', reprinted in E. Frazer, J. Hornsby and S. Lovibond (eds), *Ethics: A Feminist Reader,* Oxford: Blackwell.

Sundeen, S. *et al.* (1985), *Nurse–Client Interaction: Implementing the Nursing Process,* St Louis: C.V. Mosby.

Swanson, K. (1991), 'Empirical Development of a Middle Range Theory of Caring', *Nursing Research,* 40(3): 161–6.

Tattam, A. and M. Thompson (1993), 'Political Influences in Nursing', in M. Jolley and G. Brykczyñska (eds), *Nursing: Its Hidden Agendas,* London: Edward Arnold.

Tronto, J. (1994), *Moral Boundaries: A Political Argument for an Ethic of Care,* New York: Routledge.

Turner, B. (1995), *Medical Power and Social Knowledge,* 2nd edn, London: Sage.

Ungerson, C. (1983), 'Why do Women Care?', in J. Finch and D. Groves (eds), *A Labour of Love: Women, Work and Caring,* London: Routledge and Kegan Paul.

—— (ed.) (1990), *Gender and Caring: Work and Welfare in Britain and Scandinavia,* London: Harvester Wheatsheaf.

Vigarello, G. (1989), 'The Upward Training of the Body from the Age of Chivalry to Courtly Civility', in M. Fehr (ed.), *Fragments for a History of the Human Body,* Part 2, New York: Zone.

Warner, M. (1985), *Alone of All Her Sex: The Myth and Cult of the Virgin Mary,* London: Pan Books.

Watson, J. (1985), *Nursing: Human Sciences and Human Care. A Theory of Nursing,* Norwalk, Connecticut: Appleton-Century-Crofts.

Wilkes, L. and M. Wallis (1998), 'A Model of Professional Nurse Caring: Nursing Students' Experience', *Journal of Advanced Nursing,* 27(3): 582–9.

Young, I. (1989), 'Throwing Like a Girl: A Phenomenology of Feminine Body Comportment, Motility and Spatiality', in J. Allen and I. Young (eds), *The Thinking Muse: Feminism and Modern French Philosophy,* Bloomington: Indiana University Press.

Index